NEVILLE CHAMBERLAIN

NEVILLE CHAMBERLAIN

H. MONTGOMERY HYDE

INTRODUCTION BY
A. J. P. TAYLOR

WEIDENFELD AND NICOLSON
LONDON

For Paul and Diana

© Harford Productions Ltd 1976

Designed by Behram Kapadia
for George Weidenfeld and Nicolson Ltd

ISBN 0 297 77229 5

Printed and bound in Great Britain by
Morrison & Gibb Ltd, London and Edinburgh

CONTENTS

ILLUSTRATIONS

on page 125

The text of the Munich Agreement (Radio Times Hulton
  Picture Library)

All possible care has been taken in tracing the copyright holders
but if any have inadvertently been overlooked the publishers
will be glad of the opportunity to rectify the error.

Picture research by Juliet Scott

INTRODUCTION

WHEN Thurber was told that the women in his drawings were not attractive, he replied, 'They are to my men'. Something the same was true of Neville Chamberlain. Men either admired him greatly or disliked him intensely. No Prime Minister had more devoted followers. No Prime Minister was more completely master of his Cabinet. He had administrative gifts of a high order. He re-modelled English local government almost single-handed. He conducted the great fiscal change from Free Trade to Protection. He fulfilled the old Fabian dream of ending the Poor Law. Yet there was always hostility to him. Labour people for instance liked Baldwin and disliked Chamberlain, even though Baldwin had done little for the poor and Chamberlain did a great deal. Brendan Bracken called him 'the Coroner', and Chamberlain's melancholy appearance made the name apt. Chamberlain ought to have ranked high among successful Prime Ministers. Instead he has become a figure at best controversial and more often harshly condemned.

Chamberlain's qualities were to some extent his undoing. He had a clear efficient mind which made him impatient of muddle or hesitation. As Prime Minister he supervised the work of many departments of state and often took over affairs from the minister concerned. He dealt directly with the Dominions. He laid down the broad lines of public finance. When he became Prime Minister he intended to achieve great things at home. Events compelled him to take over foreign policy himself. He did so willingly. For all practical purposes he was his own Foreign Secretary, with Eden resentfully and Halifax contentedly as his agent and second. Abroad as at home, he sought decisive solutions and in a sense he achieved them: he made Hitler master of the European continent.

Munich can be defended as the best that could be done in almost impossible circumstances. Chamberlain's record in rearmament can also be defended, for in fact the armaments that he provided enabled Great Britain to survive. Where he failed was in inspiration. He made no attempt to conciliate the Labour opposition. He evoked no response of eager patriotism from the British people. He admitted himself that he was no war minister, and events showed that he was right.

Most of all, Chamberlain was the 'man of no luck'. He had to wait too long for the Premiership. He could not rise to the challenge of great events. In a time that demanded romantic oratory he could only offer drab prose. In the end his fall was a blessing for the country. His fate was inevitable but it was harder than he deserved. In a crisis good will and efficiency are not enough.

A. J. P. Taylor

AUTHOR'S PREFACE

As an undergraduate some fifty years ago I paid the first of many visits to the House of Commons, of which I was one day to become a Member. I recall the occasion well, since I was accommodated in a seat 'under the Gallery' and there I listened to Neville Chamberlain as Minister of Health moving the Second Reading of a Bill concerned with local government, which was then the responsibility of his department. What impressed me on that occasion was the minister's seemingly effortless mastery of his subject and the manner in which he had obviously done his 'homework'; he rarely referred to the brief which lay on the Despatch Box in front of him on the table and he was never at a loss for a fact or figure. His voice sounded a little husky, but it certainly did not have that rasping quality with which he has been credited by his critics.

I heard him speak on a number of subsequent occasions, as Chancellor of the Exchequer and later as Prime Minister, but somehow to my politically adolescent mind he never quite achieved the level of the original performance, perhaps because the subject was particularly his own and he was not so much at home at the Treasury, and at No. 10 Downing Street, as he was at the Health Ministry. From time to time I would meet him and his handsome wife, at receptions and parties at Londonderry House when I was Private Secretary to his Cabinet colleague Lord Londonderry, who was Air Minister in the MacDonald National Government, and Lady Londonderry was the leading Conservative Party hostess. I also remember Neville Chamberlain indulging his favourite pastime of salmon fishing as the Londonderrys' guest on a stretch of the river Brora, and, when he left, travelling beside the engine driver in the cab of the antiquated train which used to run between Inverness and Golspie.

A biographer may be regarded as fortunate in having some personal knowledge of his subject, however slight, and to have seen the subject in action. Neither the Oxford historian Sir Keith Feiling nor Iain Macleod, Chamberlain's successor as Minister of Health, who wrote biographies of him after his death, were personally acquainted with him, while Iain Macleod only heard his voice once, when he broadcast on the declaration of war in September 1939. However, both these authors had access to his private papers and they wrote with authority; in this book I have drawn largely on their works to which I am greatly indebted. I have also made use of the Cabinet records and other official papers in the Public Record Office which were not available at the time they wrote, and I am grateful to the Controller of Crown Copyright for permission to quote from them.

I am likewise under a heavy obligation to Neville Chamberlain's daughter Dorothy, now Mrs Stephen Lloyd, and her husband for facilitating my access to the Chamberlain family papers which are preserved in the University of Birmingham, and to the University authorities, who now own the copyright, for allowing me to see and reproduce extracts from them, notably Neville Chamberlain's diaries and letters to his sisters. I gratefully acknowledge similar permission in respect of the Baldwin and Templewood papers in Cambridge University Library.

Among the great mass of printed sources, which I have consulted, besides the works of Keith Feiling and Iain Macleod, I have found *The Chamberlains* by my friend Hope Elletson particularly helpful, and I wish to thank him for his assistance. In addition, my thanks are due to Mr Julian Amery, Mr Paul Chamberlain, Mr Maurice Cowling, Miss Hilary Lloyd Jones and Mr A. J. P. Taylor for their contributions towards the making of this book, which incidentally is not designed to be the ultimate definitive biography. For that we must await the work of Neville Chamberlain's official biographer Professor David Dilks.

H.M.H.

Tenterden, Kent

THE MAN OF BUSINESS

I

THE CHAMBERLAIN FAMILY has produced three outstanding figures in public life – Joseph Chamberlain and his two sons Austen and Neville. Both Joseph and Austen might have become Prime Minister, but largely as the result of their own actions they missed their chances of achieving the supreme prize in English politics. Joseph seceded from the Liberal Party on the Irish Home Rule issue in 1886; Austen withdrew from the contest for the Conservative Party leadership to give Bonar Law an unopposed election in 1911, and then after he had himself become leader a decade later he deliberately relinquished the leadership in order to enable Bonar Law to return to active politics. 'Austen always played the game', said his Cabinet colleague Lord Birkenhead, 'and he always lost it.' It was Neville, who lacked both his father's breadth of intellect and political foresight and his brother's charm and international *savoir faire*, who was eventually to occupy No. 10 Downing Street – the man whom Lloyd George contemptuously dubbed 'not a bad Lord Mayor of Birmingham in a lean year'.

From the beginning Joe Chamberlain's political hopes were concentrated on the elder son. Immediately after Austen left Cambridge, his father found him a parliamentary seat in the Birmingham area where the family had settled and prospered. After sitting together in the House of Commons for ten years father and son were united in Balfour's Cabinet, Joe as Colonial Secretary and Austen as Postmaster General, soon to be promoted to Chancellor of the Exchequer. Joe Chamberlain's opinion of the respective merits of his two sons at this time is of some interest. He expressed it one night in March 1902 to a friend while they sat up late waiting for news of the peace negotiations in South Africa which were to end the Boer War. 'You know, of my two boys Neville is really the clever one', Joe remarked to his friend, 'but he isn't interested in politics – if he was, I would back him to be Prime Minister.'

There have been other Prime Ministers besides Neville Chamberlain who have reached No. 10 Downing Street relatively late in life – Disraeli, Gladstone, Campbell-Bannerman and Churchill, to name a few. But they were all quite young when they first entered the House of Commons, and they spent many years there, though in some instances with occasional breaks due to loss of their seats at elections, before obtaining the Premiership. But no Prime Minister has entered the House so late as Neville Chamberlain did – he was in his fiftieth year when he became an MP for the first time in 1918.

After only four years on the back benches, he joined Bonar Law's Government as Postmaster General, the office Austen had held twenty years before. Thereafter promotion came swiftly as his administrative gifts were recognized. In Baldwin's first Government he served first as Minister of Health and then Chancellor of the Exchequer, but without ever introducing a Budget; in the second Baldwin administration he was again offered the Treasury but preferred to return to the Ministry of Health. However, on the formation of Ramsay MacDonald's second National Government in October 1931, he became Chancellor for the second time, this time serving long enough to introduce five Budgets. He continued at the Treasury after Baldwin took over from MacDonald in June 1935, and long before Baldwin resigned Neville Chamberlain had come to be recognized as his natural successor. His fateful Premiership began towards the end of May 1937 and lasted just short of three years.

After he had been in office for twenty-four hours he wrote to his sister Hilda:

You will be wondering what my own feelings are on actually taking up this post which ought to have come to the two senior members of the family and only failed to do so because the luck was against them in forcing them to choose between their natural ambition and their principles. It has come to me without my raising a finger to obtain it, because there is no one else and perhaps because I have not made

enemies by looking after myself rather than the common cause. . . .
I am grieved that so many have gone to whom this amends to Father
and Austen would have given unqualified pleasure and satisfaction.

Yet his tenure of the office was to end in disillusion and sadness.
While Stanley Baldwin retired in a blaze of popularity for his skil-
ful handling of the abdication crisis of Edward VIII, Neville
Chamberlain was forced to resign in a wave of unpopularity for his
handling of the war.

The two men differed greatly in character. Someone said that
Chamberlain had no antennae and Baldwin had nothing else.

Knowing them both [wrote Baldwin's official biographer, G. M.
Young], I always felt that, of the two, Chamberlain had the clearer
mind, Baldwin the larger vision; Chamberlain, within his own circle, the
warmer heart, Baldwin the wider affection. Instinct, insight, the most
sensitive response to what others were feeling or thinking – as dimly
perhaps as he did himself: all that was Baldwin; and to Chamberlain all
that was at times exasperating. Yet there were heights to which Baldwin
could rise and he could not; while, on the other hand, Chamberlain
could carry burdens – departmental burdens, party burdens of organisation and research – which Baldwin was only too willing to devolve on
any other man's shoulders.

Chamberlain's industry both as a departmental minister and as
Prime Minister was prodigious, unequalled by any other Premier
in this century with the possible exception of Churchill; but it was
apt to prove a delusive quality, particularly when Chamberlain as
Prime Minister began to take a personal interest in foreign affairs.
Even before he moved into No. 10 Downing Street he told Lady
Astor that 'he meant to be his own Foreign Minister and also to
take an active hand in co-ordinating ministerial policy – generally,
in contrast, with S[tanley] B[aldwin]'. The intention, when translated into action, was to have far-reaching results, not always happy
ones for himself or his fellow ministers.

A politician, and especially a Prime Minister, is apt to be judged
by the success or failure of his policies. By this criterion Chamberlain has been pronounced a failure. The verdict of history, it is
fashionable to say today, is against him – the architect of appeasement as personified in the Munich settlement. Yet the term
appeasement, with which Chamberlain's name is so strongly
linked, was not his invention. It was first used during Baldwin's

Premiership by Anthony Eden. At that time the term did not possess the pejorative connotation that was subsequently to be attributed to it. Originally it meant simply a settlement by peaceful means and as such was common political parlance of the period; only later did it mean pacification by satisfying another state's demands, thus becoming the dirty word with which the name of Neville Chamberlain has been indelibly branded.

Chamberlain's policies were destroyed in September 1939 when Hitler's Stukas and Panzers launched their lightning attack upon Poland, the country whose integrity Chamberlain in Britain's name had guaranteed. 'Everything I have worked for,' he confessed to Parliament, 'everything that I have hoped for, everything I have believed in during my public life, has crashed in ruins.' Twelve months previously he had saved the peace at Munich. How vital to Britain's ultimate survival was the breathing space then gained? The answer to this question may well be the test by which Neville Chamberlain's political record will really be judged in the light of history.

II

The name of Chamberlain is indissolubly associated with the city of Birmingham. Both Neville and his father served as Mayor and Lord Mayor. In his younger days Joe built up a successful screw manufacturing business there in partnership with his brother-in-law J. S. Nettlefold. But Joe only arrived in Birmingham in 1854, a kind of Dick Whittington in reverse. For over a century before that date the family had lived in the City of London where they were prosperous shoemakers in Milk Street. Indeed within a period of a hundred years six Chamberlains were Masters of the Cordwainers Company, the shoemakers' trade guild in the City. Although they 'occasionally conformed' to the Established Church and as such were churchwardens of St Lawrence Jewry, they were in fact Unitarians and as such worshipped at Carter Lane Chapel in the City. They are known to have come to London from the village of Lacock in north Wiltshire where for several generations they were maltsters. However, it is possible they were originally Londoners and only left the City temporarily to escape the ravages of the Great Plague in 1665. In any event the family's background, at least on the male side, was more Cockney than Brummagem.

4

In the eighteenth and early nineteenth centuries, it was the custom for the tradesmen of the City of London to live 'over the shop'. This was certainly the case with the Chamberlain shoe-making establishment at No. 36 Milk Street. Later the family moved their living quarters to Camberwell, then becoming a fashionable suburb on the south side of the river. It was here, at 3 Camberwell Grove (later renumbered 118), that Joe was born. But the shoemaking business continued to be run from the Milk Street premises.

A few doors along the street, at No. 39 at the corner of Cheapside, there was a tavern called The Dolphin kept by a family of the name of Beeton. Joe's father, Joseph Chamberlain senior, not being 'very strong in health', was 'a delicate eater' and according to the writer Harriet Martineau, who was related to the Chamberlains, the elder Joseph took his lunch every day at The Dolphin where 'he paid extra for his special cut of beef', washed down with several glasses of port wine which his doctors at that time, like the younger Pitt, 'thought to be good for his constitution'.

Samuel Powell Beeton, who helped to manage The Dolphin, had a son called Samuel Beeton who went into the publishing business, where he brought out the first English edition of Harriet Beecher Stowe's *Uncle Tom's Cabin*, and married Isabella Mayson, whose family by coincidence also lived in Milk Street. Sam Beeton also inspired his young wife to produce the best-known work on household management and cookery in the English language. First published in 1852, Mrs Beeton's cookery book cannot fail to have had a place in the Chamberlain household like countless other Victorian families. No doubt, too, it found its way to Birmingham after the Milk Street business had been wound up in 1863 and the elder Joseph Chamberlain and his wife followed their son Joe to the Midland city.

On his arrival in Birmingham, Joe Chamberlain settled in Edgbaston, then the better residential part of the town. Meanwhile he built up the business of Nettlefold and Chamberlain in Broad Street. Twenty years later, by which time the firm had a monopoly of screwmaking, Joe decided to retire from business and concentrate on politics, securing his financial independence with a fifth share of what he had made after all family claims had been adjusted, amounting to some £120,000. In 1861, he married Harriet Kenrick, daughter of Archibald Kenrick of Berrow Court;

the Kenricks came from Wales and had also prospered in Birmingham. At this time Joe and Harriet were both twenty-five. Their marriage, which lasted for barely two years, was very happy. Their first child was a girl named Beatrice, their second a boy named Austen, in giving birth to whom Harriet Chamberlain died, probably as the result of puerperal fever. Joe was devastated by the loss. 'I declare it almost seems impossible to live', he wrote at the time.

Five years later he married his late wife's cousin Florence Kenrick. With her he was equally happy. She bore him a son and three daughters, Ida, Hilda and Ethel, and she lavished the same affection on her two stepchildren as she did on her own children, treating them all alike.

The family now lived at a house called Southbourne in Augustus Road, Edgbaston, which was still green and open and where there was a field to graze a Shetland pony for the children. It was here that Florence's only son Arthur Neville Chamberlain – always known by his second name – was born on 18 March 1869.

Six years later, shortly after Joe had been re-elected Mayor of Birmingham, Florence died in giving birth to their fifth child, who survived for only a few hours and was laid to rest in the same coffin as its mother. Joe described her as 'a real helpmate and companion'. The result of this complete similarity and identity of interests, he wrote at the time, was that he could now say that 'there is no thought or action of my later years which my wife has not shared with me, and no place or ambition or desire formed for the future which has not been shadowed by her death.'

Neville's memories of his mother were vague, but he was always deeply conscious of her love. What particularly stuck in his memory was the occasion at the Kenrick home at Berrow Court when his aunt Louisa ('Louie'), his mother's twin sister who had married his father's younger brother Arthur, broke the news to the boy that he would never see his mother again.

For the next few years, while the Chamberlain children were growing up, their mother's place was taken by Clara, their father's youngest sister. Later, after Aunt Clara left to get married, his eldest daughter Beatrice kept house until Joe Chamberlain married for the third time. His second widowhood lasted nearly thirteen years, coinciding with the rapid rise of his star in the political firmament, when he was a Liberal Cabinet minister. During this period, it is said, although the fact is unconfirmed by his official biographers, he fell in love with the beautiful and richly endowed Miss Beatrice Potter, daughter of a railway and industrial magnate; they were no doubt brought together by a common interest in the pressing problems of local government such as housing and slum clearance. The philanthropist and journalist H. W. Nevinson, who was also struck by her charms, remarked at the time that they were what 'a rather hard and learned woman has when she allows a touch of the feminine to peep through, even in the delicacy of her shoes'. In her case Chamberlain's feeling was not reciprocated. Indeed she apparently disliked him to the point of loathing, although she admitted to Nevinson that 'he was the most attractive man to women she had ever known, and she had herself felt the attraction'. It was fortunate for all concerned that she did not become the third Mrs Joseph Chamberlain, but chose as her husband a fellow Fabian socialist called Sidney Webb, a much more suitable and congenial partner in every way, as their subsequent history was to show.

Although he missed his mother, Neville's early boyhood was not unhappy. There were lots of Kenrick cousins, since Joe's eldest sister Mary had married Harriet Kenrick's brother William. Indeed the Kenrick influence came out strongly in Neville, since it was from them that he inherited his love of music and flowers and his ready sympathy with suffering. Undoubtedly much of his spirit came from his mother's side, although he had his father's sloping shoulders and firm jawline. Florence Chamberlain was only twenty-eight when she died, leaving a husband twice widowed in a dozen years. 'It was to her', her stepson Austen has recalled, 'that their children owed the chief part of their intellectual tastes.' As for his father, Neville was to admit that for a good many years he respected and feared his father rather than loved him, remembering in particular that piercing eye that few could face with comfort. His bachelor uncle George Kenrick, who was his godfather, took a particular fancy to him, taught him to fish and shoot, and would later invite him to Ross-shire every summer to indulge in these pastimes, and eventually left him a substantial legacy when he died.

Early in 1877, shortly before his eighth birthday, Neville left home for a small boarding school in the sandhills round Southport, where he seems to have been happy enough. 'I like the schooll [sic] though I miss you all very much', he wrote to Aunt Clara. 'Yester-

7

day we all went to the sandhills and saw a sportsman who could not shoot anything.' The dormitory upstairs where he slept was not what he expected and he resented the lack of privacy, 'there being six little beds (with only one screen) and five little washingstands, besides which we have a bath every morning in the bathroom'. He concluded with a touch of financial acumen which he was to develop in his ministerial budgets: 'I have spent sevenpence allready [sic] but I do not mean to spend any more of it just yet.'

His next school, a preparatory one for Rugby, he liked much less, and when he went on to the public school which Dr Arnold's head-mastership and *Tom Brown's Schooldays* made famous he frankly hated it. For one thing he was bullied by a boy whom Austen had chastised when he was a pupil. Neville disliked cricket and thought the games were overdone. Finally, after he seemed to be getting on in the traditional classics curriculum, his father had him transferred to the Modern Side, a recent innovation, where he found himself thrown in with a lot of smaller boys whose superior he felt himself to be.

Unlike Tom Brown, little has been recorded of Neville's time at Rugby. He was remembered at first as 'a slender dark-haired boy, rather pale, quiet and shy', who would sometimes 'talk quickly in a low voice about things that had caught his sense of humour'.

One story is characteristic of the boy. His mathematical master expressed surprise at his skill in solving a complicated algebraical theorem. The boy replied that, as it was clear to him that he should have to learn it sometime, he might as well do it at once. 'I perceive you are something of a philosopher', was the master's comment.

On another occasion, a friend urged him to speak in the school debating society, of which he had hitherto been a silent member. 'No, I don't take any interest in politics,' said Neville. Asked why he did not, he replied: 'You don't know what our house is like before my father makes one of his big speeches. Everybody has to be quiet and even at meals conversation is subdued.' Then, after a pause, he continued on the subject of his father: 'Wretched man, he never knows what he is going to say!' Notwithstanding this exchange with his friend, Neville went to the debate and made his first political speech – but on what subject history is silent.

Neville seems to have felt his mother's loss more than Austen did his, since Neville's was really a second mother to Austen and Beatrice and they loved her dearly. But Aunt Clara does not seem

8

to have inspired the same affection in Neville. Once, when he returned from Rugby feeling thoroughly miserable, he flung himself into her arms expecting at least a few words of sympathy and welcome. But all Aunt Clara said to him was: 'Neville, your cap's crooked!'

After leaving the school, Neville never visited Rugby again, except when he had to for the purpose of changing trains on a cross-country journey.

III

Neville's father had followed up his mayoralty of Birmingham, in which he greatly improved housing and sanitation and promoted municipal reform generally, by entering the House of Commons, where he collaborated with Sir Charles Dilke in giving the Liberal Party a more Radical basis. He served in Gladstone's second and third Cabinets as President of the Board of Trade and President of the Local Government Board respectively, proving his capacity by promoting important legislative reforms relating to merchant shipping, electricity, and the law of bankruptcy. It was during Neville's last year at Rugby in 1886 that Joe resigned on the introduction of the Irish Home Rule Bill which he had consistently opposed, and led ninety of his Liberal–Unionist supporters into the Opposition lobby with the Conservatives to defeat the measure's Second Reading.

Meanwhile Joseph Chamberlain had moved from Southbourne to the Moor Green district of Birmingham where his parents lived. There he built his future home with greenhouses and gardens, calling it Highbury after the district of London to which his parents had migrated from Camberwell and where he had spent his own later boyhood. It was a huge mansion in the neo-Gothic style made fashionable by Sir Charles Barry when he largely rebuilt the Houses of Parliament after the fire in 1834. Highbury stood in ample grounds and the greenhouses were used to cultivate the orchids of which Joe was particularly fond and which he habitually wore in his buttonhole. It was also well staffed with servants, as was the Chamberlains' town house in Prince's Gardens, which Joe used when Parliament was sitting.

Austen, who was destined from the outset for a political career, went on from Rugby to complete his education at Cambridge. But, as Neville had shown no inclination towards politics, his father decided that on leaving school he must go into business and make his living. But first he must learn something of science – notably metallurgy and engineering – and for this purpose he attended lectures at Mason College, which had been founded by the philanthropist and pen manufacturer Sir Josiah Mason and was to be subsequently incorporated as the University of Birmingham.

After two years at Mason College, Neville was apprenticed to a firm of chartered accountants. Here he did well, going round the Midlands to do the firm's audits and staying in commercial hotels. The firm was so pleased with him that they offered him a permanent opening. But his father had other ideas for his future commercial career. Curiously enough, these ideas resulted from the father's visits to America at this period.

They began when Mr W. H. Smith, the Conservative Leader of the House of Commons, suggested to the Prime Minister Lord Salisbury that Mr Joseph Chamberlain should be appointed Chief Commissioner charged with the settlement in Washington of the current fishery dispute with the United States. Chamberlain accepted the offer and spent the winter of 1887–8 on the other side of the Atlantic. At a reception given in Washington by the British Minister, Sir Lionel Sackville West, for the distinguished visitor, Joe was introduced among others to Mary Endicott, the twenty-four-year-old daughter of Judge Endicott, the Secretary for War in President Cleveland's administration. In spite of the disparity in their ages they fell in love, and promptly became engaged with the blessing of the Endicott family. But they could not get married immediately since the prospective bridegroom had to go home to report progress on his political mission and also to prepare Highbury for the arrival of a new mistress. Meanwhile the news of the engagement had to be kept very quiet, since President Cleveland was going to run for office again and if it became known that a daughter of one of his Cabinet was going to marry the arch-enemy of Home Rule for Ireland he would have lost the Irish vote. However, Cleveland need not have worried, since in the event he was defeated by the Republican candidate Benjamin Harrison.

'Above all I hope you will be pleased with your new home when you come to take possession of it', Joe wrote to his fiancée on 18 April 1888. 'It is quite a new interest for me now that I constantly connect it with you and see you in imagination in every room.' Among other innovations, since Mary was fond of roses, he built a 'rose-house' for her pleasure. 'It is to be sixty feet long and on the best and latest model, but I fear we shall never equal the American roses, as our winter has so little sunshine by comparison. Still we will try and grow the American Beauties to remind you of the country you have given up for me.' In another letter he added in a note of banter: 'Take my advice and never marry a politician, but you may marry a horticulturalist – a grower of orchids, for instance!'

In the hopes that she would take to her future stepchildren, although both Beatrice and Austen were actually older than herself, he gave her an idea of how the evenings were sometimes spent at Highbury when he was at home and Parliament was not sitting. 'After dinner I got down one of the farces I wrote a long time ago and read it to the family, who proved a most indulgent audience. Then Neville played to us a *Lied* of Mendelssohn's and part of a Sonata by Beethoven.'

'It is odd how a small thing influences one's life and character', he wrote to Mary in another letter at this time.

When I was a very young man an uncle gave me a ring with the crest. I wanted a motto for it, and as there was none which the family claimed, I invented that which we all now bear: *Je tiens ferme*. It has often stood me in good stead, and I have often steadied myself by suddenly repeating this motto.

In November 1888, after the successful settlement of the fishery dispute, Joseph Chamberlain returned to Washington and married Mary Endicott in the old ivy-clad St John's Church, beyond the park in front of the White House. President Cleveland and most of the Cabinet were present, and American army officers donned full uniform in honour of the bride's father, their Secretary of War. At the reception afterwards President Cleveland proposed the customary toast, referring to the bridegroom as 'England's man with a future'.

Joe Chamberlain brought his wife home to Highbury on Christmas Eve. Later in the New Year Birmingham gave them a great civic welcome. Mary fitted perfectly into the domestic life of Highbury and all the children accepted their father's choice without question. 'She unlocked his heart and we were able to enter in as never before', said Beatrice. As for the happy bridegroom he spoke of his bride simply and truly: 'She brought my children nearer to me.'

One who was agreeably surprised, since she had detested Joe Chamberlain in his Radical Republican days, was Queen Victoria. After Mary Chamberlain had been presented to her, the Queen wrote in her journal: 'Mrs Chamberlain is very pretty and young-looking and is very ladylike with a nice frank open manner.' Nor did the Queen's opinion change. A few years later, on meeting Joe's wife again, she remarked: 'Mrs Chamberlain looked lovely and was as charming as ever.'

IV

In the autumn of 1890, Joseph Chamberlain crossed the Atlantic again with his new wife on a visit to her parents and relatives in America, taking Austen with them but leaving Neville at home to get on with his accountancy work. After a while he began to chafe from inaction and took Austen with him on a trip up the river Hudson, experiencing all the beauty of an American 'fall' as the leaves of the trees turned golden. Eventually they reached Montreal where they fell in with the Governor of the Bahamas, Sir Ambrose Shea. The Governor, whom the elder Chamberlain found 'intelligent', was full of a new discovery, which he assured Chamberlain would revolutionize the condition of the Bahamian islands.

It consists of a plant growing like a weed, which was the curse of the islands till Shea found that it would give a hemp equal to the best Manilla [Chamberlain wrote on his way back to Washington]. Now the cultivation is beginning on a large scale, and English capital is being brought in. From his account it looks as if enormous fortunes might be made out of this discovery and the prospect is so tempting that after thinking it over I wrote to Shea asking him for an option on 20,000 acres of land.

The plant was sisal.

Chamberlain had recently suffered severe financial losses from the fall in the value of Argentine stock in which he had invested heavily, and the Bahamas seemed to afford a good opportunity of retrieving his losses. Accordingly, he cabled Neville to come out, as he intended to put him in charge of the sisal plantation he had in mind after he had purchased the land. As soon as Neville arrived, he and Austen were sent off to Nassau, the colony's capital in New Providence Island, where they spent the next few months exploring the out islands. The brothers made the tour in a twelve-ton cutter, of which the only cabin – which was four feet high – was just large enough to allow one person to sleep on the deck and another on the seat. To make matters worse the weather was abominable, and the boat continuously shipped water; both brothers were constantly seasick, though they were normally good sailors. In addition one of the crew was washed overboard, but was fortunately recovered alive.

Ambrose Shea, the voluble Irish Governor, favoured Inagua for the site of the new enterprise, but this island turned out to be full of wild horses and clouds of mosquitoes. After going home to report, Neville returned to Nassau in May 1891; the same day he learned from the government surveyor that there was a large tract of land on Andros Island which held out the best possibilities, being only twenty miles from New Providence. The land was covered with pine trees, broken by belts of good coppice and on the whole of excellent quality, very level and unbroken by large 'swashies' or ponds. 'I am confident that I have secured the best site in the Bahamas', he reported to his father.

Neville Chamberlain was to spend the next seven years in the Bahamas, running the Andros Fibre Company, which had its head-quarters near Mastic Point. When he arrived, the island boasted no town, no cattle and few roads. But with the help of a willing over-seer named Knowles and local labour which was quite abundant – there were 3000 inhabitants on Andros – he succeeded in clearing 1500 acres after a year's work. By the end of 1893, 4350 sisal plants had been grown. By April 1895 there were 6000, the number of labourers rising to a maximum of 800. But the work was hard and enervating in the tropical heat, and the millions of mosquitoes made life almost unbearable after four o'clock in the afternoon.

Towards the end of 1892, Austen paid another visit to Andros to see how his brother was getting on. On his return to Highbury, he wrote to his stepmother in America:

I left Neville very well and in the best of spirits. I feel much more comfortable about him and his way of life now that I have seen him 'at home'; my admiration for the tact and skill he has shown is increased. The Colonial Secretary, *not* a gushing man, said to me: 'He is exactly the kind of man we want. His example is invaluable for the native whites. He shows them both what can be done and how to do it.'

It was very pleasant to see the feelings of the darkies towards him, and how much he has improved their work and discipline. They respect him and they trust him, and that is a good deal to be able to say without dwelling on their affection for him, which I believe to be genuine, tho' it would not stand much of a strain.

At first Neville lived in a negro's house which he rented while his own was slowly taking shape. He would rise at five, go down to the field, superintend the landing of lumber at the wharf and direct the men who were at work clearing, sometimes taking an axe or machete himself to help the labourers. Then, after twenty minutes for breakfast at nine, he would hurry off to the pineyard to measure out ground before paying wages at noon. 'I hadn't been there an hour,' he wrote to his sister Ida in September 1891, 'when down came sheets of rain which soaked me in my thin clothes in an instant.'

I would not go in however and continued measuring for three mortal hours in the hardest rain I have ever experienced. About 3 o'clock I paddled back to the store to find Knowles still counting lumber and the people all waiting for the wages. From 3 to 7.30 I sat in a thorough draught, paying wages till my limbs were cramped and my nails were blue with cold. Then I gathered myself up and stumbled home, cold wet hungry and tired in the pitchy darkness.

One day all he had to eat was two biscuits with nothing since breakfast. Then when he got home he had to sit up working on accounts which his father insisted should be meticulously kept. And all for what Neville described as his 'absurdly large salary' of £200 a year.

In the autumn of 1893, Joe Chamberlain visited Andros and gave orders for pushing on with new roads and building a railway, all of which added considerably to his capital expenditure. On his return to England he decided on a debenture issue to raise the additional capital, not a prudent decision in the circumstances when the success of the enterprise hung in the balance. Nevertheless the Andros Fibre Company was turned into a limited company with a capital of £100,000, and a debenture issue of £20,000 which was privately subscribed. Unfortunately this operation was to furnish ammunition for Joe Chamberlain's political opponents and the debenture issue was to be used with damaging effect against him during the 'Khaki' Election in 1900. About the same time, Neville's father wrote to him:

> I feel that this experience, whatever its ultimate result on our fortunes, will have had a beneficial and formative effect on your character. At times, in spite of all the hardships and annoyances you have had to bear, I am inclined to envy you the opportunity you are having to show your manhood. Remember, however, now and always that I value your health more than anything, and that you must not run any unnecessary risks either by land or sea.

In spite of his preoccupation with work, Neville was desperately lonely and homesick, increased by occasional spells of home leave. Besides reading a wide range of books from Prescott to George Eliot and Carlyle, his principal delight was his house, light and airy, with a fine view of the sea through vines and coconut palms. For servants he had a native woman cook and a houseboy; at first, too, the overseer's wife kept an eye on his health, but unfortunately she died, which sent her husband crazy from sleeplessness so that he kept entreating Neville not to shoot him.

At last the terrible truth dawned on Neville Chamberlain, and he communicated it to his father in a sad letter which he wrote in February 1896. 'The plants don't grow. . . . I don't see how we can possibly last out longer than the end of March and then we must wait till the plants are ready to cut again. . . . Meanwhile everything will be disorganised. All the order and discipline that I have worked up will be lost, all the people will go away.' For this he blamed himself, quite unjustly. 'In spite of all that you and Austen said before, this is *my* failure. I can't bear to think of it. . . . Meanwhile I find it very hard to work with energy and enthusiasm while I have this ominous outlook before me all the time.'

His father had invested £50,000 in the venture. To lose this 'would indeed be a catastrophe', his father admitted. But they had to face realities. 'If the worst comes to the worst, we will all make the best of it, and remember our motto, *"Je tiens ferme"*.' It was 'with the most bitter disappointment' that Neville advised the abandonment of the ill-fated project. 'I no longer see any chance of making the investment pay', he wrote to his father in April 1896. 'I cannot blame myself too much for my want of judgment. . . . No doubt a sharper man would have seen long ago what the ultimate result was likely to be.'

'No hope of saving anything from the wreck,' he told the Governor's secretary before he left the colony. 'I asked my father to allow me to begin again with better land; but he refused, and on the whole I think he is right. It would be a waste of time for me to spend another ten years in that hole.' And to his friend, the local clergyman, he also wrote at this time: 'There is the financial loss which is heavy, and the failure to succeed in what I have given five years of hard work to do, and the thought that all my people will relapse into what they were is extremely distressing to me.'

After a brief visit to Highbury to discuss the details of the winding up with his father, he returned to Andros the following winter to find that thieves had broken into the store and to see his plant and engines knocked down to a solitary bidder for £560. Then he said his final goodbyes. 'People came and sat in my office and sobbed.' One letter he preserved was from thirty-three of his labour force addressed to 'Mr Chimblin' and thanking him for the school and bank which he had founded for their benefit and for always treating them 'like a true gentleman'.

Later, on reflection, when the Bahamas seemed far away, he told his friend the Bahamian clergyman that he often thought of the island 'and with very grateful recollections'. 'For in spite of all the disappointments it was a great experience', he added, 'and I know I am much the better and stronger for it'.

V

The Birmingham to which Neville Chamberlain returned from the West Indies was busily expanding and consolidating its position. Already a county borough and a city, the first Lord Mayor took office in the same year that Neville came back from Andros. Meanwhile Neville had to find a place for himself in the new fast-growing community in the Midlands, and he was already twenty-eight years old, late enough at which to begin another career. His uncle Arthur Chamberlain, a younger brother of Joe's, offered to provide an opening for him in Kynoch's, the armaments and explosives firm which he controlled. But Joe considered this to be 'too dangerous politically'. Instead an opening was found for him in

Elliot's who manufactured copper, brass and yellow metal at Selly Oak, work for which his technical studies in Mason College stood him in good stead. The firm, of which he became a director, was a substantial one, employing between 700 and 800 men and doing a profitable business with Benares. Eventually Neville became chairman of Elliot's, but his work never occupied the whole of his time. His principal commercial interest lay in another concern, of which he secured the controlling interest with the help of capital provided by the family.

'I told you that I had become a director of some copper works,' he wrote to Alfred Greenwood, the secretary to the Governor of the Bahamas who was anxious to know how he was getting on since his return to Birmingham. 'Since then I have bought another business which I am going to smash up all by myself. It is concerned with the manufacture of cabin berths, not the bedding but the metallic part, and is in Birmingham, so I shall be transformed from a colonial to a provincial.'

Thus the firm of Hoskins & Son became Neville's main business interest. Every weekday, he cycled the two miles from Highbury to the works in Upper Trinity Street, hanging up his bicycle on the wall of the loading bay when he got there, arriving never later than 9 a.m. and leaving between 5.30 and 6 p.m. The firm's main advantage over its only two competitors was the patent it held for folding berths for emigrants, so that cargo could be loaded for the homeward voyage. Minor activities included the making of ammunition racks for warships. It was a typical small Birmingham firm with old-fashioned engineering shops and a strong sympathy existing between management and men. At no time did it ever employ more than 200 men, and often less than half that number. Eventually with the changing times it switched over to making hospital beds for the National Health Service. Neville, like his cousin Arthur (his uncle Arthur Chamberlain's son), was a great believer in bonus incentives, and at Hoskins's he introduced a 5 per cent bonus on output and also a pensions scheme. At Elliot's he was also responsible for the introduction of a surgery, welfare supervisors and subsequently benefits for injured men and their dependants. 'He was a real man in all his doing', wrote one pensioner, looking back many years later. 'I do hope and pray I shall meet him in the next life.' Neville Chamberlain, like Stanley Baldwin in his iron works nearby, was proud of never having a strike.

17

'My time is divided between business and local work with now and then a short holiday, and then business again', he wrote to a friend after he had been home for a few years. 'I haven't quite found *my* mission and feel a bit dissatisfied with it.'

His local work included teaching in Sunday school, being active in the Chamber of Commerce and becoming secretary of the city Liberal Unionist Association. He also acted as chairman of the newly formed committee for territorial army units. He was active too in the management boards of the local hospitals, and as an original member of the governing body of the new university, of which his father was the first chancellor, he threw himself wholeheartedly into raising money for endowments and buildings, and championed its claim to assistance from the city rates. Often he would come straight from Hoskins's to visit the casualty ward of the Birmingham General Hospital, of which he was eventually to become chairman. By 1904 he was serving on no less than fourteen important committees. Finally he joined the famous Birmingham and Edgbaston Debating Society, which held fortnightly debates. Like his father he served a term as president, and in that particular term it is worth noting that the society deplored the growing tendency towards State action as 'destructive of the moral fibre of the nation', applauded the House of Lords for rejecting Lloyd George's Budget, and on the president's initiative debated the congenial view that 'business men make better rulers than lawyers'.

Although he campaigned at election time, particularly in the General Elections of 1900 and 1906, 'speaking as often as my nervousness and laziness permit me (which is not much)', he admitted that he had not begun to think of politics as a career. For a time both his father and his brother sat in Balfour's Cabinet, Joe as Colonial Secretary and Austen as Postmaster General, and that seemed to Neville enough for one family. As a consequence of the reshuffle which took place at the end of 1903, when Joe and those who shared his views on imperial preference left the Government, Balfour promoted Austen to be Chancellor of the Exchequer.

By making this novel appointment the Prime Minister hoped that the breach between the elder Chamberlain and himself on the tariff issue should not be widened unnecessarily. The idea was that Austen should serve as a link between them, although in the event it was to be a link subject to increasing strain, since Austen was precluded from applying his father's protectionist principles which he had come largely to share, and in framing his Budgets he had to keep them within the confines of the existing accepted fiscal policy. Nevertheless it was a remarkable achievement in all the circumstances for Austen to have reached No. 11 Downing Street when he was barely forty, the first evening (as he told his father) that he was 'away from your roof in a house for the time being my own'. Neville shared his elder brother's gratitude to their father for the close friendship he had encouraged between them. As Austen expressed it, 'I do not think there are many fathers who have been and are to their sons all that you have been to me; and my prayer is . . . that I may do something to help you in the great work which you have undertaken.'

To his old friend, the Rev. F. B. Mathews, the Rector of Andros, Neville wrote at this time:

Don't you think it is pretty plucky of my father, after coming home in a blaze of popularity from South Africa, to risk it all by starting this great controversy? I need hardly say that I am an ardent adherent – in fact I have been so for some years – and I am confident that we shall win. But whether we shall win at the next election is a much more doubtful affair.

It was indeed, since the Liberals won a landslide victory at that election, while the Tories remained disunited and temporarily without a leader in Parliament, since Balfour had lost his seat, although another was to be found for him shortly afterwards. 'The majority of our party both in and out of the House are in favour of Tariff Reform, and would gladly follow if Balfour would only lead,' Neville wrote to his friend Greenwood immediately after the election. 'Unfortunately there are still in the House and in the machine representatives of the old Tories who would never follow my father's lead even if he were willing to give it.' He added that he had 'been doing more speechifying than usual this time, sorely against my will'.

Joseph Chamberlain's personal campaign came to an end a few months later. On 9 July 1906, the day after his seventieth birthday, he made the principal speech at a huge open air meeting at the Bingley Hall, which Neville and the rest of the family all attended to hear what turned out to be his political testament. It was also his swansong embodied in a peroration which has never been forgotten in Birmingham:

The union of the Empire must be preceded and accompanied by a better understanding, by a closer sympathy. To secure that is the highest object of statesmanship now at the beginning of the twentieth century; and, if these were the last words that I were permitted to utter to you, I would rejoice to utter them in your presence and with your approval. I know that the fruition of our hopes is certain. I hope I may live to congratulate you upon our common triumph; but, in any case, I have faith in the people. I trust in the good sense, the intelligence, and the patriotism of the majority, the vast majority of my countrymen. I look forward to the future with hope and confidence, and

'Others I doubt not, if not we
The issue of our toil shall see.'

But it was not given to him to see the issue of his toil. Two days later, in London, while dressing to go out to a dinner given by Lady Cunard, he collapsed in his dressing room and was found on the floor with his right side paralyzed. He had suffered a stroke, and although he recovered his faculties to some extent after he had been brought back to Highbury, the manner in which his speech was affected made any return to public life impossible. He lived on for some years, a pathetic invalid lovingly cared for by his wife Mary and his three daughters, Beatrice, Ida and Hilda, spending the winters in Cannes when on fine days he would be wheeled up and down the promenade in a bath chair. An additional affliction was that his eyesight began to fail.

'He who had been so self reliant was now dependent on a woman for every common act of life,' wrote Neville of the last months of his life in 1914.

Yet he submitted with amazing patience and allowed himself to be dragged out to walk his daily round panting and sweating with the exertion, to be thrust into his coat and piled up with rugs on the hottest day, to have his gloves pulled on and off, to have his cigars cut down and to be sent to bed early, in short to endure humiliations and discomforts without end every day of his life.

His only real pleasure was in watching his grandchildren. He could not even talk to them. He could only make uncouth noises which often frightened them, and it was touching to watch his efforts to attract them.

After a farewell garden party at Highbury to his constituents in May 1914, he insisted on going up to London to be available in case his advice should be sought on the question of Irish Home Rule, since the Liberal measure had passed the Commons three times and been thrown out by the Lords, so that under the provisions of the Parliament Act it would automatically become law later in the year. The two Unionist lawyers Lord Halsbury and Sir Edward Carson came round to Prince's Gardens to seek the advice of the stricken giant. 'Don't give in,' he said. He could hardly get out his words, but as he sat in his chair he thumped the floor with his stick to help him utter: 'If – I – were – you – I – would – fight – it – out – to – the – end!'

A few days later he had a slight heart attack and stayed in bed. On the night of 1 July, his wife, who slept next door, heard noises coming from his bedroom. She went in, and as she stood beside him she heard him making a speech in his sleep, replying to the Prime Minister Mr Asquith on some aspect of fiscal policy. Oddly enough, his speech which had been slurred and thickened since his stroke seemed to her that night to have recovered all its old clarity.

Next morning he seemed a little better, and as usual she read the news from *The Times* to him. The leading article dealt with the murder of the Archduke Ferdinand at Sarajevo. After a short time he stopped her, since he saw that the world was on the brink of war.

That afternoon Joseph Chamberlain suffered a second and more serious heart attack. The family were summoned, and when Neville saw his father in the evening it was clear the end was near. He was unconscious and breathing loudly, while oxygen was being administered. Gradually his breathing became fainter and fainter. 'He never recovered consciousness,' Neville noted, 'and he passed away peacefully in Mrs Chamberlain's arms. . . . I think he was partly conscious that his end was approaching. I am sure that he was ready for it.'

'What life will be without him I do not care to think but I can truly say that I would not have him back', wrote his widow when it was all over. 'He had so much to bear that the thought he was spared any further suffering gives peace to us all.'

The Dean of Westminster offered burial in the Abbey, but the offer was declined. His wish to be buried in Birmingham was respected and he was laid to rest with other members of the Chamberlain family in the Key Hill Cemetery after a simple funeral service in the Unitarian Church of the Messiah.

'I am glad to think his trials are over', Neville wrote to his friend Greenwood. 'But to us it means the break up of the family life. Austen cannot afford to live at Highbury, which must be pulled down and the land developed, unless it were bought as a memorial which I suppose is very unlikely.' In fact, Highbury was acquired by the Corporation of Birmingham, and the land sold for 'development'. Austen, who had inherited the property, received £27,000 from the proceeds of the sale.

In 1916, Joseph Chamberlain's widow Mary married the Rev. William Carnegie, Canon of Westminster and Chaplain to the Speaker of the House of Commons. She remained on good terms with her stepchildren, particularly Austen, but she never returned to Birmingham. However, she was to live to attend her first husband's centenary celebrations in the Albert Hall in London in 1936, along with Austen, Hilda and Ida.

It was perhaps fitting that Neville should take charge of the centenary celebrations in the Town Hall in Birmingham on this occasion.

The greatest service of Joseph Chamberlain to local government was the setting it on a new pedestal of dignity and honour [his younger son remarked]. Joseph Chamberlain always upheld municipal work as one of the most honourable and useful avocations that any man or woman could follow. In honouring him today, Birmingham is honouring herself and falsifying the saying that a prophet is not without honour except in his own country.

2

COUNCIL HOUSE TO DOWNING STREET

I

IN SEPTEMBER 1911 Neville Chamberlain was adopted as Liberal Unionist candidate for the All Saints' Ward in his father's constituency of West Birmingham. He was elected to the Council two months later. His decision to interest himself in local government politics had been foreshadowed by Parliament's decision to extend Birmingham's municipal boundaries and so make it 'the second city in the Empire'. Neville was returned as the second of three councillors. In his election address he had dwelt on town planning and open spaces, the need for more technical education, and the extension of the canal system. 'I am only following out the traditions in which I have been brought up', he concluded, 'and which it is my earnest desire to maintain.' Thus besides being the second city in the empire he wished to make it the best governed.

Earlier that same year in which he was elected to the Birmingham Corporation, Neville Chamberlain took an important step in his private life. He got married. His bride was a beauty in her late twenties named Anne de Vere Cole, daughter of an officer in the 3rd Dragoon Guards who came from a Norfolk family of farmers and small squires and had died of cholera in India. She had been brought up by her grandparents who lived in an attractive Inigo Jones house in Berkshire called West Woodhay. Anne's mother was Irish, from Curragh Chase in County Limerick. Her brother Horace was famous for his practical jokes, one of which was disguising himself and some friends as workmen and digging up Piccadilly Circus on the pretext of urgent repairs, roping off the result and holding up the traffic, leaving the authorities to clear up the mess and get the traffic moving again.

There was nothing of the Chamberlains in Anne Cole, but it was a Chamberlain link that led to their first meeting. Anne's uncle Alfred Cole had married Lilian Chamberlain, the widow of Joe's younger brother Herbert, and it was when visiting her aunt in Cannes that Anne made the acquaintance of the Joseph Chamberlains and the elder daughter Beatrice who together used to winter on the Riviera after Joseph's stroke. When they returned to London Beatrice organized a dinner and theatre party and invited Anne to meet Neville. Her plan worked like a charm. Neville and Anne immediately fell in love, and a few weeks later their engagement was announced. It was decided to postpone the wedding until after the second election held in 1910, in which Neville was to be busy campaigning. The election over, they got married in St Paul's Church, Knightsbridge. After their honeymoon, spent in Algeria and Tunisia, Neville brought his lovely bride home to Birmingham.

Here they made their home in Westbourne, a solid comfortable house in Edgbaston, looking out over the fields to King's Norton and the university. On Christmas Day 1911 their daughter Dorothy was born, and two years later a son Frank completed the family. It was an ideally happy marriage, and Neville never tired of paying tribute to his wife and telling how he owed such success as he achieved to her. 'I'd never have done it without Annie', he used to say.

In 1914 Neville became an alderman and in the following year Lord Mayor – a rapid promotion, even for one with the name of Chamberlain. It matched his father's swift rise in local government politics and it maintained the tradition of local government service among other members of the family, since five of his uncles and ten other relatives had all sat in the mayoral chair in the Birmingham Council House. Neville's prime object, he declared in his inaugural speech in the council chamber, was 'the transference of the working classes from their hideous and depressing surroundings to cleaner, brighter and more wholesome dwellings in the still uncontaminated country which lies within our boundaries'. That this work could not be pressed forward with the speed he would have liked, he blamed the German Emperor and the horrors of war which the Kaiser had let loose upon much of the world.

Besides the usual routine war work in the way of recruitment and entertainment for the forces, helping the hospitals and organizing crèches for the children of mothers working in munitions factories, the forty-six-year-old Lord Mayor made several significant personal contributions to the war effort. For instance, he seized on the opportunity of a visit by the Hallé orchestra in March 1916 to make a revolutionary proposal on the future of orchestral music in Birmingham, when he addressed the audience during the interval. As he told his sister Beatrice, 'I dropped a little bombshell by suggesting that we should have a first-class local orchestra, and contribute to its support out of the rates.' Thanks to his initiative the Birmingham City Orchestra (the first of its kind in England) was formed with municipal support three years later when the war was over. Only by large concert halls and cheap seats could music be made at once paying and democratic, the function of this art as he put it 'having always been to purify, encourage and comfort'.

Another of his pet projects was a municipal savings bank, and here he encountered formidable opposition from the financial establishment. 'I'm beat and the Savings Bank is dead', he wrote in a fit of depression in May 1916. 'The selfishness of the banks and the apathy of the Treasury together make an impenetrable entanglement.' But he refused to accept defeat and working through his brother Austen and with the aid of the Friendly Societies and some of the Labour leaders the Treasury eventually capitulated, although only boroughs with a population of a quarter of a million or more could qualify, and depositors might only invest through their employers.

'I think my position has been still further strengthened in the town', Neville wrote in his diary in June 1916. 'It is generally recognised that a new atmosphere of initiative and energy has been imported into the administration.' It came as no surprise that he should have been elected to serve a second term in November.

The following month saw the fall of the Asquith Coalition and its replacement by a new Coalition under the leadership of David Lloyd George.

On 19 December 1916, Neville Chamberlain went up to the offices of the Local Government Board in London for a conference on municipal borrowing. Afterwards he noted with satisfaction: 'I had got everything I wanted to the delight of the L.G.B. who said, "This is due to you. Birmingham is leading again." ' He was about to board the train at Paddington station to return to Birmingham when a government messenger appeared summoning him to the India Office where Austen was installed as Secretary of State. Austen told him the Prime Minister wished to see him immediately, and without further ado he was immediately ushered into Lloyd George's office in Downing Street. Would he become Director of National Service, a new department which was being formed to aid the war effort? His decision was required immediately, said the Prime Minister, since Lloyd George wished to make a statement in the House of Commons the same evening, as the House was about to begin the Christmas recess.

After a few minutes' reflection, Neville accepted, although he did so with some reluctance. 'It is an appalling responsibility', he confided to his diary. 'If it was only my own career that was at stake I wouldn't care a rap, but the outcome of the war may depend on what I do.'

Lloyd George made his announcement the same evening, and the House dispersed for Christmas, confident that the manpower problem would be solved by the time members returned from their constituencies.

We have been fortunate in inducing the Lord Mayor of Birmingham, Mr Neville Chamberlain, to accept the position of Director-General under this scheme [the Prime Minister declared]. It was with very great difficulty that we induced him to undertake this very onerous duty. He will immediately proceed to organise this great new system of enrolment for industrial purposes, and I hope that before Parliament resumes its duties in another few weeks we shall be able to report that we have secured a sufficiently large industrial army in order to mobilise the whole of the labour strength of this country for war purposes.

The circumstances in which Neville Chamberlain was offered the appointment and in which he subsequently accepted it were curious. Apparently he was not the first choice. The War Cabinet wished to offer it to Mr E. S. Montagu, who had been Minister of Munitions and whom they considered the best man to undertake the duties of Director.

We duly offered him this post [Lloyd George afterwards wrote in his *War Memoirs*], but he did not at the time feel prepared to undertake it, and we eventually fell back upon Mr Neville Chamberlain. He was appointed in a hurry, as I had to announce the appointment in the House of Commons in my speech on the policy of the new Government.

I had never seen him, and I accepted his qualifications for the post on the recommendation of those who had heard of his business and municipal experience.

According to Leopold Amery, who was then Assistant Secretary of the War Cabinet, one of Lloyd George's foibles was to fancy himself a phrenologist, judging a man by the shape of his head. Apparently when Chamberlain presented himself at 10 Downing Street, Lloyd George at once took a dislike to him, and, in particular, jumped to the conclusion that his head was not big enough. 'When I saw that pin-head', Lloyd George remarked to Amery not long afterwards, 'I said to myself he won't be any use.' There was a curious sequel to this incident, as Amery has recalled. In 1940, after Chamberlain had resigned as Prime Minister, Winston Churchill proposed to invite Lloyd George to join his Cabinet. Chamberlain, who was Lord President of the Council, objected, but later withdrew his veto. When Churchill so informed Lloyd George, the latter then refused the offer, bubbling with indignation at the thought of being admitted to the Cabinet 'by leave of that pin-head'. Such were the fateful consequences for Lloyd George, as Amery subsequently expressed it in his memoirs, of a feud originating in a hasty phrenological judgment. 'You treated my brother very badly', Austen Chamberlain told Lloyd George long afterwards, 'and you have never forgiven him.'

Lloyd George admitted that 'it was not one of my successful selections'. For this the Prime Minister had only himself to blame. In the first place it was a fatal mistake not to find a seat in the House of Commons for the new Director of National Service, so that he could answer directly to Parliament for his department. He was not even sworn a member of the Privy Council which would have at least given him some standing as a departmental chief responsible for both the military and the civil side of the recruitment of manpower. 'I have never had even a scrap of paper appointing me or giving me any idea of where my duties begin and end', he told his sister Ida at the time. 'I don't know whether I have Ireland and Scotland as well as England. I don't know whether I have munitions volunteers. I believe I am to have a salary but I don't know what.'

No doubt there were faults on both sides. Lloyd George, for instance, wished to second three senior civil servants to the new department which was established in St Ermin's Hotel next door to Caxton Hall, Westminster, while the new Director insisted on bringing down his own officials from Birmingham, in particular the ex-Town Clerk, who did not know the ways of Whitehall as well as the Prime Minister's suggested nominees. On the other hand, Chamberlain should have insisted on being in the House of Commons, and no doubt if he had put his foot down at the outset a place would have been found for him. As it was, a multiplicity of ministers had to answer for him in the House, of whom one was the Minister of Labour John Hodge, who gave him little or no support. As the Irish Member John Dillon put it in the House, 'if Mr Chamberlain were an archangel, or if he were Hindenberg and Bismarck and all the great men of the world rolled into one, his task would be wholly beyond his powers.'

The net result of setting up the new department at St Ermin's and the expenditure of some £60,000 on publicity, together with the appointment of officials all over the country to attract volunteers, was that fewer than 3000 men were placed in employment. As Neville Chamberlain later told the Birmingham Unionists, 'the mistake about National Service was fundamental. What was needed was not a campaign for volunteers; what was wanted was a careful and thorough survey of the whole resources of the nation in manpower and woman power, followed by a decision of the Cabinet as to the best method and the best manner in which those resources should be allocated.'

On 1 July 1917, after he had been in the job for barely seven months, Neville Chamberlain made up his mind to resign with effect from 27 July, but the Prime Minister persuaded him to delay his departure for a short time. Neville wrote to his sister Hilda at this time:

Now I hate the idea of resignation under present circumstances; you know I like to stick to things even after there seems no chance of success, but when I have made up my mind that the thing is hopeless I generally cut the loss with rapidity and determination. Now I am in a position that reminds me of the Bahamas when the plants didn't grow. With all the Departments against me and a chief who won't help, I see no chance of success, and if so it would be folly to let slip an opportunity of getting out on a principle.

So he resigned and went back to Birmingham. Here the family advised him to seek a parliamentary seat as soon as practicable. 'It *must* be a Birmingham seat', said Ida, 'but surely if it were known that you wanted to go in someone would make room for you.'

The upshot was that Neville wrote to the chiefs of the party machine in Birmingham and in the event was adopted for the Ladywood division, a largely working-class constituency in the middle of the town. Nevertheless he felt despondent about the future, as he wrote in his diary (17 December 1917):

My career is broken. How can a man of nearly 50, entering the House with this stigma upon him, hope to achieve anything? The fate I foresee is that after mooning about for a year or two I shall find myself making no progress. . . . I shall perhaps be defeated in an election, or else shall retire, and that will be the end. I would not attempt to re-enter public life if it were not war-time. But I can't be satisfied with a purely selfish attention to business for the rest of my life.

Chamberlain was succeeded in the Department of National Service by Sir Auckland Geddes, who not only entered the Commons but was given a seat in the Cabinet. Meanwhile Chamberlain was the recipient of several compliments in Parliament. 'I have no special friendship with Mr Neville Chamberlain, but I think that he had under the circumstances a hopeless task', remarked the Conservative leader Mr Bonar Law, at that time the Prime Minister's closest political confidant, 'and I listened with the greatest pleasure to what was said in this House as to how he had worked and how difficult his duty was.'

The Order of the British Empire had recently been instituted, chiefly as a means of recognizing the services rendered by civilians in the war. It consisted of five grades, of which the highest (G.B.E.) was offered to Neville Chamberlain. 'Last night,' he noted in his diary on 27 December 1917, 'I received a letter from the P.M. saying that the King had approved his recommendation that I should receive the honour of a G.B.E. Today I declined it.' When he saw the list he was glad he had done so. 'I wonder what you thought of the Honours List,' he wrote to his political agent in Birmingham early in the New Year. 'I have never ceased to congratulate myself that I did not figure among that rabble.'

The war and its immediate aftermath brought two family sorrows. The first was the death of his cousin Norman Chamberlain (his uncle Herbert's son), who was killed in action in Flanders. They had been colleagues together on the Birmingham City

Council and shared many interests, particularly in the formation and encouragement of youth clubs. 'I feel frightfully depressed over his loss and discouraged too', Neville wrote at the time. 'I was counting and depending on him more than I realised and he was in fact the most intimate friend I had.' Neville thereupon set himself the task of collecting Norman's letters and papers. The result was *Norman Chamberlain: A Memoir*, the only book Neville ever wrote.

The second family loss was the death, in the influenza epidemic which swept Europe at the end of the war, of his half-sister Beatrice ('Bee'). 'She was a wonderfully gifted woman of brilliant intellect and the highest moral character', he wrote in his diary on 22 November 1918. 'She had the warmest heart and her love for children and genius for amusing them made her always a favourite. It is an awful gap in our family circle.'

The General Election was fought on 14 December 1918 and the votes were counted a fortnight later. Neville Chamberlain did not relish the strain of electioneering. 'I do wish speaking didn't make me so unhappy beforehand', he noted during the campaign. 'About teatime I begin to feel unwell – by dinner my appetite has completely gone, and if I have an exciting meeting I can't get to sleep for ages afterwards.' In Ladywood there was a three-cornered contest, Neville Chamberlain's opponents being Mrs Corbett Ashby, an Asquithian Liberal, and Mr J. W. Kneeshaw, who though nominally Labour was a pacifist and had been denounced by his party leaders. Thus the issue was never in doubt and Chamberlain romped home with a majority of 6833.

Already before the election his sister Hilda had forecast a great future for him. 'You *are* a natural born leader of men', she told him, 'and I believe you will shortly be recognised as such. I don't mean you will be P.M., for many things may open or bar the way to such a post, but that you will be a leader with a devoted following before long I am sure.'

II

During the General Election of December 1918, the respective party leaders, Lloyd George for his large Liberal following and Bonar Law for the Conservatives and Liberal Unionists – they were now generally referred together simply as Unionists – issued a joint manifesto advocating the continuance of the war-time

Coalition. Favoured Coalitionist candidates – and they amounted to a majority – received a letter from Lloyd George and Bonar Law endorsing their candidatures, the letter being described by Asquith as a 'coupon', the term having been suggested by the recently discarded food ration book. Certainly the possession of the 'coupon' proved a most effective passport to Westminster, since 474 Unionists altogether were elected. The residue in the form of the Opposition consisted of 59 Labour members and 26 Asquithian Liberals, although Asquith himself was defeated. In the new Government Bonar Law continued as Leader of the House of Commons with the titular office of Lord Privy Seal. He had previously been Chancellor of the Exchequer, an office which was now given to Neville's half-brother Austen, although the Prime Minister insisted, somewhat to Austen's chagrin, that Bonar Law should be allowed to continue to occupy the Chancellor's official residence at No. 11 Downing Street on the ground that it was necessary for the Leader of the House 'to have constant access to me'.

The new House of Commons met for the first time early in February 1919. Its members were described in a phrase attributed to Stanley Baldwin, the Financial Secretary to the Treasury, as consisting for the most part of 'hard-faced men who looked as if they had done well out of the war'. Although the name of Chamberlain served Neville as a useful introduction to his new surroundings, the fact that his brother was Chancellor of the Exchequer he regarded as a mixed blessing. At what turned out to be a rather acrimonious interview between them, Neville came away with the impression that with the pressing need for economy in public expenditure Austen might well thwart Neville's housing schemes in Birmingham – he was still an alderman – and put a stop to the continuance of the Birmingham Municipal Bank. 'The fact is I always said that if I went into the House we should differ', Neville told their sister Hilda at this time, 'and we are bound to do so because our minds are differently trained. He thinks me wild and I think him unprogressive and prejudiced.'

Neville Chamberlain made his maiden speech as soon as he practically could, the occasion occurring on 12 March 1919 when he spoke for ten minutes without notes on the Rent Restriction Bill which was taken in a Committee of the whole House. His speech was in support of an amendment providing that the proposed increase of 10 per cent could not be obtained by the landlord unless he produced a certificate certifying the house fit for human habitation. The Attorney General, Sir Gordon Hewart, had already rejected the point, but he seems to have been so impressed by what the maiden speaker said that he changed his mind and undertook to insert words in the Bill to meet Neville's argument. It is rare for a maiden speech to achieve anything, but this in its small way was an exception, although the achievement did not commend itself to the Birmingham Property Owners' Association. However the *Birmingham Post* described the member's maiden effort as 'an admirable performance, good in substance, in form and in delivery'.

A week later, unusually quickly for a newcomer, he spoke again, this time on his pet subject of canals and waterways. In July, on the Committee stage of the Electricity Bill he actually defeated the Government when he carried an amendment to a new clause proposed by the Home Secretary. Finally, before the House rose in August, he took a leading part in a debate on Treasury control in a speech which Winston Churchill, who followed him, described as 'a very important and helpful speech'. None of these speeches is worth quoting verbatim from Hansard, well reasoned though they were if on humdrum topics. But the cumulative achievement of the new MP was that he had established himself as an influential backbencher in the chamber, although he was less successful on the social side, seldom being seen in the Members' Smoking Room, exchanging the latest gossip. He was more often attending in one of the committee rooms upstairs arguing some issue of local government. But his work did not go unnoticed by the Unionist Whips.

One afternoon in March 1920, after he had been barely a year in the House, he received a message from the Chief Whip that Bonar Law would like to see him in his room. Neville described the meeting in a letter to Hilda:

He asked me to sit down and with some diffidence opened up cautiously, saying that I have been head of a great department and that he didn't know what I should think of a lower place, but it had been suggested to him by [Sir Robert] Horne [President of the Board of Trade] that perhaps I might be willing to take an Under-Secretaryship. He thought I was worth more but didn't see how anything more could be offered just now. He suggested Health but said there were a number of places to be filled.

Bonar Law added that he had spoken to the Prime Minister and 'he would be very glad if I would take it'.

It is possible that this was an olive branch which Lloyd George was holding out. However Neville Chamberlain, with whom his treatment over the Department of National Service still rankled, asked for a little time to consider the offer, and then turned it down. If it was an olive branch, its rejection may throw some light on the outcome of an approach made a few months later.

Some of the Irish Nationalist MPs thought that Neville Chamberlain would make a good Chief Secretary for Ireland in view of the solution to the Irish troubles which was being put forward in the Government of Ireland Act. John Redmond, Joe Devlin, T. P. O'Connor, and Jeremiah McVeagh, with whom the idea apparently originated, were all enthusiasti cand converted some of the English ministers such as H.A.L. Fisher and the Attorney General Sir Gordon Hewart to their way of thinking. But Lloyd George's reaction probably showed pique when the proposal was conveyed to him. 'Oh, I don't like that fellow!' he said. And that was the end of the matter. So long as Lloyd George remained Prime Minister, Neville Chamberlain could not hope for political office.

Nevertheless the Coalition was beginning to show signs of strain. For one thing it was weakened when Bonar Law withdrew because of ill-health and Austen Chamberlain took his place as the Unionist party leader. There was also increasing discontent with Lloyd George, and his frequent absences made itself evident among the Conservative and Unionist rank-and-file. There were, too, unsavoury rumours of corruption and the sale of honours to which the Prime Minister was privy and which were to erupt into a national scandal. Few of his supporters thought that Bonar Law would be fit to resume the party leadership, but when things became so alarming on both the foreign and the home front he was persuaded to return to active politics, and Austen Chamberlain once more sacrificed his chances of becoming Conservative Prime Minister. Eventually the Coalition broke up in October 1922 following the famous Carlton Club meeting of Conservatives and Unionists, when the motion to fight the next General Election as an independent party was carried by a majority of more than two to one.

Neville Chamberlain was not present on this momentous occasion as he had gone off to America and Canada on a tour. But Austen was there and voted against the motion, thus remaining faithful to the Coalition and thereby excluding himself from office in the event of Lloyd George's resignation and an exclusively Unionist Government being formed by Bonar Law.

Three days after the historic Carlton Club meeting, Neville was on the high seas returning to England when he learned the news of Lloyd George's resignation, and that Bonar Law had been invited by the King to form a Government prior to the dissolution of Parliament and a General Election. 'My mind begins to clear on the political situation', he noted in his diary on 22 October.

I cannot imagine myself leaving the Unionist party for Lloyd George when there is no fundamental difference of policy. My only difficulty is Austen, and I have wondered whether I should go out of politics altogether. But that does not seem fair to the constituency or the party in Birmingham, which ought to be kept united. I don't want to do anything embarrassing to Austen, but it seems to me that he is unlikely to leave the party either, tho' he could hardly take office under Bonar Law.

By the time he arrived in England, Neville found that Bonar Law had virtually completed his Government, keeping open a post for him – that of Postmaster General, a prospect he viewed with some doubts as he knew he must first have a difficult interview with his brother.

I told him that in my view my acceptance would not be regarded as putting us in opposite camps, but rather as a link between him and the new government ... facilitating his acceptance as one of the leaders, if not the leader, in the event of Bonar Law being unable to carry on.

But Neville failed to convince his brother of the truth of this view, upon which Neville said he would refuse the office, as he cared more for their personal relations than for politics. 'But I felt bound to tell him', Neville added in his diary, 'that I should consider my political career ended, for one cannot go on refusing office when one does not differ in principles. . . . I said this in justice to myself, but not as an argument. However, it proved too much for him.' He put it more briefly to his sister Hilda: 'I went to him as soon as I had the offer and he took the idea very badly, feeling that if I accepted it would be the last drop of bitterness in the cup.'

In the event Austen withdrew his opposition and now urged Neville to accept it, which he did. Although Neville was not in the

Cabinet, his post was one of Cabinet rank, and in consequence he was sworn of the Privy Council. It was indeed a rapid rise, since he had been in the House for less than three years. His progress thereafter proceeded apace. A few months later he was promoted to be Minister of Health with a seat in the Cabinet, and Stanley Baldwin, who was now acting Prime Minister, when Bonar Law went on a health cruise in the following spring, reported that Neville Chamberlain had so far done 'extraordinarily well in his new post and the Labour men are beginning to appreciate him'.

Bonar Law returned through Paris, where he was examined by a doctor who reported that his condition was so serious that he had little time left to live – he was suffering from cancer of the throat. To the surprise of many, who had expected Lord Curzon, the Foreign Secretary and senior Conservative minister, to succeed, the King sent for Stanley Baldwin, the Chancellor of the Exchequer, and invited him to form a Government, which he undertook to do. 'I had rather hoped that Curzon would have been P.M., but I had not realised the extent of his unpopularity in the country', Neville wrote to his sister Hilda. 'The new P.M. asked me to go and see him . . . he is the nearest man we have to Bonar in the qualities of straightforwardness and sincerity.' The object of this meeting was to ask Neville Chamberlain to continue as Minister of Health, which he agreed to do, since he thoroughly liked the work of this department. But in the event it was not to be for long.

At the time Baldwin became Prime Minister, he was Chancellor of the Exchequer, but he felt unable to carry both offices. A prolonged search was undertaken to find a new Chancellor, as Robert Horne and Reginald McKenna both refused. McKenna, who was chairman of the Midland Bank, would have had to have a seat found for him in Parliament, if he accepted, and this presented difficulties. Baldwin then wrote to Neville Chamberlain, who was on a fishing holiday in Scotland, and asked him to take on the job. 'What a day', Chamberlain replied. 'Two salmon this morning and the offer of the Exchequer this afternoon!' However, although he regarded the Prime Minister's offer as 'the greatest compliment I have ever received in my life', he asked Baldwin not to press it.

'I do not think that I have any gift for finance which I have never been able to understand,' he explained with unexpected candour, 'and I feel that as Chancellor I should not fulfil your expectations'. But, on the offer being repeated, Chamberlain cut short his holiday and came back to London where, after a long interview with Baldwin, he agreed to become Chancellor. The consideration which eventually broke down his resistance was the Prime Minister's admission that he felt the need of a colleague with whom he could discuss affairs as he used to do with Bonar Law at their morning talks when he himself was Chancellor, and passed through No. 10 Downing Street on his way to the Treasury. He added that McKenna had himself suggested Chamberlain for the post. Nevertheless Chamberlain, who was looking forward to at least two more years as Minister of Health, 'thought it revealed a certain weakness in the government since the P.M. feels there is no [other] choice open to him'.

Thus it came about that Neville Chamberlain attained the second position in the Government at the age of fifty-four, and with less than four years' experience in the House of Commons. It was a record without parallel in modern English parliamentary history.

III

Neville Chamberlain moved into No. 11 Downing Street on 2 October 1923. At this date the Baldwin Government had a dependable majority in the House of Commons of around 80, and in the ordinary nature of things could look forward to a relatively long spell of power. Thus Neville Chamberlain could expect to spend three or four years at the Treasury. Yet as events turned out he had barely time to take his place as Chancellor on the Government Front Bench, let alone introduce a Budget. In fact, he remains one of the very few Chancellors in history who never did introduce a Budget, the only other whose name immediately comes to mind being, by a tragic coincidence, that of his biographer Iain Macleod.

Three days after he had moved into his official house, the new Chancellor of the Exchequer was invited to meet Baldwin at Chequers. Of this meeting he wrote to his sister Hilda on 7 October from the Prime Minister's official country residence:

I find the P.M. very seriously considering the party policy and disposed to go a long way in the direction of new duties with preference designed to help the Dominions and to develop Empire sugar, cotton and tobacco, all of which we now have to buy from the U.S.A. I need hardly say that I warmly welcome this disposition and believe it will be the salvation of the country and incidentally of the party. . . .

Look out for Baldwin's speech to the Party Conference on October 25th.

The trend of Baldwin's political thinking was greatly encouraged by the Imperial Economic Conference of Dominion and Colonial Prime Ministers which Bonar Law had convened in London at the beginning of October, and which it now fell to Baldwin as his successor to preside over. As the conference got under way, various new preferences were proposed by the President of the Board of Trade, Sir Philip Lloyd-Greame, who undertook on behalf of the Government to bring them forward in Parliament in due course. The other two strong protectionists in the Cabinet were Amery and Neville Chamberlain; these all combined to influence Baldwin's mind in the direction of tariff reform, not least as a means of reducing the unemployment figures which were rising. At the same time Bonar Law had given a pledge that there would be no fundamental change in the country's fiscal arrangements without consulting the electors. 'That pledge binds me and in this Parliament there will be no fundamental change', Baldwin declared at the Party Conference at Plymouth, 'and I take those words strictly. I am not a man to play with a pledge. . . . But at any time I am challenged, I am willing to take a verdict.'

Neville Chamberlain, who had accompanied the Prime Minister to Plymouth, addressed an overflow meeting in the Guildhall, at which he went rather further than his leader, when he stated that, if the unemployment situation were to be dealt with adequately 'next winter', it would be necessary 'that we should ask to be released from that pledge'. This was taken by *The Times* to imply

a definite decision on the part of the Cabinet to go to the country on the question of tariff reform, and it is already obvious that there is to be a great struggle between those who want an early election and those who believe that the appeal to the country should be deferred until as late as possible next year.

Two days previously Baldwin had told the Cabinet the gist of what he said at Plymouth, and the Free Traders like Lord Salisbury and the Duke of Devonshire, Lord Robert Cecil, and the Hon. Edward Wood (later Lord Halifax) were certainly taken aback and registered strong protests. But Baldwin's mind was virtually made up. Three weeks later he asked the King to dissolve Parliament, and a General Election was announced for 6 December.

What finally led Baldwin to this decision which, as he confided to his friend Tom Jones, the Assistant Secretary of the Cabinet, was 'a long-calculated and not a sudden' one? The most plausible explanation is what he described to Jones as the prospect of dishing 'the Goat' as he called Lloyd George. At this time Lloyd George was on his way back from America where he had been on a lecture tour. 'I had information that he was going protectionist and I had to get in quick', Baldwin admitted to Jones some years later. 'Otherwise he would have got the Party with Austen [Chamberlain] and F.E. [Lord Birkenhead] and there would have been an end to the Tory Party as we know it.'

Perhaps this is a convenient point at which to cite the opinion which the Chancellor's private secretary, an able young civil servant named P. J. Grigg who twenty years later was to become Secretary of State for War in Churchill's war-time administration, formed of his chief at the Treasury, and in particular of the manner in which 'he readily mastered briefs on the most complicated subjects and could expound them cogently and persuasively'.

He was a pleasant chief though shy and reserved, so that those who worked for him could rarely discover the humanity and kindliness that were undoubtedly there. Sometimes they shone through the cloud, particularly when one happened to touch on one of the Chancellor's private enthusiasms such as birds or the topography of Rome or his relations with his family. Nevertheless, reserve was the normal attitude and I am not sure that it did not lead to a certain fallibility in his judgment of persons and as a corollary to a lack of sureness in appraising political situations. Of the latter, his share in Mr Baldwin's decision to appeal to the country in October 1923 was probably a very good example and I remember an instance of the former just as he was on the point of leaving the Treasury. An old and experienced member of the House of Commons had asked to see him urgently, and when I told him this, Mr Chamberlain wondered what he wanted. I said cynically 'a peerage of course', but my master was more charitable and guessed that what was coming was an invitation to rejoin the board of a company with which he had been connected some years earlier. When the interview was over, Mr Chamberlain confessed somewhat sadly that I had been right.

Conservative Central Office was confident from reports from the constituencies that the Tories would get an overall majority of 87.

In the event they found themselves in a minority of 97, a swing of 11.8 per cent against the Government. As in 1906, the Tories had been defeated by the cry of 'dear food'. They were still the largest party in the House of Commons with 257 seats, Labour coming second with 191 and the Liberals getting 158. Baldwin had asked the country for a mandate for tariff reform, he told the King's Private Secretary Lord Stamfordham after he had consulted Neville Chamberlain and his close confidant John Davidson; this had been refused and the honourable thing would be for him to resign at once, he argued. However, the King inclined to the view that Baldwin should first meet Parliament. In the event the Government was defeated by a hostile Labour amendment to the Address on the King's Speech, the majority of the Liberals voting with Labour. Baldwin resigned early next day and the King invited Ramsay MacDonald, as the leader of the next largest party in the Commons, to form an administration. This he was able to do, thus becoming the first Labour Prime Minister in British history. But he headed a minority government and could be turned out any time the Liberals chose.

Baldwin was conscious that he was the target for a good deal of discontent on the part of many of his followers for his disastrous decision over the election. Astute politician that he was, he realized that, if he was to maintain his position as party leader, he must reunite the Tories by bringing back the Coalition dissidents such as Austen Chamberlain and Birkenhead to the Unionist fold. Consequently, as soon as Neville Chamberlain had returned from a ski-ing holiday towards the end of January, Baldwin asked him to go for a walk with him in St James's Park. According to Chamberlain, Baldwin seemed reluctant to come to the point, talking about the pelicans in the park and the beauty of spring at his country home in Worcestershire. Finally, in the interests of reunion he suggested that, as he had not written to Austen, not wishing to take such a step without letting Neville know, the three of them should dine together in the Atheneaeum Club. 'Better dine with me', Neville countered. 'Then no one will know anything about it!' Baldwin agreed, and the dinner was fixed for 5 February at Neville's house in Eaton Square.

Before they parted Neville gave his leader some good advice as to how to break the ice when they met. 'Say "I have decided to ask you *and your friends* to sit with us on the Front Bench and to invite you to join our councils on just the same footing as if you had been members of the late Cabinet." ' Neville emphasized that Baldwin should not show the slightest hesitation. Otherwise Austen might say that Baldwin did not know his own mind and was only playing with him. Again Baldwin agreed, saying he thought Neville's suggestions were on the right lines. Nevertheless Neville remained uncertain until the night of the dinner how far Baldwin would adopt them.

The dinner took place as arranged, the only other person present being Anne Chamberlain, who left the others to their port and cigars as soon as the meal was over. Austen was rather stiff at first, since he was still feeling sore that he had not been included in the first Baldwin Government. But he gradually thawed, and by the end of the evening it was 'my dear Stanley' and 'my dear Austen', as if they had never parted.

'Well', said Baldwin after Mrs Chamberlain had left them, 'I think that in the present circumstances and in the position in which we are now it is time for all of us to get together.' To Neville's considerable relief Baldwin took exactly the line he had suggested at their previous meeting, inviting Austen to sit on the Opposition Front Bench and also to come to the first meeting of the Shadow Cabinet which he had summoned for two days hence, and to which (he said) he would also invite Birkenhead and Balfour.

Austen Chamberlain replied, after a moment's hesitation, that to such a proposal, so made, he could give only one answer. He accepted, and he added that he was in a position to say that his friend Lord Birkenhead would do the same. 'So reunion has come at last', Neville noted in his diary, 'thanks I may say to me.'

At the meeting of the Shadow Cabinet, the presence of Austen and the other Coalitionists such as Horne was tacitly accepted and everything went smoothly. It was agreed by all except Amery that the tariff question should be dropped for the present, and Neville was asked to keep a particular eye on the likelihood of any developments.

During the short-lived Labour Government, Neville Chamberlain wisely put himself forward as the Opposition spokesman on health and housing, where he gave a good account of himself in debating with the minister John Wheatley, a militant Clydesider and perhaps the ablest departmental head in Ramsay MacDonald's

administration. Although he was an ex-Chancellor, Neville intervened much less in financial debates, leaving this to more experienced colleagues who had been at the Treasury, such as his brother
Austen and Robert Horne. The fiercest tussle took place over the
Rent and Mortgage Bill, Clause 1 of which proposed that if rent
was in arrears because the tenant was unemployed, the Court could
authorize the tenant to withhold it *unless the landlord could prove
that he would thereby suffer the greater hardship.* Neville had little
difficulty in annihilating this proposition. Why should it be confined to housing? If an unemployed man were coatless, had he not
a right to the Minister of Health's coat? And if a landlord were also
a tenant, could he refuse to pay his rent, if he had been deprived of
his income? And who, under these circumstances, would ever
willingly let his house again?

Asquith followed and announced that the Liberals could not
support the controversial clause. J. R. Clynes, the Lord Privy Seal
and Deputy Leader of the House of Commons, tried to save the
principle of the Bill embodied in this clause – the other clauses
were uncontroversial and unimportant. He promised to bring forward an amendment which would place on public funds the cost of
maintaining the tenant in his home. But when the Prime Minister,
after pondering over the clause for a week-end, produced a new
clause no one could understand it, and Ramsay MacDonald, who
clearly could not understand it himself, gave up the effort to
explain. Consequently the division on the second reading of the
measure was carried against the Government. Although the Prime
Minister had declared on taking office that he would only resign on
a major issue and this could hardly be regarded as such, nevertheless it was only a matter of time before the Liberals would turn
the Government out. The opportunity came in the early autumn
over the question of the prosecution of the editor of a Communist
organ called *The Workers Weekly*, as a result of which the Government was defeated. At the ensuing General Election the Conservatives were returned by a large majority, substantially increased at
the last moment by a 'Red scare' in the shape of a letter allegedly
written by Gregory Zinoviev, the head of the Third International,
and designed to create disaffection in Britain's armed forces. (Years
later the letter was proved to be a forgery.)

The General Election of October 1924 was a resounding Tory
triumph, the Conservatives outnumbering the other two parties by

more than 200, and the Liberals being largely wiped out, losing 116 seats, mainly to the Conservatives, and over a million votes compared with the 1923 election – a mere rump under the uneasy leadership of Lloyd George. Asquith lost his seat and was compensated with a peerage by the generously disposed Baldwin.

Ironically enough, one of the hardest fought contests was for Ladywood, Neville Chamberlain's seat in Birmingham. This was due in large measure to the outstanding abilities and energy of the Labour candidate Sir Oswald Mosley, who had only been adopted six weeks previously for this largely working-class constituency. But his oratory made an extraordinary impression. In the result Neville Chamberlain only succeeded in holding the seat by 77 votes after four recounts.

Mrs Chamberlain worked magnificently on the other side in street canvass [Mosley has recalled], but when it came to demagogy Neville was not in the ring. An able administrator . . . he had no great appeal to the masses. During the count he sat huddled up in a corner, either exercising an iron self-control or in a state of near collapse; his agents did everything and he never moved. The count was a drama . . . Chamberlain was declared the winner, we left the Town Hall at six o'clock in the morning to find an enormous crowd in the square outside which had waited up all night to hear the result; they were singing the Red Flag. They seized me and carried me around with an enthusiasm which deeply moved me. I decided to remain in Birmingham. . . .

For anyone who has witnessed, or better still as a candidate has experienced, an electoral count after the ballot boxes have been opened, the experience can be trying and indeed agonizing. It is at the discretion of the returning officer who shall be admitted to the count as spectators. On this occasion the Labour candidate's supporters appeared in some strength. 'The galleries of the Town Hall were filled with Socialists, who booed at us, even invaded the floor with yelled insults,' Chamberlain noted afterwards. 'We hated the idea of being beaten, especially by that viper.' So much for 'the peaceful co-operation of all classes' for which Chamberlain had pleaded during his campaign.

However, in spite of his near setback in his native city, Neville Chamberlain was quick to appreciate the significance of the composition of the new House of Commons. 'What alarms me now is the size of our majority, which is most dangerous,' he confessed to his sister Ida. 'Unless we leave our mark as Social Reformers the country will take it out of us hereafter. But what we do will depend on how the Cabinet is made up. Poor S.B.!'

IV

The life of the first Labour Government was formally terminated on 4 November 1924 when Ramsay MacDonald went to Buckingham Palace and tendered his resignation as Prime Minister. Later the same day the King sent for Baldwin and entrusted him with the formation of a fresh Government. In doing so, the King urged the new Premier to get to grips with such questions as housing, education, unemployment and the cost of food, and to select for this purpose 'able, efficient and energetic administrators'. The King added that he would welcome it personally if Austen Chamberlain were chosen for the post of Foreign Secretary.

The new Prime Minister immediately agreed to the elder Chamberlain's appointment to the Foreign Office. Indeed he already had it in mind, he said. At the same time, he told the King that he proposed to invite Mr Winston Churchill to join the Government at once. This would have to be done sooner or later, he said, and he thought 'it better to give him office now rather than run the chance of his having a grievance and being disgruntled at being omitted'.

As one of the leading Coalition Conservatives whom Baldwin was anxious to include in his new administration, Sir Robert Horne was an obvious choice as Chancellor, since he had previously held the post with some distinction in the last Lloyd George Government. However, Baldwin wanted to have Neville Chamberlain back at the Treasury, since his previous tenure had been so brief. Accordingly he wrote to Horne offering him the Ministry of Labour, but without saying anything about either raising the status or the salary of the office, thus failing to make it clear whether it carried a seat in the Cabinet. Horne was consequently very upset and he complained to Austen Chamberlain about it. Austen passed on Horne's complaint to Baldwin.

You have cut an old friend to the quick. You will remember that the fairest reason you gave me for not offering Horne the Treasury was that you wanted Neville there. I told you that Horne would accept the Treasury, but that I did not think he would take Labour, whilst Neville would gladly go to Health if Horne went to Exchequer. I am afraid my opinion carries no weight with you.

Baldwin had not heard from Horne when Neville Chamberlain called upon the Prime Minister, at the latter's request, at Conservative Party Headquarters where Baldwin spent most of 5 November 1924 completing the principal posts in his ministry.

'Needless to say I want you to go back to the Treasury', the Prime Minister began after Neville had been shown in. Neville made no comment, and Baldwin went on to say that he had offered Horne the Ministry of Labour and was awaiting his reply. At this moment a letter was brought in and handed to Baldwin. It turned out to be from Horne. The Prime Minister read it and said: 'He won't take it'. In his letter Horne carefully chose the phrase 'personal circumstances' to indicate that his refusal was not due to his business commitments, thus delivering a calculated snub. As Horne told Austen Chamberlain, he 'would not be forced upon a man who did not want him'.

Later in the course of the conversation Churchill's name came up, and Baldwin told Neville that he had decided to take him in at once. 'He would be more under control inside than out', he remarked, adding that he thought of making him Minister of Health. According to Neville, Baldwin then asked him what post he would like. Neville replied that he had given the matter full consideration, and that he would like to go back to Health, since this department included responsibility for housing in which he had a particular interest. 'But who then could be Chancellor?' Baldwin asked. After Neville had suggested Sir Samuel Hoare, a former Air Minister, and Baldwin had turned this down, what happened was described by Neville in his diary.

He [Baldwin] mentioned Winston but said he supposed there would be a howl from the party. I said I thought there would but that would be so if he came in at all, and I did not know if it would be much louder if he went to the Treasury than to the Admiralty. On the whole I was inclined to say that Winston Churchill for the Treasury was worth further consideration.

The Prime Minister did not say who his next visitor was, but on the way out Neville immediately discovered his identity when he

44

recognized one of Churchill's unmistakable hats in the waiting room. Apparently Churchill was shown into Baldwin's room by another entrance so that he should not encounter Chamberlain on his way in.

The Prime Minister immediately asked Churchill if he would serve as Chancellor. According to Baldwin's official biographer, G. M. Young, Churchill thought he was being offered the Chancellorship of the Duchy of Lancaster, a sinecure post sometimes given to elder supporters whom the Prime Minister wished to have in the Government with little to do apart from offering occasional advice, and administering the Duchy of Lancaster through the departmental officials. When he realized that it was the Exchequer that the Prime Minister had in mind, Churchill was completely taken aback and showed it by his emotion. Tears came into his eyes, as he stammered his acceptance of Baldwin's surprising offer. He thereupon pledged his loyalty to his new chief, adding: 'You have done more for me than Lloyd George ever did.'

It has been suggested that Baldwin's interviews with Neville Chamberlain and Churchill were part of a deliberately stage-managed drama, and that Baldwin intended all along to send Churchill to the Treasury, since he had already been told by Austen Chamberlain that his brother would like to go back to Health and Housing. ('I ought to be a great Minister of Health', Neville remarked at the time, 'but am not likely to be more than a second-rate Chancellor.') According to Tom Jones, who spent the following weekend at Chequers, Baldwin told him (Jones) that the idea of making Churchill Chancellor originated with Neville Chamberlain. Whatever the truth of the matter may be – and there seems no reason to doubt Baldwin's word – the appointment was a clever move on his part. Furthermore it seems to have been made more or less on the spur of the moment.

On the advice of his principal Treasury officials and the leading City financiers and bankers led by Mr Montagu Norman, the Governor of the Bank of England, Winston Churchill, with Baldwin's assent, made the momentous but (as the economist Maynard Keynes accurately predicted at the time) disastrous decision in the spring of 1925 to return to the gold standadr at the pre-war parity. This caused the pound sterling to be fatally over-valued in terms of foreign currencies, with the result that exports were penalized and imports encouraged, to the detriment of the balance of trade. Looking back many years later Churchill described it 'the biggest blunder' of his life. It was this decision that dominated his first Budget, in itself a strictly orthodox affair, which in the Prime Minister's view followed 'the soundest lines of prudence and Conservative finance', reducing income tax by sixpence, giving some relief to surtax payers and, somewhat surprisingly for a wholehearted free trader like Churchill, imposing duties on artificial silk and lace. The object of these latter duties was to meet the cost of the new contributory old age pensions scheme, which was really Neville Chamberlain's brainchild, rather than doing this by direct taxation.

There is an illuminating entry in Chamberlain's diary written when he and Churchill were discussing the pensions scheme, for which in fact it was thought that Churchill got too much credit and Chamberlain too little.

He [Churchill] wished to treat the subject free from personalities (I gathered that he meant he wasn't going to claim *all* the credit for himself), it would have to be my bill but that he would have to find the money and the question was would I stand in with him, would I enter partnership and work the plan with him *keeping everything secret*?

Chamberlain assured the Chancellor that he liked his idea and would consider it favourably, that personalities did not enter into the question so far as he was concerned and that he would communicate with him again on the subject. 'It seemed plain to me that he regretted still that he was not Minister of Health', Chamberlain noted in conclusion, 'a man of tremendous drive and vivid imagination'.

In fact, the Widows, Orphans and Old Age Pensions Act was introduced in fulfilment of the Party's election pledges, as Chamberlain made clear when he moved the third reading in the Commons. There was nothing to be ashamed of in this, he argued, and it ought not to be regarded as something in the nature of an election bribe. 'It is because we believe that a measure of this kind, a contributory scheme of pensions, was right and good', he declared, 'because we believe it would have a great effect in strengthening the moral character of the nation, that we have advocated it at Election times and that we are now carrying it into effect.'

If the Pensions Bill was the highlight of the session and caught the popular imagination – even the King congratulated Chamberlain on the 'remarkable skill, patience, and courtesy' with which he piloted it through the House – the Minister's most substantial achievement, forming as it did the keystone of his future work for local government, was the revolutionary change in the system of rating and valuation of property which had been in use since Elizabethan times. Broadly speaking, the purpose of Chamberlain's Rating and Valuation Bill was four-fold – firstly, to transfer rating powers from the poor law guardians in the parishes to 'the real living bodies of today', that is the county, borough and district councils; secondly, to achieve a single basis of valuation, including that for income tax, instead of three or four; thirdly, to standardize assessment instead of having a network of differing deductions and contradictory methods in different districts; and fourthly, to keep rating up to date by a single system of quinquennial valuations. Thus there would be a single rating authority with uniform methods.

The measure involved 12,000 parish overseers losing their powers to 648 new rating authorities, and 600 poor law boards of guardians to 343 new assessment areas. It aroused considerable opposition, particularly among the Tory county members who complained that the Bill 'nationalised local government and seriously affected the liberties of our English country people'. And so in a way it did. But with an autumn parliamentary session and help from the Labour benches it eventually became law. 'I slaved away at it day and night till one in the morning', Chamberlain noted, 'so that when the time came I had mastered the beastly thing.' His worst ordeal came when both it and the Widows, Orphans and Old Age Pensions Bill were in Committee at the same time and Chamberlain was in charge of both.

Here is how he described his experience in a letter to Ida dated 5 July 1925:

On Tuesday I started on the R. and V. Committee at 11 and on the Pensions Bill at 4 and then sat right on till 7 a.m. At 9 a.m. I got out of bed again and went to the office, where I arrived soon after 10. At 11.30 we had Cabinet till 1.30.

At 2.30 I addressed the International Congress of Radiologists and at 3.45 I began Pensions again and sat on till 6 a.m. on Thursday. At 11 I got out of bed, having breakfasted, and went to the office; I lunched at the House and answered my questions as a demonstration and then went on Pensions again till 8.15.

Chamberlain's easy relations with Churchill were fortunate; they necessarily had to be in frequent consultation, since Churchill had to find the money which Chamberlain needed for his schemes of social reform. In a private letter which Chamberlain wrote to the Prime Minister shortly after Parliament rose for the summer recess in 1925, Chamberlain gave an interesting assessment of Churchill's character and record:

Looking back over our first session I think our Chancellor has done very well, all the better because he hasn't been what he was expected to be. He hasn't dominated the Cabinet, though undoubtedly he has influenced it: he hasn't tied us up to pedantic Free Trade, though he is a bit sticky about the safeguarding of industries. He hasn't intrigued for the leadership, but he has been a tower of debating strength in the House of Commons. And taking him all round, I don't think there can be any dispute but that he has been a source of influence and prestige to the Government as a whole . . . .

There is no doubt that you made us both happy, and I for one have never for a moment regretted the decision I made or envied Winston his pre-eminence. What a brilliant creature he is! But there is somehow a gulf fixed between him and me which I didn't think I should ever cross.

But cross that gulf Chamberlain succeeded in doing, because he liked the man. 'I liked him', he told the Prime Minister. 'I liked his humour and his vitality. . . . But not for all the joys of Paradise would I be a member of his staff! Mercurial! a much abused word, but it is the literal description of his temperament.' One reason for their affinity possibly lies in the fact that neither was a Tory, or at least only one in the sense of that 'Tory democracy' which both their fathers had endeavoured to fashion. 'Our policy', Chamberlain declared in introducing the Pensions Bill – and here he spoke for Churchill as well as himself – 'is to use the great resources of the state, not for the distribution of an indiscriminate largesse, but to help those who have the will and desire to raise themselves to higher and better things.'

It was typical of Neville Chamberlain and his immense powers of application and industry that on taking office as Minister of Health he should have sketched out a programme of legislation including twenty-five Bills to be introduced under a definite time-table during the next three years. And it was a great tribute to his determination that no fewer than twenty-one of his contemplated measures should have been enacted during this period. 'I should never be a favourite with the press, like Father was or Winston is', he remarked when he began at the Ministry of Health. But he hoped nevertheless to make a substantial contribution to the field of local government. And in great measure he was to succeed. Indeed the historian A. J. P. Taylor rightly regards him as the most effective social reformer of the inter-war years, although in the field of foreign affairs his brother Austen enjoyed a much more popular if in the event less solid reputation as the author of the Treaty of Locarno which marked the end of the first year of Baldwin's second term as Prime Minister. Incidentally Austen's acceptance of the honour of Knight of the Garter for his accomplishment at Locarno at first shocked Neville, since the acceptance of honours was very much against the Chamberlain family tradition; but Neville eventually came round and jocularly suggested to his brother that he ought to take a peerage on the ground that 'if one was to have a title, one might as well go the whole hog and have a good one.'

It is not possible here to enter into all the detail of Neville Chamberlain's legislative achievements as Minister of Health at this period. By securing the full co-operation of private builders as well as of the local councils, he solved the immediate housing problem: by the time he left office before the General Election in 1929 nearly one million houses had been built. Fifty-eight slum clearance schemes were confirmed at the same time.

Shortly after Highbury was sold, the Chamberlain sisters Ida and Hilda moved to Hampshire, partly because they wanted to be near their brothers and partly because they wished to take part in some public work in a country area conveniently near London. While Hilda became a local school governor, Ida was elected to the County Council, becoming an alderman a few years later and remaining one until her death in 1943. She became something of an authority on rural housing, and Neville frequently took her advice. Austen Chamberlain wrote at this time that both the sisters were

very pleased because with the aid of Neville's rural housing act they are gradually getting all the bad cottages in the neighbourhood put into good repair and made weatherproof and decent sanitary arrangements made. . . . What with impoverished and careless landlords and speculators, the cottage property in the neighbourhood was in a really shocking condition and it delights them to see in their walks now this cottage, now that taken in hand and made decent for the poor old folks to live in.

49

Best of all, perhaps, Neville Chamberlain was mainly instrumental in passing the important Local Government Act of 1929 which completed the work of the Rating and Valuation Act by abolishing all the remaining poor law boards of guardians and recasting the financial relations of the State and the local authorities. His speech in the House of Commons in moving the Bill's second reading, which contained over a hundred clauses, lasted two and a half hours, and when he sat down the House cheered continuously for several minutes – one Cabinet colleague said he had never known anything like it in all his eighteen years' membership of the House. 'What particularly struck and touched me', Neville noted in his diary that night, 'was that Liberals and Labour men joined with great heartiness in paying their acknowledgements.'

The final accolade was conferred by *The Times* which wrote in a leading article on 27 March 1929:

It may safely be predicted that when the history of the present age is written the Local Government Act of 1929 will take its place as one of the outstanding legislative achievements of the twentieth century. Hardly ever in the whole course of our Parliamentary history has a Government in its last year of office ventured to initiate a measure which, while containing so little to attract the popular favours so eagerly pursued by the party tacticians, appeals so profoundly to all that is solid and statesmanlike in the judgment of the country.

The credit for this remarkable achievement must be accorded in the first place to Mr Neville Chamberlain.... Nor should it be forgotten how much these great reforms owe to the imagination and courage of Mr Churchill.

Baldwin had arranged that the General Election should take place in May 1929. Again it did not occur to him that he would be defeated when the country went to the polls. Almost up to the start of the campaign he was thinking of the composition of his new Government and sounding out his particular friends and advisers. Some months previously he had discussed the possibilities of leadership, 'if anything happened to him', as he told Neville Chamberlain. 'He did not want to go out', Neville noted at the time, 'for he doubted if the party was ripe for a successor', and he 'thought the party would select Hogg or myself, probably myself'. In fact, Sir Douglas Hogg, the Attorney General, was popular with the Tory rank and file in the Commons and was a better debater than Neville. However, owing to a misunderstanding consequent upon the offer of the Lord Chancellorship to Hogg and the time given to him by the Prime Minister to decide whether or not to accept, the die was cast and the Attorney Generalship, which Hogg was presumed to have vacated, was given to Sir Thomas Inskip. 'Poor Douglas was very unhappy,' Neville wrote to Hilda on 31 March 1928, 'for his political career, and of course the tragedy is that he is now barred from the chance of becoming P.M. when S.B. retires.'

To my mind this is a great misfortune for I believe he would have a very good chance and I am sure he is the best man we have for such a position. . . . He and I have been very close together on nearly every point that has arisen and I have a very high opinion of his character and judgment. I would gladly serve under him as I believe he would under me, but I have never regarded him as a rival, *having no ambition to become P.M. myself* [Author's italics].

Earlier the same month Baldwin had asked Neville which he would prefer, the Colonial Office or the Exchequer. Neville replied that he would be pleased to become Colonial Secretary as his father had been before him, but that if it suited Baldwin better that he should go to the Treasury he would not refuse to consider it. 'His comment was that it would be an extraordinarily popular appointment in the party', Neville noted in his diary. 'For one thing they liked to have the next man to the P.M. in that office.'

We discussed the possibility of a stalemate between Socialists and Conservatives with L[loyd] G[eorge] holding the balance . . . S.B. said the King's government must be carried on, but that he personally would not serve with L.G. I said I was in the same position, and S.B. said in that case he supposed the leadership would go to Winston.

'I am trusting to the decency of the British public', Baldwin remarked to Tom Jones on the eve of the poll. 'I believe they will recognise the good work we have done and will not be deluded by Lloyd George.' In the event he was wrong. It was 1923 all over again. As in 1923 the Liberals held the balance, with 59 seats, between Labour's 287 and the Conservatives' 261, although owing to the peculiarities of the British electoral system slightly more people voted Tory than Labour. This time Neville Chamberlain was home and dry, since he had transferred from the uncertainties of Ladywood to the safe middle-class haven of Edgbaston, which he was to continue to represent until his death.

'The election has come and gone in disaster', Neville noted in his diary on 8 June 1929. 'We are out and R. MacDonald has formed his second Cabinet. After all, S.B. dallied so long with reconstruction that it never came. . . . I thought perhaps the general respect and affection with which he is regarded would have overborne everything else, but it was not so.'

Neville Chamberlain's assessment of the situation and his forecast of the future were to prove remarkably accurate.

L.G. finished up with less than 60 seats. His effort to revive his party has failed, thank Heaven, and we may hope that the process of disintegration will now continue until it is absorbed by others. But I am convinced that the explanation of the result of the election is to be found in the ceaseless propaganda that has been going on for years among the working classes to the effect that things would never be right for them till a 'Labour' came in. . . .

There is no conversion to Socialism. It is merely the present discontents showing themselves in a desire for change. And since L.G. is not in a position to dictate terms and dare not yet ally himself openly with Socialists, what has happened is perhaps the best thing for the country that could have occurred.

R[amsay] M[acDonald]'s game is clear enough. Keep very moderate, and quiet suspicions and fears for two years. Then say to the proletariat, 'if we have not been able to do all you like, that is because we have not had a majority. Here is a budget which really offers you a good taste of the millenium, and all at the expense of the rich. Give us real power, and it is yours.'

I think it quite possible that he may succeed. In that case we are out for 7 years, and then if we come back I shall be 67 if I were alive, and I daresay politics will have ceased to interest me. On the other hand, the new government may make such blunders that, before two years are up, the country will be glad to be rid of them.

The day after he wrote these words Neville recorded that he had already received an offer of the chairmanship of a new company at a salary far exceeding that of a Minister of Health. 'I fear that so big a bribe portends a risky transaction', he opined, 'and I can't afford to risk my reputation.' Whatever the offer was, he refused it.

V

For the second time in less than six years Baldwin had led his Party to electoral defeat. It was hardly surprising that some of his followers should have begun to murmur and as the months passed to talk in the clubs and in the lobbies increasingly of a need for a change in the leadership. The movement was to escalate, more perhaps to Neville Chamberlain's embarrassment than to Baldwin's since Chamberlain, though coming more and more to be acknowledged in the Party as the heir-apparent, was too loyal to Baldwin to entertain any design to supplant him. The two met after the summer recess in 1929 and Neville spoke frankly to his leader, as he told Hilda in a letter he wrote to her on 26 October:

I told him of the criticisms that were reaching me from all quarters about his want of leadership and told him that he must give a lead and be a bit more aggressive if the Party was to be held together. . . .

It was all very depressing and particularly embarrassing for me because everyone I meet tells me of S.B.'s failings and many suggest that I should do better in his place. Heaven knows I don't want the job. It is a thankless one at any time and never more now when the Party is all to pieces. Moreover S.B. is my friend as well as my leader and I would not on any account play L.G. to his Asquith.

Neville added in this letter to his sister that he was thankful he was going to leave the country for a time. He had arranged a tour of East Africa which was to occupy the greater part of two months and take him through Kenya, Uganda and Tanganyika. There was the usual round of inspecting schools and hospitals and railway workshops and agricultural research laboratories as might be expected for a visiting VIP. Nevertheless he managed to get a little fishing, catching rainbow trout at Nyeri. Once when his car got stuck in a donga on the plains of Athi, they were stranded for four hours in pitch darkness to the accompaniment of the snorting and roaring of wild animals before rescue came. Speaking at Dar-es-Salaam he took as his text his father's two lines of conduct, 'trusteeship for the backward races and development of undeveloped estates'. In regard to the latter he noted with a touch of humour how many settlers had come out to East Africa 'with a little capital and no experience and now had a little experience and no capital'. On his return home he stressed how some closer union of

53

the territories would help development plans to go forward, a dream which was to fail in projected Federation and has yet to be realized in the Organization for African Unity.

Tory discontent was also vented on the head of the Party Chairman John Davidson, who was somewhat unfairly blamed for the loss of the election and relieved of his post by Baldwin, who persuaded Neville Chamberlain to take on this rather thankless task. 'The tide is flowing our way strongly', wrote Austen a week or so after his brother was installed in Davidson's chair in Palace Chambers, 'but shall we escape fresh blunders? Both Neville and I are driven nearly to despair by S.B.'s ways, but between us we are getting order into our affairs by degrees, greatly to the satisfaction of our colleagues. Neville does the heavy work and I do the trimmings.'

At the same time Austen was anything but pleased that his brother had become saddled with the Party Chairmanship, and he wrote in this sense to their sister Ida:

I am more than ever vexed that S.B. should have prevailed upon him to take the Central Office. It requires too much time and what is worse it involves him in difficulties and enmities which ought not to be his affair. So much do I feel this that I even sounded him as to my undertaking to bell the cat and gently indicating to S.B. that it was time for him to go, but Neville thought I should do more harm than good and asked me not to try it. So there we are – none of us happy except S.B. and his cronies and Neville's future chances being seriously jeopardised by his new office and his old leader.

At this time both the powerful Press barons Rothermere and Beaverbrook were vigorously attacking Baldwin in their newspapers and calling for his resignation. In fact Rothermere, who owned the *Daily Mail*, went further and made it known to Neville Chamberlain that both he (Rothermere) and Beaverbrook were prepared to give the Conservative Party '100 per cent' support provided Neville Chamberlain were substituted for Baldwin as leader.

Austen Chamberlain's reaction was very much in character and expressed in a letter he wrote to Ida:

On the other hand, I doubt whether Baldwin can recover his position. For one thing he seems to be living in a fool's paradise and to deceive himself completely about the state of things. For another, he is, I fear, incapable of giving that active fighting lead which is so essential.

However, Neville was more cautious in his assessment. 'If any move is made', he told Austen, 'it should really come from the House of Commons which makes, and can presumably unmake, leaders.'

Fortunately for Baldwin, he struck the right note at Caxton Hall, although he was apprehensive before the meeting began. 'Photograph me now', he told the Press photographers who crowded round him at the entrance. 'It may be the last time you will see me.' However, as his private secretary Geoffrey Fry told Tom Jones, he had 'a marvellous reception, made a very good speech, very dignified . . . there was no question of his resigning. All the niceness of the man came out.' The 'free hand' on fiscal policy, for which Baldwin asked at Neville Chamberlain's prompting, was endorsed with only one dissentient – Lord Beaverbrook; and the meeting went on to pass a vote of confidence in the Leader by 462 votes to 116. 'I was not surprised at the size of the minority', W. C. Bridgeman, a former First Lord of the Admiralty and strong supporter of Baldwin, wrote to Neville Chamberlain a few days later. 'If only people knew who were there, they would realise that if we were 4 to 1 in numbers we were 20 to 1 in intelligence.' At the same time, Bridgeman added, 'I have already hinted to S.B. that he must keep on fighting as a party leader, and you are right in thinking that he should see and talk to as many people as possible.'

Baldwin's tendentially unpredictable behaviour at this time proved a sore trial to Neville Chamberlain, who was trying hard as Chairman to keep the Party together in face of continuing dissensions. Baldwin would suddenly cancel meetings without letting any of his colleagues know, and once, when he cried off making a short appearance in a film about Disraeli on the pretext that he had strained a ligament in his foot during his sleep, Chamberlain commented sardonically: 'Any ordinary mortal would have telephoned to save me going round to his house, but the poetic temperament doesn't work that way.' Then, after a Party luncheon to the Australian delegation at the Imperial Conference, Chamberlain complained: 'S.B. would only make jokes about his leg and couldn't be got into general conversation.' A few weeks later, Chamberlain wrote despondently in his diary:

The question of leadership is again growing acute. . . . I am getting letters and communications from all over the country. . . . Sam Hoare . . .

reports that the feeling in the House could not be worse. I cannot see any way out. I am the one person who might bring about S.B.'s retirement but I cannot act when my action might put me in his place.

The trouble about Baldwin was that, as a believer in what is usually termed today consensus politics, he was a failure as a Leader of the Opposition. Lord Derby, a strong Conservative who carried great influence in industrial Lancashire, wrote to Neville Chamberlain a few days after the diary entry quoted above, incidentally echoing what Austen had said about living in a fool's paradise.

The worst of Baldwin is his leadership. His policy is good: he makes, as a rule, very excellent speeches, but after that he fails as a leader. He has no hold on his party; he doesn't seem to want to keep in touch with them. He listens to all the agreeable things that are said, and not to any of the disagreeable ones, and he never seems to want to cultivate the good opinion of the younger members of his party.

Between ourselves, I think Mrs Baldwin has done him incalculable harm. She may be quite right to spare him as a general rule, but surely she ought to let him know some of the criticisms which I know she hears herself but which she keeps from him. The worst thing for a man like that is to be allowed to live in a fool's paradise.

At the beginning of March 1931, the King's Private Secretary Sir Clive Wigram, who had succeeded Lord Stamfordham, saw Baldwin and asked him what he thought of the political situation. 'He said he thought it was distinctly rocky', according to Wigram, 'and, with a wink, added that his own situation was not too bright.' Wigram asked him if, supposing Ramsay MacDonald resigned and the King sent for Baldwin, he would be able to form a Government? 'No, certainly not', he answered without hesitation. 'Lloyd George would have me out in a week on a vote of confidence on tariffs. If the King sent for me, I could only recommend a dissolution.'

At this crucial moment in the Conservative leader's political fortunes, two things happened which affected the demand for his resignation. There was a by-election pending in the St George's Division of Westminster, where the Press lords Rothermere and Beaverbrook were putting up an anti-Baldwinite candidate with the object of splitting the Conservative vote. Baldwin's first stroke of luck was when Mr Duff Cooper, who had been a junior minister in the last Baldwin Government but had lost his seat in the 1929 General Election, now gave up the safe seat he was nursing at Winchester and offered himself to the official constituency association at St George's where he was warmly welcomed and adopted as the official candidate.

Baldwin's second stroke of luck arose over India, where the Viceroy Lord Irwin (later Earl of Halifax) had been able to reach an understanding with the Congress Party leader Mahatma Gandhi, which had resulted in Gandhi calling off his campaign of civil disobedience. This gave Baldwin the opportunity of publicly complimenting the Viceroy on pledging eventual Dominion status for India, which he did in the House of Commons. 'The unchanging east has changed, is changing with alarming rapidity, and there are many people who are blind not to see it', he declared in a speech which his friend Tom Jones regarded as one of the best he had ever made. 'The ultimate result depends not on force, but on good will, sympathy and understanding.' Incidentally, it was on this declared policy towards India that Winston Churchill had recently resigned from the Conservative Shadow Cabinet, dismissing the Indian claims as 'absurd and dangerous pretensions'. Meanwhile Baldwin proclaimed that 'the great work of Lord Irwin is that he has bridged the gulf by ability and character, and when the history of the time comes to be written, his name will stand out as one of the greatest Viceroys, and as a Viceroy I had the honour of myself sending to India.'

This for the moment has confirmed him in the Leadership [wrote Tom Jones a few days later], but the Party is honeycombed with faction and disloyalty and how long he can hold his position no one can tell. Much will depend on the way the St George's election goes. There are, I need hardly say, many aspirants for the leadership. . . . Winston at the moment is the darling of the diehards.

Austen Chamberlain stirred up some trouble at a meeting of the Conservative Shadow Cabinet at this time by asking Baldwin bluntly when he was going to release his brother from the Party Chairmanship. He did so on the ostensible ground that the Opposition Front Bench debating strength had been considerably depleted, particularly by Churchill's defection. 'It was pretty plain what he had in mind', noted Neville in his diary, namely a need for a change in the leadership, and this immediately determined

Neville to ask to be relieved of his Central Office job. Thus he wrote to his leader:

There was always the consciousness that my name is one of several who might succeed you if you decided to retire and although I do not think I have been ever influenced by any such considerations it is intensely disagreeable to think that interested motives might be attributed to me by others.

Another cause of irritation was the fact that the St George's election campaign had been or was being planned without enlisting Chamberlain's help and knowledge as Party Chairman. It appeared that contrary to the usual practice by which a leader keeps aloof from by-elections, Baldwin intended to intervene in this one and his intention had come to Chamberlain's ears. 'Of course I could not make any plans (nor have I yet begun to) until I had talked it over with the Chairman', wrote Baldwin, apologizing for any apparent and unintentional discourtesy. 'Very few things in politics have the power to hurt me'; Baldwin added: 'it would hurt me if I felt a shadow of misunderstanding between us.'

Duff Cooper easily defeated the Press lords' candidate by over 5000 votes, a victory to which Baldwin contributed in a speech in the Queen's Hall embodying a phrase which subsequently became famous – said to have been suggested by his cousin Rudyard Kipling – in which he denounced what the proprietorship of these papers was aiming at, namely 'power, and *power without responsibility – the prerogative of the harlot throughout the ages'*.

Baldwin's leadership was never again to be challenged by members of his own political party. Neville Chamberlain, who might have grasped the palm, resigned himself to the prospect of waiting for it to be handed to him by Baldwin – in the event, more than seven years later. Meanwhile both men had a touching reconciliation. 'We spoke very frankly to one another', Neville noted in his diary on 25 March.

S.B. professed no grievance against me. . . . I then told the story of my own grievance. . . . He pleaded in excuse his shyness and reserve . . . and the general distress he had suffered during the last fortnight, and he declared his warm appreciation of all I had done and his sorrow at having hurt my feelings. . . . We parted shaking hands, and with the clouds removed.

Before handing over the Party chairmanship to his successor, Lord Stonehaven – he agreed to continue to look after the running of the Conservative Research Department – Neville Chamberlain also reached an accommodation with Beaverbrook, who conceded that 'the cause is infinitely greater than the quarrel' and consequently undertook to support the official Party line at the next General Election. For this achievement Chamberlain was 'overwhelmed with congratulations which have come from all quarters', as he told his sister, adding 'except S.B. who can't bear the thought of making it up with the Press Lords and doesn't see how it has helped his own position'.

I am not quite sure what will happen to negotiations of this kind when I am no longer Chairman. But I daresay I shall still be wanted to take part in them, must as I don't expect to part entirely from the Office. The staff who seemed most genuinely grieved over my departure are anxious to maintain contact after I go and my retention of the Research Department will make it easier to ensure this.

VI

'I thoroughly enjoyed hitting those two rascals', Baldwin wrote of Rothermere and Beaverbrook after his Queen's Hall speech, 'and it has done a lot of good. . . . However, *if* there isn't an election, one hopes for a good holiday in August. I don't think the Government can last beyond October. . . .' In the event Baldwin's prediction was realized through the economic crisis which convulsed the country and led to the break-up of the Labour Government in the holiday month of August.

The history of the crisis with its political overtones has frequently been related, and it is only necessary to describe it briefly here in the context of Neville Chamberlain's role in it. As the result of a Liberal amendment to a Conservative motion in the Commons calling for the appointment of an independent Committee to make recommendations for 'effecting forthwith all practicable and legitimate reductions in the national expenditure', the Government set up such a body under the chairmanship of Sir George May, who had been secretary of the Prudential Assurance Company and was one of the leading actuaries in the country. By this date (March 1931) unemployment figures had risen to $2\frac{1}{2}$ million, and Philip Snowden, the financially orthodox Labour Chancellor of the Exchequer, hoped that the economies recommended by the May

Committee coupled with proposals for increased taxation would balance the drastic Budget, which he planned to introduce in the autumn, following on a stop-gap Budget in the spring. Meanwhile the collapse of the American stock market was followed by a similar collapse in Austria and Germany, where the banks were obliged to repudiate their international liabilities by declaring a moratorium. This was bound to affect the Bank of England and hit sterling, which in fact happened in mid-July when £33 million in gold and a further £33 million in its foreign currency holdings were withdrawn.

Meanwhile, Ramsay MacDonald began to think more and more of an all-Party coalition as the only way to surmount the impending crisis. Early in July Lord Stonehaven, the new Conservative Party Chairman, reported to Neville Chamberlain that the Labour Premier had sounded him out in this sense. 'He thought a national government should be formed', since 'they did not wish to be forced to vote against the two things they thought necessary, viz. reform of unemployment insurance and a tariff.' Chamberlain passed on this news to Baldwin and, as he noted in his diary on 6 July, 'we agreed that our party would not stand it for a moment'. Speaking at Hull eleven days later, Baldwin publicly rejected 'the idea that a national government such as existed during the war should be set up in the present difficulties'. He had brought down one Coalition government and he had no wish to join in the establishment of another. That would be all very well where it was a question of helping Germany out of her financial troubles, Chamberlain pointed out when they met again on 24 July, but MacDonald would not ask him to coalesce for that. As the pressure on sterling mounted, the possibility that Chamberlain foresaw was 'a panic in the City, a hundred million deficit in the Budget, a flight from the pound, and industry going smash'. It was then that MacDonald would come to him, Chamberlain argued, 'because he would not be able to count on his own people to support him'. However, Baldwin remained unconvinced that there was any immediate need for a coalition of the kind Chamberlain as well as MacDonald had now come to envisage. As Baldwin walked across Palace Yard on the last day of Parliament, he said to the Secretary of the Cabinet, Maurice Hankey: 'I will do everything I can to help the Government in making economies, but I will not enter a Coalition Government.'

When Chamberlain spoke to Baldwin, he had been informed in advance of the main recommendations of the May Committee, whose Report was published on 31 July, the day after Parliament rose for the summer recess. In Neville Chamberlain's words, 'the May Report confirmed the most pessimistic views circulating abroad as to the insolvency of the Budget. . . . The credits had to be encroached upon, and they began to melt away at such a pace that it was only a matter of days before they disappeared completely. Enquiries in Paris and New York showed that there was no chance of a loan in either quarter.' In these circumstances the London bankers bluntly told Ramsay MacDonald that 'the cause of the trouble was not financial but political, and lay in the complete want of confidence in His Majesty's Government existing among foreigners', and that 'the remedy was in the hands of the Government alone'. Consequently the Cabinet Committee appointed to consider the implications of the May Report decided that the Budget must be balanced at all costs, but 'there must be equality of sacrifice'. It was a grim prospect.

Baldwin and his wife had planned to motor the whole way to Aix-les-Bains for their usual holiday, but they had only got as far as Angers in Normandy when Baldwin received a telephone call from Davidson on the evening of 11 August urging him to return to London immediately, as 'the Government was breaking up'. Baldwin hesitated, since he was always reluctant to alter his plans, but an immediately following telegram from Geoffrey Fry decided him to return at once; this he did next day. Warned by Davidson that the idea of a 'Government of All the Talents to rescue the Labour Party from its dilemma' was being widely mooted, his reaction was quite definite. 'Well, they got into this mess, let them get out of it. As the situation develops I may or may not have to take some part in it, but that time hasn't arrived.'

This seems to have been his attitude when he and Chamberlain went to Downing Street the same afternoon to see the Prime Minister and Snowden, who said they had decided that the Budget must be balanced and that economies must be made to the extent, though not necessarily in the precise ways, recommended by the May Committee. 'If they could be assured of our general support', wrote Chamberlain to his sister Hilda at this time, 'they propose to summon Parliament in the first fortnight in September to pass a supplementary Budget and an Economy Bill.' He continued:

To secure such a measure of relief and to do it through a Socialist Government seems to me so important in the national interest that we must give it our support provided the proposals for 'equal sacrifice' do not imperil British credit or too brazenly affront ordinary rules of justice and fair play. And I don't think they will do either. . . .

Anyway the decisions are left to me as S.B. is not coming back. I think he would agree that crises of this kind are not his forte. He had apparently given no thought to the situation, asked no intelligent question, made no helpful suggestion and indeed was chiefly anxious to be gone before he was 'drawn into something'. He left a final message for me that he was most grateful to me for sparing him the necessity of returning and he would 'back me to the end'!

An urgent telephone call from Chamberlain on the evening of 10 August summoned Baldwin back to London, this time for good. Judging by the size of the crowd which turned up at Victoria Station to greet Baldwin when he arrived the same evening, between three and four hundred people thought so, their feelings expressed by one inebriated gentleman who shouted, 'You'll save the country!' Since Baldwin's house was closed, Davidson put his own house in Great College Street at his leader's disposal, and after dining there with Davidson Baldwin went to the Conservative Research Department in Old Queen Street for a meeting with Neville Chamberlain, Hoare and such other members of the Shadow Cabinet as Chamberlain had been able to reach in the holiday season. There Chamberlain confirmed what Baldwin had already heard from Davidson, namely that MacDonald had decided to resign and to advise the King to send for the leaders of the other two parties for consultation as to the next step with a view to forming some kind of three-Party government.

Hoare's impression of Baldwin on this occasion was that 'the last thing in the world that he wished for was either a return to office or the end of his holiday'. Having destroyed one coalition, he kept repeating, he did not wish to form another. 'Only if a National Government was really inevitable', Hoare later recalled, 'was he ready to take his part in it. Chamberlain and I were inclined to be impatient when we saw him so reluctant to take the only course that seemed to us possible. Our impatience became irritation when the King, on MacDonald's advice, sent for him the next morning and he could not be found.' He was eventually run to earth at the Travellers Club where he was lunching with Geoffrey Dawson, the editor of *The Times*. He was told that the King wished to see him at three o'clock that afternoon in Buckingham Palace.

At the afternoon audience, the King asked Baldwin whether he would be prepared to serve in a National Government under MacDonald. Baldwin replied that he would. To the further question whether he would be ready to carry on the Government himself in the event of MacDonald declining, Baldwin agreed, provided he could be assured of Liberal support in putting through the economy programme. After the Tory Leader had left the Palace, Wigram noted that 'the King was greatly pleased with Mr Baldwin's readiness to meet the crisis which had arisen, and to sink Party interests for the sake of the country'.

Shortly after ten o'clock that night Ramsay MacDonald went to the Palace looking 'scared and unbalanced', according to Wigram. He informed the King that at the Cabinet which he had just left eleven members had voted in favour of the economies, including a 10 per cent cut in the dole, and eight against. In view of this irrevocable split, MacDonald felt that he had no alternative but to tender his resignation. On the King assuring him that 'he was the only man to lead the country through the crisis' and hoping he would reconsider his decision, since 'the Conservatives and Liberals would support him in restoring the confidence of foreigners in the financial stability of the country', MacDonald asked whether the King would confer with Baldwin, Samuel and himself in the morning. (The Cabinet had already agreed to this proposal.) The King replied that he would gladly do so, and MacDonald returned to Downing Street where Samuel was waiting for him. Shortly afterwards, in response to urgent telephone messages, they were joined by Baldwin, Neville Chamberlain and several financial experts from the Bank of England.

After the bankers had outlined the minimum economy measures necessary, they left, and the politicians got down to business. What happened then was recorded by Chamberlain in his diary, from which it is clear that the Prime Minister was still intent on resignation. 'For himself, he would help us to get these proposals through, though it means his death warrant, but it would be no use for him to join a Government. He would be a ridiculous figure unable to command support and would bring odium on us as well as himself.'

Chamberlain then intervened. Had the Prime Minister

considered, he asked him, that while he might not command many votes in the House of Commons he might command much support in the country? And would not a Government including members of all Parties hold a much stronger position than a two-Party combination? To this MacDonald replied that his mind was not fully made up but his present mood was for resignation. The account given by Chamberlain in his diary continues:

I then suggested that many people would not understand why, if he supported the new Government, he refused to enter it and would criticise him on that ground. He replied that was a worrying point, but people would say he had stuck to his office for the sake of the salary, to which I replied that if several of his colleagues accompanied him the odium would at least be spread.

Finally I asked him if he had considered the effect on foreign opinion which was all important. . . . This argument took him in a weak place. He said without egotism he thought his name did carry weight in America. . . .

Samuel supported me strongly though S.B. maintained silence and we did not pursue the matter further then.

When Baldwin left this meeting, he shared Chamberlain's impression that MacDonald still intended to resign and that he would not serve under a Tory Premier. 'Last night it looked as if I should have to form a Government', Baldwin wrote to his wife next day (24 August). 'The P.M. said he couldn't join me.' The impression persisted as he walked with Davidson to Buckingham Palace for his meeting with the King. 'Nor did he think this a bad thing', remarked Davidson later, 'since he had little love for Coalitions.'

During the next two hours the situation changed dramatically. 'This morning the King, Samuel and I met', Baldwin told his wife afterwards; 'and Ramsay, with real courage, deserted by some of his leading colleagues and by his Party, offered to form an *ad hoc* Government to put through the financial legislation necessary and then dissolve for a general election which will come probably in October.' The offer, endorsed by Samuel and Baldwin, was warmly welcomed by the King. Later the same day Ramsay MacDonald returned to the Palace and kissed hands on his appointment as Prime Minister of a new 'National' Government.

MacDonald limited his Cabinet to ten members; and, although as Prime Minister he knew he could not count on the support of more than a handful of his own Party followers, he insisted on

Labour having four places, the same number as he allotted to the Conservatives, leaving the balance of two to the Liberals. He also insisted that Snowden should continue at the Treasury and he vetoed the suggested inclusion of Hailsham whom he described as 'particularly obnoxious to the Labour Party', no doubt on account of the part he had played in getting the Trade Disputes Act through Parliament. Besides MacDonald and Snowden, Labour was represented in the Cabinet by Sankey who remained Lord Chancellor and J. H. Thomas who combined the portfolios of Dominions and Colonies. 'I am going to be Lord President of the Council', Baldwin wrote to his wife. 'Politically I think it is the best thing for me.' The other Conservatives in the Cabinet were Neville Chamberlain and Cunliffe-Lister (formerly Lloyd-Greame), who returned respectively to the Ministry of Health and the Board of Trade, and Hoare who got the India Office. The two Liberals were Samuel and Reading, who took the key posts of Home Secretary and Foreign Secretary. Incidentally, Neville Chamberlain's brother Austen was bitterly disappointed at not being given the Foreign Office; but he agreed instead to become First Lord of the Admiralty without a seat in the Cabinet, feeling that he appeared (as he put it) 'not as someone who gives all he can to help in a crisis but as an old party hack who might be dangerous outside and so must have his mouth stopped with office'. In short, he said, he had allowed himself to be 'deeply humiliated' and 'with no advantage to the Government or the country'. And, as he wrote to his sister Hilda, 'you can imagine that I have found my position almost intolerable. For thirty years or more I have been at the very centre of events. After such an experience it is not easy to adjust oneself to the position of the fly on the wheel.'

The Cabinet met for the first time on 26 August and appointed small committees to deal with finance, taxation and economics. This was preceded by a meeting of the full senior ministerial team of seventeen, at which Samuel paid tributes to Baldwin for 'serving with a Prime Minister whose views had been different from his own in many matters', and also Austen Chamberlain and other Conservative ministers, 'who had put all other considerations aside in the interests of public security'. Upon this Baldwin remarked that he and his colleagues 'would do their best'. One difficulty which MacDonald asked Hankey to resolve was the question of precedence at Cabinet meetings in the event of his absence.

Hankey suggested that the order of precedence should be as follows: the Prime Minister, Baldwin, Snowden, Samuel, Reading and Sankey. However, MacDonald insisted on Sankey, the Lord Chancellor, coming fourth. Then Chamberlain objected to Reading being added to the Cabinet finance committee, which consisted of Snowden, Samuel and himself, on the ground that the balance of parties would be upset. He also objected to Lord Cecil of Chelwood continuing to represent the Government at Geneva and leading the British delegation to the League of Nations Assembly. These were the kind of differences which Baldwin's tact, added to Hankey's, were required to smooth out with the Prime Minister during this critical period.

Meanwhile the King had gone back to Balmoral. 'I wish you and your colleagues every success in the difficult task imposed upon you', he wrote to Ramsay MacDonald on 27 August. 'I am happy to feel that I have been able to return to my Highland home without changing my Prime Minister, in whom I have full confidence.' This confidence, it may be added, was not shared by the Chamberlain brothers. 'It is really hard lines', Austen wrote at this time, 'after being led for these last two years by a man so unhelpful and inert as S.B., Neville should now be driven to exclaim to me that Ramsay is "infinitely worse".'

The House of Commons met on 7 September to pass the emergency Budget and Economy Bill. There was little opposition to Snowden's proposals for meeting the anticipated deficit of £170 million, which he did by raising £76 million in increased taxes, including income tax at 5s., and the balance by suspending national debt redemption and imposing cuts in state salaries and benefits including the unemployment 'dole' by 10 per cent. Both the King and the Prince of Wales voluntarily surrendered £50,000 each from their incomes as a contribution to the emergency. These measures had the effect of temporarily staying the drain on gold from London. Unfortunately some naval ratings of the Atlantic Fleet at Invergordon refused to obey orders as a protest at the cuts, some of which by a misunderstanding exceeded 10 per cent. This incident assumed the proportions of a naval mutiny in foreign eyes, and investors, thinking it was the prelude to a revolution in Britain, began to withdraw more gold from the vaults of the Bank of England.

Under pressure from the Bank, the Government immediately

rushed through Parliament in a single day a Bill suspending the Gold Standard, which had the effect of relieving the Bank of its statutory obligation to sell gold on the international money market. The pound fell by a quarter in terms of dollar and other foreign currencies, although the man in the street who had no occasion to buy foreign exchange noticed little or no difference, since he had been using paper money since 1914 when gold sovereigns had disappeared from circulation.

Meanwhile *The Times* had come out with a powerful leading article from the editor's pen urging that a General Election should take place as soon as possible. 'Is there any reason', asked Geoffrey Dawson, 'why the appeal to the country, whenever it may come, should not be made – on a broad programme of reconstruction which will include a tariff – by the National Government as such?' This view was echoed by the evening papers, and many Conservatives declared their support for it, including the powerful 1922 Committee of Conservative backbenchers in the House of Commons. Neville Chamberlain was strongly in favour of a tariff as the only practical means of reversing the adverse trade balance and this was endorsed by the Conservative Business Committee which included Baldwin. Chamberlain noted in his diary on 24 September:

All were in favour of the national appeal by a national government under MacDonald, provided the programme embodied the full tariff. All agreed that the elections should be held at the earliest moment. All agreed that, if we went to election with R[amsay] M[acDonald] as P.M., we must accept him as P.M. when we come back, though we might well have an understanding as to the filling of the posts in the new Government.

MacDonald and Thomas in the Cabinet were disposed to go along with the Conservatives, but Samuel and Reading, the two Liberals, being convinced Free Traders, were not, while Snowden and Sankey hesitated to commit themselves. This seeming deadlock greatly worried the King, who was afraid that if the Liberals resigned MacDonald would follow suit and that would be the end of the National Government.

On 28 September Wigram reported to the King, who was still at Balmoral, that while the Prime Minister did not actually turn down a General Election he had no heart for it. 'Without doubt he is sentimental and an idealist. He does not like the idea of smashing

67

up the Labour Party at the head of a Conservative organisation. He does not know how to run with the hare and hunt with the hounds.'

In view of these developments the King returned to London. When MacDonald saw the King on 3 October, he told him that 'he was beginning to feel that he had failed and had better clear out'. The King's immediate reaction was to say that in this event he would not accept the Prime Minister's resignation and that it was his positive duty to find a solution. He spoke quite bluntly to MacDonald who, he said, 'must be more patient and brace himself up to realise that he was the only person to tackle the present chaotic state of affairs'.

MacDonald went back to the Cabinet. At last, shortly before midnight two days later, a formula was reached to which all ten members of the Cabinet agreed. The National Government would go to the country and ask for a 'doctor's mandate' to apply every remedy they could agree on to cure the country's ills, each Party issuing its own manifesto with a general pronouncement from the Prime Minister signed by him alone. This was to lay its emphasis on party co-operation as long as the crisis lasted. Parliament was immediately dissolved, and polling in the General Election fixed for 27 October. The King declared himself to be 'very pleased', and congratulated the Prime Minister when he came to the Palace to ask for a dissolution.

'I never fought an election under such a difficulty', Neville Chamberlain wrote to his sister Hilda at the start of the campaign:

We are now committed to this extraordinary proceeding under which we go to the country as a united Government, one section of which is to advocate tariffs while the other declares it has an open mind but is unalterably convinced of the virtues of Free Trade. . . .
I hope we may win the victory we anticipate but if we do I foresee a peck of troubles as soon as the election is over, first in the formation of the Government and then in the formulation of policy.

In Birmingham, his own election address was brief and decisive. 'I must frankly say that I believe a tariff levied on imported foreign goods will be found to be indispensable', he wrote. 'The ultimate destiny of this country is bound up with the Empire. . . . I hope to take my part in forwarding a policy which was the main subject of my father's last great political campaign.'

The resultant Tory gains – 200 at the expense of Labour – were far greater than either Chamberlain or Baldwin anticipated. The Conservatives won 473 seats, including all 12 in Birmingham, which together with their 'National' Labour and 'National' Liberal allies, led respectively by Ramsay MacDonald and Sir John Simon, enabled them to count on a total strength of 521 in the new House of Commons. Orthodox Labour came back with a mere 52, the whole of their Front Bench having been defeated with the exception of George Lansbury. In the aggregate returns the Liberals were split three ways – the 'pure' Liberals led by Samuel, who gained 33 seats, the Simonite Liberals, so-called National Liberals, who gained 35 seats, and the Lloyd George family, consisting of Lloyd George, his son, his daughter and his son-in-law who preferred to sit as an independent group. MacDonald and his National Labour following only captured 13 seats, but these included the Prime Minister's at Seaham.

Baldwin took the results of the election calmly. 'The workers throughout the country have put their trust in the National Government', he declared. 'We must not fail them.'

VII

At a hurriedly summoned meeting of the Cabinet on 29 October 1931, Ramsay MacDonald announced that he proposed to reconstruct his Government and asked that the offices of all ministers might be put at his disposal 'in order to give a free hand in the reconstruction', in which he would invite the co-operation of the other party political leaders. He also proposed to enlarge the Cabinet to its normal size, since it would be necessary to refer a number of 'complicated and technical questions' to Cabinet Committees.

The troubles foreseen by Neville Chamberlain in the reconstruction were soon embarrassingly apparent. 'Stan very worried by office seekers', noted Mrs Baldwin as soon as the election results were known. 'He does so hate saying no to his friends.' At an audience he had with the King on 2 November, Baldwin said that the Conservative Party 'might kick if they did not have some of the key positions, such as the Exchequer, Home Office, Foreign Office and Dominions Office'. The King remarked that he thought

Baldwin himself should go to the Treasury in preference to Neville Chamberlain who was 'so good as Minister of Health' and 'would be suspected of ultra-protectionist views' if he became Chancellor of the Exchequer. But Baldwin did not want any portfolio for himself; he preferred to carry on as Lord President of the Council, a job without any departmental responsibilities which would give him plenty of time to advise on the formulation of policy. He thought Neville Chamberlain might do as Foreign Secretary, but he really wanted him back at the Treasury, although he did not pursue the point further on this occasion.

Since the Conservatives were by far the largest Party in the Commons, it was inevitable that they should have the lion's share of the jobs going. In the event they were allocated eleven out of the twenty places available in the normal-sized Cabinet, while the Simonite and Samuelite Liberals together got five places and the National Labour (MacDonaldites) four. Baldwin was content to continue as Lord President, but since his salary was only £2000 compared with £5000 attached to the other senior offices he was given as compensation the use of the Chancellor of the Exchequer's official residence at No. 11 Downing Street. 'It was very comfortable', he remarked later, 'and I could always keep my eye on my Prime Minister.'

Neville Chamberlain got the Exchequer minus the official residence, which he does not seem to have minded as much as his brother Austen did when he had to yield it to Bonar Law in 1918 when Lloyd George was Prime Minister and wanted Bonar next door as Leader of the House. Otherwise the Tories secured most of the plums except the Foreign Office and the Home Office, which went to Simon and Samuel respectively, and the Woolsack which Lord Sankey continued to occupy. The three service ministries – War (Lord Hailsham), Admiralty (Sir Bolton Eyres-Monsell) and Air (Lord Londonderry) – all went to Conservatives. Chamberlain was anxious to have Cunliffe-Lister carrying on at the Board of Trade, but MacDonald could not stomach the idea of an ardent protectionist at Trade as well as the Treasury, and consequently the office went to the Liberal Walter Runciman, who soon turned protectionist, while Cunliffe-Lister got the Colonial Office instead, which was separated from Dominions which went to the Labour J. H. Thomas. Meanwhile Hoare agreed to carry on at the India Office. Lloyd George's exclusion was inevitable for health reasons: anyhow he had broken with both Samuel and Simon, and Baldwin would not have him at any price. Churchill was also kept out on account of his stand over India.

Ramsay MacDonald, although he showed himself at first to be a conciliatory and resourceful chairman of the Cabinet, could seldom afford to take a strong line, since he had such a small personal following in Parliament, and in effect he became the prisoner of the Conservatives. His jailers were Baldwin and Chamberlain, of whom the Liberal leader Herbert Samuel has left a vivid pen picture at this time:

> The attractive personality of Stanley Baldwin contributed to the smooth handling of affairs. The real power lay with him, but he was careful not to let the fact appear. Reticent in Cabinet, one might almost say taciturn, Baldwin rarely, if ever, initiated a proposal; but often, when a discussion was taking an awkward turn, he would intervene at the end with some brief observation, full of common sense, that helped us to an agreement.

> Neville Chamberlain, on the other hand, was always ready to take the lead, particularly on economic questions which then held the field and which had always been his special province. His ideas were positive and clear-cut; he was tenacious in pursuit of them, whether in the Cabinet itself, or its Committees, or in the conversations that, as in all governments, were continually proceeding among its members. Courteous and agreeable in manner, Chamberlain was always willing to listen to arguments with a friendly spirit – but a closed mind.

The question of overriding urgency, if Britain was to be set on the road to economic recovery, was the extent to which a protectionist policy should be adopted by the National Government. With this Baldwin was particularly concerned, although he was content to leave the details to be worked out by Chamberlain and Runciman. The Conservative Party as a whole wanted protection, and the rumour which spread abroad that tariffs were to be imposed began to flood the country with foreign goods. To stem this flow and halt further unemployment, the Government immediately introduced an Abnormal Importation Bill imposing a 100 per cent duty on 'excessive imports'. This was passed by Parliament without opposition from Samuel and his Liberal National followers. A Cabinet committee was thereupon set up with Neville Chamberlain in the chair to examine the whole question of the balance of trade, and since the committee had a protectionist majority its recommendations were bound to lead to a clash with the Samuelites.

Meanwhile, the Cabinet trade committee under Chamberlain had recommended that a general 10 per cent tariff should be imposed on all imported goods, with a number of specified exceptions, including all imports from the Dominions which were to enjoy preferential treatment, the details to be worked out at a conference later the same year in Ottawa. When the committee's report came before the Cabinet on 21 January 1932, the Liberals and Snowden threatened to resign, since they regarded the committee's recommendations as amounting to full protection. The same night MacDonald telephoned Sandringham and told the King's Private Secretary that in view of what had happened he might have to tender his own resignation and that of the whole administration. However, this possibility was averted when the Cabinet met again next morning and the Free Traders accepted a suggestion from Hailsham that to prevent the National Government from breaking up so early in its life it would be better to sacrifice the rule of collective responsibility and to accept a majority decision in the Cabinet. Snowden urged that the dissentients might be allowed to speak and vote against the committee's recommendations in Parliament, and this was duly agreed.

'Frankly, although the burden is heavy, I rejoice at it,' Neville Chamberlain wrote to a friend on 8 January 1932. 'To be given the chance of directing such great forces where I am convinced they should be applied, is such a privilege as one had no right to hope for; and I intend to make the most of it.'

A few weeks later, on 4 February, 'the great day of my life', as he described it to his sister Hilda, he unfolded his ideas to a crowded House of Commons for over an hour in the presence of his stepmother and other members of the family. As he took his place on the Front Bench, he placed in front of him the battered old despatch box which had belonged to his father when he was Colonial Secretary, and took his notes from it reverently. A general tariff, he claimed, would help to correct the balance of payments, raise fresh revenue, prevent an unchecked fall of the pound, and reduce unemployment by transferring 'to our own factories and fields work which is now being done elsewhere'. He therefore moved that with effect from 1 March there should be charged a duty of 10 per cent on all goods imported into the United Kingdom, with certain specific exceptions. For the time being, at any rate until after the forthcoming Ottawa Conference, none of the new duties would apply to goods from the Dominions, 'since we desire to mark at every stage our wish to approach this conference in the true spirit of Imperial unity and harmony'. Thus by the use of this 'system of moderate Protection' the Government hoped to encourage greater efficiency in industry and to secure a bargaining factor in tariff negotiations with other countries.

When he came to the peroration of his speech, his voice began to falter with emotion and he had difficulty in controlling it as he conjured up his father's image and the prospect of his life's work achieving a measure of fruition.

There can have been few occasions in all our long political history when to the son of a man who counted for something in his day and generation has been vouchsafed the privilege of setting the seal on the work which the father began but had perforce to leave unfinished. Nearly 20 years have passed since Joseph Chamberlain entered upon his great campaign in favour of Imperial Preference and Tariff Reform. More than 17 years have gone by since he died, without having seen the fulfilment of his aims and yet convinced that, if not exactly in his way, yet in some modified form his vision would eventually take shape. *His work was not in vain.* Time and the misfortunes of the country have brought conviction to many who did not feel that they could agree with him then. I believe he would have found consolation for the bitterness of his disappointment if he could have foreseen that these proposals, which are the direct and legitimate descendants of his own conception, would be laid before the House of Commons, which he loved, in the presence of one and by the lips of the other of the two immediate successors to his name and blood.

It was a touching moment when Neville sat down, and Austen came down from his usual corner seat on the third bench below the gangway to the Treasury Bench and silently shook his brother by the hand to the accompaniment of prolonged cheering. Next day the post brought masses of letters and telegrams of congratulations, from all over the country 'ranging', as Neville put it, 'from the King to my tailor'. Thus the free trade system, initiated eighty-six years before with the repeal of the Corn Laws, was ended in 1932. The principle has not since been seriously challenged, although it has been modified by the coming into being of the European Economic Community. On the other hand, all that emerged at Ottawa, in spite of the hard work put into it by Chamberlain, was a declaration that the lowering or removal of empire tariff barriers would facilitate the flow of trade and that the individual agreements made in the Canadian federal capital were 'a step forward which should in future lead to further progress in the same direction'.

With the resignation of the Free Traders from the National Government in 1932 Chamberlain hoped that the Government supporters would now become a more homogeneous team, and might 'move towards that fused Party under a National name which I regard as certain to come', thus reflecting and reinforcing his hope, which he had earlier expressed, that 'we may presently develop into a National Party and get rid of that odious title of Conservative which has kept so many from joining us in the past'.

Besides his measure of 'moderate' tariff reform and his work at the Ottawa Conference, Neville Chamberlain was particularly associated at this period with three other measures – his Budget, the conversion of £2000 million of 5 per cent War Loan to 3½ per cent stock, and the international conference held at Lausanne to settle German reparations.

In the austere Budget, his first, which he opened on 19 April, the Chancellor with the object of holding adequate reserves of gold and foreign exchange made a decision of great future importance, namely to borrow up to £150 million to establish a new Exchequer Equalization Fund. The deficit of £35 million which he anticipated due to a heavy fall in the coming year's income tax and surtax would be partly made good by his tariff and partly by a tax on tea. But there could be no remissions. The revival of public confidence which his policy had already engendered coincided appropriately with the conversion scheme which he announced in the Commons on 30 June and which was a great success, resulting in a saving to the Exchequer in interest charges of about £23 million a year, while further conversions in the course of the year brought the total annual saving in interest to £40 million. This had a tonic effect on the economy and strengthened the position of the Government.

On the other hand, the Lausanne Conference, from which Chamberlain returned to announce the conversion scheme, accomplished less than he hoped. At the opening session on 17 June, he came out flatly for cancellation all round of both war debts and reparations. But this proved unacceptable to the French, and what had to be accepted instead was a lump sum from Germany in lieu of reparations, accompanied by a declaration that a new order was about to begin, 'since financial confidence depended on a sense that political relations were really improved'. For this Chamberlain had to work very hard.

'The P.M. is I think getting to rely on my help very much', he wrote to Ida about Ramsay MacDonald, who led the British delegation. 'He has a good deal of difficulty in following the more technical side and he doesn't understand French, so he likes to have me about and in fact he won't now conduct any conversations with the other delegations without having me there too.'

'I get on very well with the French', Chamberlain added. 'The Wigrams* declare that Herriot [the French Prime Minister] "adores" me, and also with the Germans, though I must say the latter, especially von Papen [the Chancellor], are incredibly stupid.'

Because of his adhesion to the principles of orthodox finance, Chamberlain's strictly balanced Budgets were rated 'dull' and received with little enthusiasm except from Montagu Norman and the City bankers. However the economic tide gradually turned. By 1934, Chamberlain could report a small but distinct rise in wholesale prices, new low records in the rate of short-term interest, Consols standing higher than they had before the war, an increase in the volume of industrial production, and something like equilibrium in the balance of payments. 'We had finished the story of *Bleak House*', he said, 'and could now sit down to enjoy the first chapter of *Great Expectations*.'

The Budget surplus was £29 million and he could now restore the whole of the cut in the unemployment benefit and half the reduction in the pay of State and local government employees. The 6d increase in income tax was likewise removed and a year later he completed the process when the pay cuts were restored in full and the smaller income tax payers were helped by changes in their allowances, although some of his expenditure had to come from 'raiding' the Road Fund, a move which aroused the Transport Minister Leslie Hore-Belisha to fury.

Above all, unemployment steadily fell. In his 1935 Budget

* Ralph Wigram was 1st Secretary at the British Embassy in Paris and a rising star in the Foreign Service. His untimely death at the age of forty-six in December 1936 was described by Winston Churchill as 'an irreparable loss to the Foreign Service'. He married Ava, daughter of the historian J. E. C. Bodley.

statement, the Chancellor could point with pride to the fact that improvement had been 'solid, continuous and steady', a process to which tariffs, conversion operations, cheap money, balanced Budgets and remissions of taxation had all contributed. For example, the British people had 'sweetened their lives' with 80,000 more tons of sugar than in the previous year, smoked the equivalent of 2600 million cigarettes and spent £2¾ million on entertainments, and 'washed away their troubles' with 270 million more pints of beer, a statistic which was loudly greeted with shouts of 'Hear, hear' in the Commons when he announced it. 'Broadly speaking', he concluded, 'we may say that we have recovered in this country eighty per cent of our prosperity.' Or as the historian C. L. Mowat put it, 'The National Government's financial policies made the best of both worlds: they seemed sufficiently deflationary to restore confidence; they were in fact sufficiently inflationary to assist recovery by maintaining the purchasing power of the people.'

Chamberlain's position as Chancellor of the Exchequer, Chairman of the Conservative Research Department and *de facto* Chairman of the Cabinet Consultative Committee, a policy-making body which Chamberlain persuaded Baldwin to set up early in 1934, made Chamberlain the most powerful member of the National Government after Baldwin. Soon he began in effect to supersede Baldwin as the leading Conservative and the Party's chief policy-maker. As early as October 1932 he told his sister Hilda: 'It amuses me to find a new policy for each of my colleagues in turn.'

So much for Cabinet colleagues. But with junior ministers he could on occasion be sternly admonitory, as when Duff Cooper was appointed Financial Secretary of the Treasury by Ramsay MacDonald in 1934, thus becoming in effect parliamentary under-secretary and Chamberlain's deputy in the Commons. 'At our first interview', Duff Cooper later recalled, 'he reminded me that I had a reputation for indiscretion and warned me that while the unguarded words of most junior ministers mattered little, an indiscretion by the Financial Secretary to the Treasury might bring down the Government.' It was a warning which Duff Cooper took to heart.

The usual formula embodied in the minutes of the meetings of the Cabinet Consultative Committee showed an unintentional humour in its invariable opening: 'At Mr Baldwin's request, Mr

Chamberlain opened the proceedings *as usual.*' By the spring of 1935 it was clear that Chamberlain was shouldering the main burden of government. 'I am more and more carrying this government on my back', Chamberlain noted in his diary on 8 March. 'The P.M. is ill and tired and won't apply his mind to problems. It is certainly time there was a change.'

It certainly was. Ramsay MacDonald had already indicated his intention to retire after the King's Silver Jubilee in May. The change came on 7 June, when MacDonald changed places with Baldwin, who moved from No. 11 to No. 10 Downing Street, while Chamberlain at last took possession of his official residence. The Cabinet reshuffle had already been foreshadowed by an entry dated 17 May in Chamberlain's diary, from which it is clear that the interim changes which Baldwin made pending a General Election were mainly due to Chamberlain's prompting. 'By constant prodding I have got things moving at last', he had written, 'greatly aided by the general dissatisfaction with the conduct of the Air Ministry as well as the Foreign Office.' MacDonald, although his health was failing, stepped down to become Lord President; Simon, whose tenure of the Foreign Office had not been an unqualified success, went to the Home Office; while Hoare became Foreign Secretary, the job he had always coveted, and Londonderry was demoted to Lord Privy Seal and Leader of the House of Lords, thus giving way to Cunliffe-Lister who went to the Air Ministry. (Chamberlain wanted to sack Londonderry altogether.) There was some talk of bringing Lloyd George into the Government, but nothing came of this idea as Chamberlain deliberately kept him out.

Chamberlain himself carried on as Chancellor, but soon he had to see financial prudence thrown to the winds by the necessity to provide for national defence to the tune of £1500 million, to be spread over the next five years.

These changes made one thing very clear. Neville Chamberlain was now firmly established as Prime Minister-designate, although in the event two more years were to elapse before he succeeded Baldwin and assumed the titular office.

3

PRIME MINISTER AND APPEASEMENT

I

ALTHOUGH BY JUNE 1935 Neville Chamberlain had served nearly four years as Chancellor of the Exchequer, his official residence, No. 11 Downing Street, had been occupied for almost the whole of the time by Baldwin as the result of a special arrangement with the Prime Minister. Indeed it was only for the few weeks when he had his first spell at the Treasury in the latter part of 1923 that he enjoyed the amenities of the Chancellor's official residence. But with Baldwin's succession to the Premiership in June 1935 he was able to move in at last, and with No. 10 now in prospect he decided to sell his own London house, letting it first as an experiment. 'Did I tell you that we have let Eaton Square to Ribbentrop?' he wrote to one of his sisters at this time. 'Amusing, considering my affection for Germans in general, and R. in particular.' Ribbentrop was now Hitler's special emissary despatched to conclude an Anglo-German naval treaty, and he was soon to become ambassador. Chamberlain had never been fond of the Germans. 'How I loathe the Germans', he remarked during a holiday in the Black Forest some years previously. With increasing news of Hitler's aggressive intentions, including the admission made openly that Germany had an air force contrary to the Treaty of Versailles, he liked the Germans and their official representatives even less.

The first problem which Baldwin and his reconstructed Cabinet had to face was how to reconcile the rearmament programme with the public demand that the Government should lend support to the policy of collective security. This was reflected in the result of the misleadingly named Peace Ballot, which was declared on 28 June 1935. For some months the League of Nations Union had been carrying out a number of public opinion polls which were then becoming fashionable. Question 5 asked whether an aggressor should be stopped by economic measures and, if necessary, by war. Over 10 million answered yes, while over 2 million said no and another 2 million did not reply. Thus the ballot, which had been originally designed as a ballot for international disarmament and collective security, was in effect a substantial vote for the enforcement of collective security by all means short of war, and even in some measure for war in the final resort.

'Terribly mischievous', Chamberlain called the ballot when it was first announced, and later he wrote of 'the League of Nations cranks' who had been 'infuriated' by the White Paper on defence which had been published in March 1935 and which Chamberlain had a hand in drafting, notwithstanding that his brother Austen as the architect of Locarno was one of the League's foremost champions. 'What I shall work for', Neville wrote to Ida in August, 'is a Britain strong enough to make it impossible for her wishes to be flouted as Mussolini has flouted them now.' However, in spite of the warning by Sir Samuel Hoare, the Foreign Secretary, in a speech at Geneva that Britain stood with the League 'for steady and collective resistance to all acts of unprovoked aggression', the Italian army and air force launched an attack upon Abyssinia, which Mussolini had long coveted, at the beginning of October. Economic sanctions were immediately applied against Italy by most members of the League, but force was ruled out. However the sanctions failed to stop the Italian occupation of the country and the flight of its emperor, and eventually sanctions were called off after Neville Chamberlain had realistically described them as 'the very midsummer of madness'.

On consulting Chamberlain, the Prime Minister decided to go for an autumn General Election. The question was, what would be the main issue to put before the electors? In view of the peace ballot it would be necessary to proceed with great circumspection, since Chamberlain realized that, if the Government came out strongly in favour of rearmament, Labour would accuse them of warmongering and perhaps of concealing their plans in this respect from the people.

On 2 August 1935, Chamberlain wrote in his diary:

As a matter of fact we are working on plans for rearmament at an early date, for the situation in Europe is most alarming. Germany is said to have borrowed over £1,000 millions a year to get herself rearmed and she has perfected a wonderful industrial organisation capable of rapid expansion for the production of the materials of war. With Mussolini hopelessly tied up in Abyssinia and Great Britain disarmed, the temptation in a few years to demand territory etc. might be too great for Goering, Goebbels, and their like to resist. Therefore we must hurry our own rearmament and in the course of the next 4 or 5 years we shall probably have to spend an extra £120 millions in doing so.

We are not yet sufficiently advanced to reveal our ideas to the public, but of course we cannot deny the general charge of rearmament, and no doubt if we tried to keep our ideas secret until after the election we should either fail or if we succeeded lay ourselves open to the damaging accusation that we had deliberately deceived the people.

Parliament was dissolved in the latter part of October, so that polling could take place on 14 November and thus cause a minimum of interference with Christmas shopping. Baldwin was cautious on the question of rearmament; indeed he was frightened of making defence the *prime* issue. 'I give you my word that there will be no great armaments', he announced at the outset of the campaign. At the same time he begged the electors not to 'fear or misunderstand when the Government say that they are looking to our defences'. Chamberlain loyally supported this view coupled with the probability that the country was in 'for a long and anxious period in foreign affairs in which it was essential that we should have a stable Government with the authority of the nation behind it'. Indeed the idea was already embodied in the Conservative election manifesto, of which Chamberlain was the chief draftsman. 'We have made it clear', he wrote, 'that we must in the course of the next few years do what is necessary to repair the gaps in our defences.' Needless to add, Chamberlain was branded by his political opponents as a warmonger, and one of Labour's eye-catching posters featured a baby in a gas-mask.

'I am bound to recognise', wrote Neville to Hilda at the close of the campaign, 'that if I supply the policy and the drive, S.B. does also supply something that is perhaps more valuable in retaining the floating vote.' There is no doubt that Chamberlain bore the brunt of organizing the campaign on his own shoulders, although the Prime Minister may not have fully appreciated this. 'The fact is that you and I are complementary', Baldwin told Chamberlain.

Neville Chamberlain, aged six months, with his mother.

below Joseph Chamberlain, Neville's father, about 1877.

below right The young Neville Chamberlain in 1887.

Highbury, the Chamberlain family home in Birmingham, built by Joseph Chamberlain.

A family group at Highbury, 1889. From the left: Neville Chamberlain, Ethel Chamberlain, Hilda Chamberlain, Mrs Endicott, Beatrice Chamberlain, Mr Endicott, Mrs Joseph Chamberlain, Ida Chamberlain.

Nassau as it was at the time of Neville Chamberlain's visit in 1891.

Baled sisal ready to be shipped abroad from the Bahamas. The man in the white suit and straw hat is possibly Mr Knowles, the overseer employed by Neville Chamberlain in the Andros Fibre Company.

Austen Chamberlain when Chancellor of the Exchequer, 1903–5: 'Austen always played the game and he always lost it' (Lord Birkenhead).

Neville Chamberlain in 1915: 'Not a bad Lord Mayor of Birmingham in a lean year' (Lloyd George).

Neville Chamberlain as Chancellor of the Exchequer in his room at the Treasury. The battered-looking red box on the table was traditionally used by Chancellors when introducing their Budgets and had once belonged to Mr Gladstone.

Fishing the River Don at Castle Forbes in Aberdeenshire. Lady Forbes and Mrs Chamberlain look on.

The United Kingdom delegation to the Imperial Conference at Ottawa in 1932. Left to right: Stanley Baldwin, Neville Chamberlain, J.H. Thomas, Lord Hailsham, Sir Philip Cunliffe-Lister, Walter Runciman, Sir John Gilmour.

Walking with his wife in St James's Park.

Facing the dictators.

With Hitler at Godesberg, 22 September 1938. On the left is Hitler's interpreter Dr Schmidt.

With Mussolini at Munich.

Heston airport, 30 September 1938. Chamberlain is waving the paper, signed by Hitler and himself earlier that day in Munich, recording 'the desire of our two peoples never to go to war with one another again'.

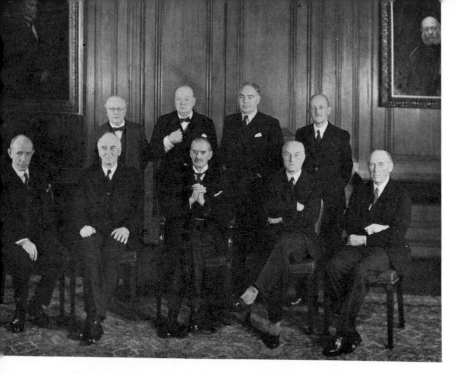

The Chamberlain War Cabinet, September 1939. Left to right standing: Sir Kingsley Wood (Secretary of State for Air), Mr Winston Churchill (First Lord of the Admiralty), Mr Leslie Hore-Belisha (Secretary of State for War), Lord Hankey (Minister without Portfolio). Left to right sitting: Viscount Halifax (Secretary of State for Foreign Affairs), Sir John Simon (Chancellor of the Exchequer), Mr Neville Chamberlain (Prime Minister), Sir Samuel Hoare (Lord Privy Seal), Lord Chatfield (Minister for the Co-ordination of Defence).

Highfield Park. Chamberlain spent the last months of his life in this house and died here on 9 November 1940.

'Each puts into the pool his own contribution and we make a jolly effective unit!'

Conservative Central Office estimated the Tory majority at 100, perhaps somewhat higher. In the event the Conservatives won 432 seats, which gave them a majority of 247 over the combined Opposition. Both the MacDonalds lost their seats to official Labour which increased its representation to 154.

'I am not biased by friendship when I say that the triumph is a personal one for S.B.', wrote Tom Jones on learning the results.

He has made no mistakes. He timed the election correctly in his Party's interest. Six months hence and it is certain the results would be less favourable to him. He has only very slowly and with obvious reluctance proclaimed the need for more armaments; he has avoided all trace of the *Daily Mail*'s lust to arm the nation to the teeth and has also kept clear of Winston's enthusiasm for ships and guns. He has strictly confined the extent to which he was prepared to move against Italy and distinguished Mussolini from the Italian people. . . . Over all he has thrown that halo of faith and hope, free from meretricious ornament, which inspires confidence. The effect is to gather to the Tories a large voting strength of Liberals and unattached folk who like his sober and sincere accents, and who are afraid of the menace to small owners and investors associated with Socialism.

Baldwin's first task on the morrow of electoral victory was to review the composition of his ministerial team. He had previously hoped to make considerable changes, but this had been ruled out by the size of his majority since each member of the Cabinet tended to regard the result as a vote of confidence in himself as well as in the Cabinet as a whole. There was also the consideration whether it would not be preferable in a time of international crisis to keep the Cabinet substantially intact with the balance of parties unaltered. The changes, which in the event he did make, Baldwin reduced to a minimum. He even retained the two MacDonalds, though well aware that the problem of finding them seats in the new Parliament would not be easy. In the Government, however, Malcolm MacDonald changed places with J. H. Thomas, whose removal from the Dominions Office was necessitated largely by general dissatisfaction with his handling of Anglo–Irish relations. Chamberlain carried on at the Treasury, while Halifax took over from Londonderry as Lord Privy Seal and Leader of the House of Lords. This last change made it possible for Duff Cooper, whom

81

Baldwin wished to promote and whom Chamberlain also thought worth advancement, to become War Minister with a seat in the Cabinet.

Meanwhile Hoare was working out a plan with the French Foreign Minister Pierre Laval for the settlement of the Abyssinian question to the advantage of Italy. When the plan was prematurely 'leaked' by the French press, there was a violent reaction in the British newspapers to what seemed a *volte-face* to Hoare's Geneva pledge of support for the League and sanctions. In Hoare's absence through illness, Chamberlain put his (Hoare's) case to the Cabinet which at first was inclined to accept the Hoare–Laval plan as a workable compromise, but afterwards had second thoughts and rejected it. In the result Hoare resigned. He was succeeded as Foreign Secretary by the thirty-eight-year-old Anthony Eden.

With continued evidence of aggression from the Japanese in the Far East as well as from the Germans and Italians in the West, foreign affairs and defence occupied much of the time in the Cabinet in which Chamberlain played a leading part. While naturally regretting the abandonment of his prudent financial policy in his first years as Chancellor in the National Government, Neville Chamberlain as Prime Minister-designate in effect now became the chief architect of the policies put forward in the Defence White Papers of 1936 and 1937. For the Navy these two White Papers provided for the laying down of five new capital ships, twenty cruisers and four aircraft carriers, besides a steady replacement programme for destroyers and submarines. For the Army they provided for the raising of four new infantry battalions, in addition to the modernization of equipment and expansion of the Territorials, and for the Air Force, a front line strength of 1750 aircraft exclusive of the Fleet Air Arm. In addition there were to be 'shadow' factories for the construction of aircraft and manufacture of munitions, as well as local government schemes for air raid precautions. This new defence expenditure was estimated to total £137 million. At the same time, in what was to be his last Budget, Chamberlain put up income tax to five shillings in the pound and proposed a graduated tax upon the growth of business profits which he called the National Defence Contribution. The NDC caused such a furore in the City and influential Party circles that it had to be abandoned and a straight tax on profits ('a simpler tax with a larger yield') imposed instead. 'What a frightful bill we do owe to Master Hitler, damn him!' Chamberlain wrote at this time. 'If it only wasn't for Germany, we should be having such a wonderful time just now.'

Hitler's occupation of the demilitarized zone of the Rhineland, which took place in March 1936, foreshadowed the appointment of a minister with responsibility for defence. Baldwin thought Chamberlain should have it, but he refused to consider it. After a number of other names had been canvassed and ruled out for various reasons, such for example as Churchill and Hoare, the task was assigned to the Attorney General, Sir Thomas Inskip, a relatively obscure lawyer with no pretensions to knowledge of the subject, although in the event he was to prove much more of a success in the job than was anticipated by many critics at the time of his appointment. It was generally agreed that Inskip would be 'safe but not inspiring'. He would create no jealousies, as Chamberlain put it. 'He would excite no enthusiasm but he would involve us in no fresh perplexities.'

Meanwhile, as Chamberlain himself admitted, there 'appears to be a general acceptance of my position as heir apparent'. At the annual Party conference, which took place at Margate, he deputized for Baldwin who was unwell. 'I am sending for people', Chamberlain noted in his diary at the time, 'and endeavouring to conduct business as if I were in fact P.M.' At the same time he could not forget the tricks which fate had played upon his father and also upon Austen. 'I wonder', he wrote with a sense of foreboding to his sisters, 'whether Fate has some dark secret in store to carry out her ironies to the end.' But the end, as he was eventually to acknowledge, was to witness his progress to 'the highest pinnacle of his career'.

The other great event in which he played a part as the heir apparent before this came about was the abdication of King Edward VIII. When George V died in January 1936, Chamberlain looked forward with some anxiety to the rule of his successor. 'I do hope he "pulls up his socks" and behaves himself now he has such heavy responsibilities', Chamberlain wrote after the new monarch's Accession Council had been held, 'for unless he does he will soon pull down the throne.' It quickly appeared to Chamberlain that Edward VIII was not 'doing the boxes', that is reading the state papers which were submitted to him daily in the traditional red boxes, with the patient care that his late father had habitually shown.

The story of the King's determination to marry Mrs Simpson, which culminated in his abdication of the throne, does not properly belong to this narrative. The part which Chamberlain played in the affair is not always clear, largely because the Cabinet minutes on the abdication are officially closed until the year 2037. However, it is known that Chamberlain drafted a memorandum for Cabinet circulation, urging that the King should 'settle down', wear conventional clothes, work at his 'boxes' and not make remarks in public, which were apt to be reported in the newspapers, about such topics as the slums and unemployment. It is also known that the Prime Minister thought it wise to suppress this memorandum.

When the King had virtually made up his mind to abdicate, Walter Monckton, his legal adviser, warned him that he would still have to face the prospect of a prolonged separation from Mrs Simpson before her divorce decree became absolute and they were free to marry. Accordingly he suggested that, in addition to the Abdication Bill, the King should ask the Government to present a second Bill simultaneously to Parliament which would make the divorce absolute forthwith.

When the proposal came before the Cabinet for consideration, there is some evidence that Chamberlain was disposed to accept it. On the other hand, it was strongly opposed on religious grounds by ministers like Halifax and Inskip. However that may be, when Monckton was summoned to hear the Cabinet's decision, the duty of communicating it to him was delegated to Chamberlain instead of being carried out by Baldwin as might have been expected. It was hardly a task which Chamberlain could have relished.

In the event Monckton was informed of the decision that the proposed Divorce Bill was unacceptable on several grounds. This was done in the Cabinet room on the morning of Sunday 6 December 1936, after Monckton had been kept waiting for two hours while the matter was being debated behind closed doors. The grounds were as follows:

(1) it could not be denied that the King regarded the Bill as a condition of abdication, and it would therefore be denounced as an unholy bargain;
(2) it would irretrievably damage the moral authority of the Government at home and in the empire;

(3) it would be looked on as an injury to the marriage law in general; and

(4) it would injure the respect for the monarchy.

Someone asked Monckton what would be the King's reaction to the decision. Monckton replied that His Majesty had hoped that both Bills which the Prime Minister 'had looked upon with favour' would be acceptable. 'This decision will greatly disappoint him', he added. 'In the light of the present circumstances, he will undoubtedly ask for additional time for further thought.'

At this point, Ramsay MacDonald spoke up. 'How much time will the King ask for? How many days?'

'Hardly days', answered Monckton. 'I anticipate he will require weeks.' It would be necessary for him to consult his advisers, Monckton went on, since 'a divergence of view had arisen'.

Baldwin, who had hitherto been silent, now interjected: 'This matter must be finished before Christmas.' Some other ministers remarked that this was too long to wait and the matter should be settled immediately. One minister was heard to say that the continued uncertainty was hurting the Christmas trade. According to Monckton, this observation emanated from Neville Chamberlain.

Finally Monckton said he would report to the King what had happened. When he did so later that day it was with some feeling. 'I was more philosophical', the King admitted, 'although it did seem to me that the Chancellor of the Exchequer was being a trifle more mercenary than his office demanded.' According to Monckton, 'Baldwin was ready to resign but I told him the King would not wish that'.

'S.B. as I anticipated', wrote Chamberlain to Hilda, 'has reaped a rich harvest of credit which has carried him to the highest pinnacle of his career.' He was still on the pinnacle five months later when he formally handed over the office of Prime Minister to his designated successor. His last parliamentary gesture was to announce an increase in MPs' pay of £200 a year. 'This means a lot to the Labour members and was done with Baldwin's usual consummate taste', noted Harold Nicolson, who was present. 'No man has left in such a blaze of affection.'

Next morning, 28 May 1937, Baldwin went to Buckingham Palace and formally tendered his resignation to the King. A few minutes later Neville Chamberlain kissed hands and took his place as Prime Minister and First Lord of the Treasury.

II

In his appointment as Prime Minister Neville Chamberlain appreciated an important 'contributory factor'. This was the help he had always received throughout his public career from his wife. 'I should never have been P.M. if I hadn't had Annie to help me', he told his sister Hilda.

It isn't only that she charms everyone into good humour and makes them think that a man can't be so bad who had a wife like that. She has undoubtedly made countless friends and supporters . . . and she has kept many who might have left me if I had been alone but who are devoted to her. But besides all this she has softened and smoothed my natural impatience and dislike of anything with a whiff of humbug about it, and I know she has saved me often from making an impression of harshness which was not intended.

Yet his satisfaction was not wholly unalloyed. There were some regrets that neither his father, his eldest sister nor his brother had witnessed his success. Austen had suddenly died two months before, while in the act of taking down a book from a shelf in his library. 'I don't regret so much the fact that Austen just missed the actual consummation', he told his other two sisters, ' – he knew it was coming. But I wish our Bee [Beatrice] could have lived to be aware of it, for it would have meant an enormous lot to her.'

As he told the Party meeting which formally elected him leader, Neville Chamberlain was entering upon the duties and responsibilities of the Premiership 'at an age when most people are thinking of retiring from active work'; but, he added amid laughter, he had hitherto led 'a sober and temperate life' and was consequently 'sound in wind and limb'. Gladstone once said that sixty should be the maximum age for Prime Ministers, although he was eighty-three when he filled the office for the fourth time. With the exception of Sir Henry Campbell-Bannerman, who was two years older when he became Prime Minister in 1906, Neville Chamberlain at sixty-eight was the most senior statesman of this century to reach No. 10 Downing Street for the first time. And it was with becoming modesty that he accepted the supreme political honour. 'I know you will rejoice that a Chamberlain of sorts has got the position that others ought to have had', he told a kinsman a few days after his election. 'I have been given a good start, but I am not going to boast when I am putting on my armour.'

The only painful physical ailment which afflicted him was gout, in his case a hereditary complaint. But in spite of this probably no Prime Minister has worked harder since Peel. Ernest Brown, who served as Minister of Labour under him, paid tribute to 'the comfort it had been to hard pressed departmental ministers to know that, when their subjects have to be discussed, whoever else has not read their papers and digested them, one man had – the Prime Minister'. A similar tribute came from Sir John Simon, whom Chamberlain appointed Chancellor of the Exchequer in his place in May 1937.

You may learn a good deal about the attitude of a busy man to the crowd about him by noting how and where he seeks refreshment from his labours [wrote Simon in his memoirs]. Chamberlain found his relief in noting the habits of birds, in studying flowers, in the music of Beethoven, and in fishing. He was not of a gregarious nature. He was too honest to affect a personal interest which he did not feel in popular sports and would not accept suggestions to show himself at the Derby or at Lords.

('It would be a humbug and I won't be party to it', Chamberlain said.) Fishing, which he had taken up in middle age, gave him much pleasure and relaxation, and he was both expert and generous as an angler. 'That was a noble fish!' Baldwin once wrote thanking him for the gift of one. 'We had him for dinner on Wednesday, lunch on Thursday, and more will appear at our Sunday evening meal. Our blessings on you and your rod.'

Unfortunately a natural sense of shyness weakened his effectiveness as a political leader. He lacked Baldwin's popular touch, and his ungregariousness was noted in the Members' Smoking Room of the House of Commons where he was seldom to be seen, unlike Baldwin and also Churchill. Yet he was aware of his shortcomings. 'I suppose it is a good thing to see oneself as others see us, but it is a very painful process', he remarked after seeing himself in a film in 1937. 'If I had not previously seen the person who addressed us from the screen, I should call him pompous, insufferably slow in diction and unspeakably repellent in person.' Chamberlain could sometimes cast a spell over his audience. Churchill has admitted that on the occasion of the one intimate conversation he had with him on a social occasion during twenty years' acquaintance – about his time as a young man in the Bahamas – he was 'fascinated by the way Mr Chamberlain warmed as he talked'. On the other hand, his chauffeur once told Hoare that 'you can't know Mr Chamberlain till you have been with him five years'.

It should be remembered too that Neville Chamberlain was a product of the Victorian age. Indeed he was over thirty when the old Queen died. Thus there were many Victorian traits which persisted in his character, such as the punctilious and rather old-fashioned dress with the stiff wing-collar he habitually wore, not to mention the umbrella he usually carried. He liked to describe 'the late Victorian age before the days of motors and telephones' as the period to which he looked back with a sense of nostalgia. New-fangled inventions were often not to his liking. For example, he could not abide the use of the fountain pen, and all his life he wrote his letters and speeches with an old-fashioned steel-nibbed pen which he would dip into an inkwell every few minutes. He found Stanley Spencer's pictures 'hideous, distorted, grotesque productions', and as for Epstein's *Christ* he felt it must be a joke produced 'for the cynical satisfaction of hearing fools exhaust their vocabulary of admiration over it'.

Although he used the Cabinet room and offices, Chamberlain and his wife did not immediately move in to No. 10 as a residence but continued to use No. 11 as their living quarters for several months. This was because Mrs Chamberlain, in making her first tour of inspection of No. 10, considered that the offices, State rooms and the living and sleeping quarters were too interwoven for convenience. She decided to move the bedrooms from the first to the second floor, adding an extra staircase since the main one only extended to the first floor.

The room at the north-western corner overlooking St James's Park and the Horse Guards Parade was converted into a comfortable bedroom for Neville, with another bedroom for his wife facing it across the passage. An adjacent bathroom was also installed. The former bedrooms on the floor below, beside the State reception rooms, were now used as additional offices. Of the two main bedrooms on the first floor, the one at the corner directly underneath the Prime Minister's was made into an extra drawing-room, thus forming a suite of three reception rooms, the other two being the small drawing-room containing furniture which had once belonged to Clive of India, and the larger State drawing-room at the other corner. A former inner bedroom became the Prime Minister's private study, and it was here that he worked late in the evenings rather than in the Cabinet room on the ground floor. Other modernization included improvements to the kitchen and the installation of a service lift.

The total cost of this renovation came to £25,000, which in view of the value of money in those days suggests that the Chamberlains hoped to occupy the house for several years at least. When it came to curtains for the bedrooms on the second floor, Mrs Chamberlain was told that she would have to provide these herself and this she did, using country chintzes, a choice which seems to have been both happy and admired. She certainly took an immense pride in the house after the alterations and improvements had been carried out, and she delighted in showing visitors round. On one occasion she delivered an informed lecture on the house and its history to the members of the Empire Parliamentary Association. Fortunately in the alterations which she carried out she had the advice and help of Sir Philip Sassoon, the Minister of Works, and a man of considerable artistic taste himself. He was also able to produce some fine pictures, which were lent by the National Gallery, while the cellars at No. 10 yielded among other finds a large landscape by Turner and another by Claude Lorrain, which likewise adorned the walls.

During each parliamentary session, Mrs Chamberlain usually gave three parties on consecutive evenings, Tuesday, Wednesday and Thursday, the entertainment being arranged in this way so that the flowers lasted and the same hired china could be used. Over the three days there were several hundred guests, including MPS (each of whom was allowed to bring two constituents), and they were given tea or coffee and cakes. Secretaries and other members of the staff were placed at the doors of the reception rooms to keep the guests moving, since the floors were then considered unsafe and only a limited number of persons could be safely accommodated at any one time. Smaller sherry parties were also held for more distinguished visitors, such as President Le Brun of France, and the Dominion Prime Ministers. Luncheon and dinner parties were few compared with present-day practice. The King and Queen were entertained to dinner along with twenty other guests in the State dining-room in March 1939, but no special arrangements were made in the kitchen, the meal being prepared by Mrs Chamberlain's cook. Incidentally it is worth noting that only twice before in this century had the sovereign and his consort dined in the house, the first time being when King George V and Queen Mary dined with the Asquiths in 1911, and the second when George VI and Queen Elizabeth dined with the Baldwins on the eve of Baldwin's retirement.

As might be expected, Neville Chamberlain took a keen interest in the garden at No. 10 and had a herbaceous border laid out along the Horse Guards wall. There had not been many flowers there before, only a lawn with two or three trees, one of them an ever-green oak. With only one entrance leading out of the house from Downing Street, apart from the area steps leading down to the basement, Chamberlain has been credited with providing an additional door giving access to the Press Office on the Whitehall side – it was found useful also for delivering the beer.

Chequers, the Prime Minister's official country residence situated in a fine wooded park near the village of Ellesborough in Buckinghamshire, not far from Wendover and Princes Risborough, deserves some brief notice in the context of the use which the Chamberlains made of it during the three years of Neville Chamberlain's Premiership. Of all the Prime Ministers who have occupied the place since it was presented to the nation by Lord Lee of Fareham in the time of Lloyd George, Neville Chamberlain was perhaps fondest of it. From the first moment he set foot in it he liked everything about the place – the lovely old Elizabethan house, the furniture, the pictures, the garden and above all the park and the trees. Like Ramsay MacDonald before him he was never happier than when he was clearing up parts of the woodlands. With his own hands he bound up one tree which was in danger of falling down. As a keen naturalist, he made a particular study of the trees on the estate, writing a monograph on the subject, which Anthony Eden who discovered it later in manuscript described as 'charming and erudite'.

During one of his early visits, about a fortnight after he had become Prime Minister, he wrote enthusiastically to Lord Lee:

We have already explored the box woods, visited Cymbeline's castle, searched (vainly) for the Druid's Maze, discovered new flowers and ascended Beacon and Coombe Hills. We have also made a tour of the house and started a preliminary examination of its pictures and other treasures. The rest must wait until we come back and I hope that won't be long.

What trees there are here! I have never seen such magnificent specimens as the yew, the tulip trees, the horse chestnut, not to speak of the oaks, beeches, limes and elms. . . .

Anne Chamberlain was similarly thrilled. 'It would have amused you could you have seen us on the downs that first morning', she wrote to Lady Lee. 'We were both so excited and thrilled with everything – Neville with moths, butterflies, flowers and birds, and I by the thought of Cymbeline's abode.'*

The Chamberlains established one precedent during their time at Chequers. They were the first Prime Minister and his wife to invite Lord and Lady Lee of Fareham to stay in the house which they had presented to the nation sixteen years before, and it was a pleasant surprise for the latter to be greeted by their old butler whom they had left behind when they handed over in 1921. The Chamberlains also liked to spend Christmas at Chequers, and they did so in each year of Neville's Premiership. No wonder that, when the time came to say goodbye, he hated doing so. 'It will be a hard wrench to part with a place where I have been so happy', he told his sisters. And so it was.

III

'Neville has reshuffled the Cabinet and postponed any radical change until the next election – when he may find himself less able to do so than he is today.' Thus wrote Tom Jones on 30 May 1937, two days after Chamberlain had assumed office.

His team is not a very loyal one to him personally. He is still rather a dark horse, especially in foreign affairs. He told Nancy [Lady Astor] last week that he meant to be his own Foreign Minister and also to take an active hand in co-ordinating ministerial policy generally, in contrast with S.B. We shall see.

Inside the door of No. 10, with its lion-headed knocker, a long corridor runs down the breadth of what were once two separate

* Cymbeline's Mount, about half a mile north-west of Chequers house, was a castle in Roman times. According to tradition it was the residence of the British King Cymbeline, who inspired Shakespeare's play of that title. However, in spite of a coin bearing his superscription which had been discovered in the estate, there is no credible evidence that Cymbeline ever lived there. Known also as Cunobelinus, he made his headquarters at Camulodunum, the modern Colchester, in the first century BC.

houses to the Cabinet room. This famous room, which has been called the nerve centre of the British Commonwealth, where so many historic meetings have been held and decisions taken, is long, narrow and lofty. In Chamberlain's time the greater part of the room was occupied by a long table about twenty-five feet in length, surrounded by sabre-legged and leather-upholstered chairs for the Cabinet ministers. Opposite each place lay a blotter of worn black leather with the gilt imprint of the First Lord of the Treasury, the title by which the Prime Minister has as a rule been officially designated. The wall recesses were filled with massive mahogany bookcases, and above the marble chimneypiece hung the only picture in the room, the portrait by Van Loo of Sir Robert Walpole, the first Prime Minister in the modern constitutional sense. The only armchair, with its back to the fireplace, was that traditionally occupied by the Prime Minister when he presided at meetings of the Cabinet.

Of course it is not necessary that Cabinet meetings should invariably take place in this room, although the majority of them have always done so. The usual time of meeting was 11.30 on Wednesday mornings, but for some reason it was not convenient for Chamberlain to hold his first Cabinet on the Wednesday morning after his accession. Accordingly it took place at four o'clock in the afternoon of that day in his room in the House of Commons. It was not especially remarkable. Anthony Eden, who was staying on at the Foreign Office, reported on a bombing incident off the coast of Spain in which the German pocket battleship *Deutschland* had been damaged and which had interfered with British plans to get foreign contingents removed from the fighting in the Civil War on the mainland. The salaries of Ministers of the Crown and a new Rating and Valuation Bill were also discussed, as well as the forthcoming conference of Commonwealth Prime Ministers to be held in London. Foreign policy was not discussed in detail, since shortly after Hitler's military occupation of the Rhineland this began to be handled by a special Cabinet committee, consisting of about half a dozen ministers. The committee had already met eleven times since its inception, and Chamberlain had made a point of being present on each occasion, thus briefing himself on current foreign affairs against the time when he should play the active part in their direction which he contemplated.

Chamberlain's admission to Lady Astor, shortly before becoming

Premier, that he intended to be his own foreign minister has already been mentioned. About the same time Chamberlain had a talk to Anthony Eden in his room at the Treasury when he told him that he was to succeed Baldwin and expressed the hope that he (Eden) would continue his work at the Foreign Office. 'I know you won't mind', he added with a smile, 'if I take more interest in foreign policy than S.B.' Eden was not at all dismayed by this remark, since (as he afterwards admitted) 'we both knew that no one could have taken less'.

Eden has also recalled in his volume of memoirs *Facing the Dictators* that some months previously Neville Chamberlain had invited him to dinner at No. 11 Downing Street to meet his brother Austen, who had recently returned from a trip to Austria and Czechoslovakia where he had met President Beneš. 'This was one of the last occasions on which I saw Sir Austen before his death', Eden wrote. He went on to record that he enjoyed his evening since Neville was 'a delightful host and food and drink were always excellent at his table'. Austen held forth at length about his visit to Beneš and what he thought of the Nazi danger to Austria, while Neville and Eden listened, Neville in particular taking very little part in the conversation. However, towards the end of the evening, according to Eden, he did venture to make certain comments on the situation as he saw it, whereupon Austen said, 'Neville, you must remember you don't know anything about foreign affairs'. Neville smiled wryly and remarked that 'this was rather hard on a man at his own dinner table'. Thereupon 'Austen made one of his sweeping, deprecatory gestures, half apologetic, and went on his way'.

It is only fair to add that, in spite of this and other rebukes which he occasionally received from him, Neville was devoted to his brother, as the latter was to him. 'From my earliest days', Neville wrote to the Archbishop of Canterbury Cosmo Lang at the time of his brother's death in March 1937, 'I have looked up to Austen with perhaps much more deference, as well as affection, than is usually the case where the difference in years was so small. He was a rare good brother to me, and the only one I had.'

Tom Jones's remark about the loyalty of the new Government to its chief or rather lack of it may have had some basis of truth. One Conservative MP (Edward Grigg) described the reshuffle as 'feeble', and certainly the overall impression was that of a somewhat humdrum collection of ministers composed largely of the 'old gang'. It would be unfair as well as untrue to describe them as incompetent – on the contrary they consisted of some able administrators, but most of them had made their reputations on the home front, although two (Simon and Hoare) had both served at the Foreign Office where they were considered to have been failures.

The changes may be briefly summarized. Simon moved from the Home Office to the Treasury, and Hoare (whom Baldwin had brought back to the Cabinet after the Laval fiasco) from the Admiralty to the Home Office. Duff Cooper, whose administration at the War Office had brought him into conflict with Chamberlain, was somewhat surprisingly transferred to the Admiralty; his place at the War Office was taken by Leslie Hore-Belisha, whose record as Minister of Transport had impressed Chamberlain, particularly his zebra crossings and orange-coloured beacons. Of the other changes, Lord Stanhope went to Education and Oliver Stanley to the Board of Trade, where he succeeded Runciman who retired with a peerage. Ramsay MacDonald also retired, refusing any honour, his place as Lord President of the Council being taken by Halifax. Eden (Foreign Office), Inskip (Defence), Swinton (Air), Ormsby-Gore (Colonies), Malcolm MacDonald (Dominions), Kingsley Wood (Health), Walter Elliot (Scotland), W. S. Morrison (Agriculture) and Lord Zetland (India) kept their former offices.

It is worth noting that five ministers, Simon (Chancellor of the Exchequer), Lord De la Warr (Privy Seal), Hore-Belisha (War), Leslie Burgin (Transport) and Ernest Brown (Labour) were Liberal Nationals, thus collectively enjoying a much greater number of posts than their party strengths in the House of Commons justified. Malcolm MacDonald was the sole representative of National Labour. Thus, although Chamberlain maintained the façade of a 'National' Government, the Government was 'National' only in name, while the great majority of Members of the House of Commons (nearly 400) was Conservative. However, taken all in all, the mixture was very much as before, although it lacked the glow which Ramsay MacDonald and Baldwin occasionally provided. There were altogether twenty-one ministers of Cabinet rank, with twenty junior ministers and Under-Secretaries not in the Cabinet. It may be noted here that there was in practice an inner Cabinet of three ministers in addition to Chamberlain, and he relied on them particularly when he did not make a major decision on his own initiative. This trio consisted of Halifax, Simon and Hoare, but even they were sometimes kept in the dark about the Prime Minister's intentions or learned of them through a close friend like Kingsley Wood who would often be taken into Chamberlain's intimate confidence.

'Make the new Government as unlike the old as you can' was Hoare's advice to Chamberlain. 'If you can, make all your changes at one moment', Hoare wrote to the new Prime Minister on 3 June 1937. 'Baldwin destroyed his first Government by merely taking over the Bonar Law inheritance. Boredom is one of the chief enemies of governments, and the country will be bored from the start if it looks as if you are only continuing the Baldwin regime.' But the advice was disregarded and Chamberlain was to live to regret it bitterly when he eventually fell from power. Men of ripe experience like Churchill and Amery were omitted, as likewise were rising young Tories with a rebel streak in their make-up like Harold Macmillan and Robert Boothby. Amery wrote afterwards in his political autobiography:

What was obvious was that he did not think it mattered what office he assigned to any particular colleague; the Civil Servants would keep him straight on ordinary administration; major policy he meant to conduct himself. That being so he had even less desire than Baldwin to include disturbing elements like Churchill or myself who might have wished to force his hand over the pace of defensive preparations or over economic policy.

After the Government had been formed and the list of ministers appeared in the press, Amery, who in his words 'realised the kind of Government he wanted', was 'distinctly annoyed' to receive a note from the Prime Minister expressing his regret that he had not been able to find room for him.

On the other hand, Churchill found Chamberlain 'alert, business-like, opinionated and self-confident in a very high degree'. He was to write of him in *The Gathering Storm*, the first volume of his history of the Second World War:

Unlike Baldwin, he conceived himself able to comprehend the whole field of Europe, and indeed the world. Instead of a vague but none the less deep-seated intuition, we had now a narrow, sharp-edged efficiency within the limits of the policy in which he believed. Both as Chancellor of the Exchequer, and as Prime Minister, he kept the tightest and most rigid control upon military expenditure. He was throughout this period the masterful opponent of all emergency measures. He had formed decided judgments about all the political figures of the day, both at home and abroad, and felt himself capable of dealing with them. His all-pervading hope was to go down to history as the great Peacemaker; and for this he was prepared to strive continually in the teeth of facts, and face great risks for himself and his country. Unhappily he ran into tides the force of which he could not measure, and met hurricanes from which he did not flinch, but with which he could not cope.

At the outset of his Premiership, Neville Chamberlain was faced with some truly daunting prospects. Rearmament at home was barely getting under way, while Germany, Italy and Japan were linked together by the Berlin–Rome Axis and the German–Japanese Anti-Comintern Pact, these three countries becoming militarily merged together in November 1937. In the following month Italy, like Germany and Japan, left the League of Nations, thus writing 'finis' to the policy of collective security. 'What country in Europe today, if threatened by a large Power, can rely on the League of Nations for protection?' Chamberlain asked at this time. He supplied the answer himself: 'None'. The truth was that world peace was being fatally menaced. Already there was war in two spheres: in China in the Far East, and in Spain in the West, where Britain's policy of non-intervention contrasted sharply with the activities of Germany and Italy on one side and Soviet Russia on the other.

Chamberlain, as Churchill has emphasized, was essentially a man of peace and he was determined to preserve it, so far as he could. His formula came to be known as appeasement, and his name has been particularly linked with it, although he was not the first to use the term and as a policy it was initially popular on a wide scale. In fact it was Anthony Eden who coined the word during a parliamentary debate following the German reoccupation of the Rhineland. 'It is the appeasement of Europe as a whole that we have constantly before us', Eden assured the House of Commons in March 1936. The sense in which he used the word was the dictionary one of meaning to settle strife, or pacify by satisfying demands. It was only later that in practice it came to mean, as the historian A. J. P. Taylor has aptly expressed it, 'endorsing the claims of the stronger and then making out that these claims were just'.

Although Chamberlain as Prime Minister must bear the chief responsibility for the policy of appeasement, as it worked out in practice, it was not exclusively his personal policy. Not only was it backed by his Cabinet colleagues and the mass of his supporters in Parliament, but it expressed the general desire of the British people. The Prime Minister, as Hoare insists in his memoirs, was not an autocrat who imposed his views on doubting or hostile colleagues. 'There is a fundamental consideration in judging his action. Nothing is further from the truth than the myth that has been invented of his intolerant omnipotence. Whilst the prime mover, he was never the dictator of the Government's policy.' Before the Munich settlement and the subsequent German occupation of Bohemia and Moravia opened the eyes of the British people to Hitler's insatiable ambitions, appeasement was generally popular, and it had influential Press support, notably from *The Times*, whose editor Geoffrey Dawson was in the van of the movement, and *The Observer* whose editor J. L. Garvin held similar views, as well as Lord Rothermere whose *Daily Mail* was all for appeasing the dictators as an alternative to war. Prominent appeasers like Dawson, Garvin, Tom Jones and Lord Lothian, and occasionally Chamberlain himself, used to meet as guests at Lady Astor's country house parties at Cliveden, near Maidenhead, and there is no doubt that the so-called Cliveden set was strongly pro-appeasement, although its members did not conspire or intrigue with Hitler's representatives as has sometimes been suggested, nor did they constitute an organized or conscious group as such. But not every guest who came to Cliveden was pro-appeasement. One of them was Eden, whom Tom Jones reported in October 1937 as having aged since he saw him six months previously, and who appeared 'dog tired at the start of the [Parliamentary] Session'. According to Jones, Eden described the Cabinet as being 'very weak and the armament programme far in arrears'.

On the other hand, he seems to argue that we can't do business with Germany until we are armed – say in 1940. This assumes that we can catch up with Germany – which we cannot – and that Hitler takes no dramatic steps in the meantime, which is unlike Hitler. We have spurned his repeated offers. They will not be kept open indefinitely. His price will mount and he will want the naval agreement revised in his favour.

It is easy with the advantage of hindsight, as reflected for instance in the revelations of Hitler's aggressive plans at the War Crimes Trials at Nuremberg, to condemn appeasement and the appeasers. In retrospect, after Munich and later during the war, most people denied that they were ever in favour of appeasement. But at the time things were rather different, as many who lived through these times can readily recall. 'In retrospect everyone was against appeasement; at the time not so many.'

IV

The policy of appeasement is generally thought of in the context of the two dictators Hitler and Mussolini, and particularly as expressed by the Munich settlement. But appeasement also found expression in other parts of the world where Britain possessed substantial interests, notably Ireland and Palestine, and it may be convenient to consider them briefly before the larger European aspect of the question.

In Ireland President De Valera had taken advantage of the abdication crisis in England to introduce a new constitution which made southern Ireland or 'Eire' independent for all practical purposes. Both the British Government and the Dominions recognized this constitution, and continued to treat Eire as a member of the Commonwealth, according British citizenship to Irishmen, a compliment incidentally which Eire did not reciprocate. But Chamberlain regarded this as not worth quarrelling about in the interests of settling Anglo–Irish differences which had persisted for centuries. Not only was the thorny question of the land annuities settled by an outright payment of £10 million from Eire, but the three naval bases in southern Ireland, which Lloyd George had insisted on retaining under the 'Treaty' of 1921, were likewise surrendered. Churchill, it is true, argued that the loss of the ports would be a disastrous handicap to the Royal Navy in time of war. On the other hand, the Chiefs of Staff held the view that the ports would be useless if Eire were hostile, and that it was worthwhile giving them up to keep her friendly and perhaps make her an ally if Britain were attacked. Undoubtedly this was Chamberlain's hope. 'I shall be accused of having weakly given way, when Eire was in the hollow of my hand', he wrote at the time of this settlement. 'Only I and my colleagues (who are unanimous) can judge of this, but I am satisfied that we have only given up the small things (paper rights, and revenues which would not last) for the big things – the ending of a long quarrel between North and South

Ireland, and the co-operation with us in trade and defence.' In the long term this gesture of appeasement proved in vain. Eire was to maintain a formal though friendly neutrality during the war between 1939 and 1945, while the use of the ports was denied to the British Navy with resulting loss of many lives. As for the 'long quarrel' between north and south, it has remained unresolved in the face of Ulster's stolid opposition to Ireland's unification.

In Palestine likewise it was Britain's traditional enemies who were appeased at the expense of the friends who had trusted her. Hostility between the Arabs and the Jews was exacerbated by Hitler's anti-semitic policy which increased the numbers of Jewish immigrants to Palestine. This in turn led to Arab rioting and violence on a scale comparable with Ireland. Eventually, after a Round Table Conference had failed, as similar conferences between native disputants had done in Ireland and India, the Chamberlain Government agreed in May 1939 to end Jewish immigration after a further 75,000 Jews had been admitted. Thus the Balfour Declaration, by which the Jews had been promised a national home without strings attached, was abandoned, since it was thought that the Arabs, being the bigger troublemakers, would be appeased. But as subsequent history has shown, Palestine remained unappeased by the prospect and realization of an independent Palestine state, and as in Ireland violence and murder have been the predominant hallmark of the Holy Land, thus mocking Christian teaching and virtues.

In spite of his brother Austen's half-joking gibe about his lack of knowledge of foreign affairs, not to mention the private opinion of Sir Robert Vansittart, Permanent Under-Secretary at the Foreign Office, that 'an earnest and opinionated provincial was bound to err if he plunged into diplomacy', the Prime Minister did know something of the subject in which he professed a genuine interest. As far back as 1928 Churchill had suggested to Baldwin that Neville Chamberlain would make a good Foreign Secretary, and in 1934 after the suggestion had been repeated by Halifax he was in fact offered the post and turned it down, because he felt he should carry on at the Treasury on account of the importance of his programme as Chancellor. However, it is doubtful whether Neville Chamberlain fully appreciated the special position occupied by the Foreign Secretary, who customarily circulates to the Prime Minister and his other colleagues in the Court hierarchy all executive telegrams, despatches from British embassies, accounts of the Foreign Secretary's interviews with the heads of foreign missions and similar confidential documents or 'prints', and in turn the Foreign Secretary is entitled to expect the support and confidence of his chief. It is true that a few Prime Ministers in the past, notably Disraeli and Lloyd George, had conducted secret negotiations behind the backs of their Foreign Ministers and Cabinets, but generally speaking Prime Ministers, although constitutionally entitled to exercise a measure of open control over foreign policy, have had no secrets from their Foreign Secretaries. 'To make things run smoothly', as Churchill has put it, 'there must not only be agreement between them on fundamentals, but also a harmony of outlook and even to some extent of temperament. This is all the more important if the Prime Minister himself devotes special attention to foreign affairs.'

Unfortunately there was little harmony either of outlook or temperament between Chamberlain and Eden. As Churchill has indicated, it would have been much better for everyone concerned if Chamberlain, in forming his Government, had sent Eden to one of the service departments and appointed Halifax Foreign Secretary, 'a colleague who seemed to share his views of foreign affairs with sympathy and conviction'. These views differed from Eden's over a wide field and in the event were to continue to do so more and more widely. The principal bone of contention between the two men was provided by Italy.

Chamberlain was anxious to get on good terms with Mussolini as well as with Hitler, and he believed in appeasement as the best method of achieving this aim while speeding up rearmament at home. To his sister Hilda he confided after he had been Prime Minister for a couple of months: 'I believe the double policy of rearmament and better relations with Germany and Italy will carry us safely through the danger period, if only the Foreign Office will play up.' On the other hand, after Hoare had left the Foreign Office over the Laval affair and his place had been taken by Eden, the latter attempted to rally the nations at Geneva against Mussolini and indeed was prepared to carry sanctions against Italy to the point of war.

Like the late Austen Chamberlain, Eden believed strongly in the Anglo–French Entente, which did not commend itself to the Prime Minister. 'She can never keep a secret for more than half an hour or a government for more than nine months!' Chamberlain wrote of France to an American cousin of his stepmother in January 1938. 'Therefore our people see that in the absence of any powerful ally, and until our armaments are completed, we must adjust our foreign policy to our circumstances, and even bear with patience and good humour actions which we should like to treat in a very different fashion.' Thus, to some extent, necessity in the Prime Minister's eyes was the mother of appeasement.

Eden was also conscious of Germany's growing power, particularly in the air, and was against any attempts to appease the German dictator. In his memoirs he has recalled a significant incident which occurred at the end of a Cabinet meeting in Downing Street. When the ministers began to disperse, Kingsley Wood was standing by the fireplace and within earshot of the Prime Minister. As Eden moved away to the other side of the table, Kingsley Wood declared in tones plainly intended to be heard by Eden as well as by Chamberlain: 'It's time that the Foreign Office thought less about France and tried to get on terms with Germany.' Eden made no comment.

Eden was anxious too for closer relations with Soviet Russia. In 1935, when he was a junior minister in Baldwin's Government, he had visited Moscow and met Stalin, the first British politician to have done so, and his reputation as a supporter of collective security which was shared by the Soviet Foreign Minister Litvinov commended him to the Kremlin. On the other hand, the Prime Minister was strongly anti-Soviet. 'I must confess to the most profound distrust of Russia', he was to write some time later when Hitler's aggressive intentions in the East became apparent and pointed more than ever to the need for a concrete Anglo–Soviet understanding.

I have no belief whatever in her ability to maintain an effective offensive, even if she wanted to. And I distrust her motives which seem to me to have little connection with our ideas of liberty, and to be concerned only with getting everyone else by the ears. Moreover she is both hated and suspected by many of the smaller States, notably by Poland, Roumania, and Finland.

The Prime Minister made his first conciliatory approach to the Italian dictator in July 1937 by inviting Mussolini's ambassador Count Grandi to meet him in Downing Street. This meeting took place with the knowledge but without the presence of the Foreign

Secretary, who in fact arranged it at Grandi's request. Chamberlain spoke of his desire for an improvement in Anglo–Italian relations, while the ambassador stressed that his master was anxious that Britain should accord *de jure* recognition to Italy's conquest of Abyssinia; he read out a despatch from the Duce emphasizing this and other points, including Britain's recent strengthening of her Mediterranean defences. Chamberlain then asked, possibly as the result of a hint from the ambassador, whether a personal note to the Duce would be appreciated. On being assured by Grandi that it would be, the Prime Minister sat down and wrote a letter in friendly terms, in his own hand. It was despatched without reference to the Foreign Secretary, who was in his office close by; in the event it produced 'a very cordial reply' from Mussolini in which, to quote Chamberlain's diary, 'he declared his readiness to open conversations with a view to the removal of all points of difference'.

When Eden heard about the letter, which he eventually did, he made no difficulty about the incident at the time, although (as he afterwards admitted in his memoirs) he would otherwise have imposed some conditions to the opening of discussions before the letter was sent, and he would have made some suggestions 'to guard the sender from appearing too gullible to the recipient'. However, he thought that there was no deliberate intent to bypass him as Foreign Secretary, but that it was what he described as 'merely a slip by a Prime Minister new to international affairs'. In this judgment he was apparently mistaken, since he did not know what he learned for the first time some years later, on the publication of Iain Macleod's biography of Neville Chamberlain, that the Prime Minister also noted in his diary at the time that he did not show the letter to the Foreign Secretary *because he had the feeling that he would object to it*. Even without this knowledge Eden's sensibilities were understandably ruffled. As he was about to leave for a holiday he wrote to Vansittart: 'I am presuming that there will be no further correspondence between No. 10 and Rome without my seeing it. I naturally attach importance to this.'

V

It is not possible to recount here in detail the course of Chamberlain's differences with Eden, which eventually led to the Foreign

Secretary's resignation seven months later. Chamberlain's biographers Keith Feiling and Iain Macleod have given Chamberlain's version based on his diaries and letters, while Eden has given his version in his memoirs. It is difficult to reconcile them in certain particulars so that the reader must judge for himself which is the more likely or reliable. In his diary the Prime Minister referred to the behaviour of the Italians and its effect upon the League of Nations prior to September 1937, when it was hoped that the Anglo–Italian conversations would begin.

At that time Eden and I both recognised (and the Italians apparently agreed) that the formal recognition of their Abyssinian conquest, to which they attached great importance, must follow on some declaration by the League that Abyssinia was no longer an independent State and that members of the League might if conversations went well be willing to make such a declaration at their next meeting; but unfortunately during the holiday months Mussolini sent a message to Franco boasting of his share in Franco's victories and a series of submarine attacks (probably Italian) were made on shipping in the Mediterranean, which produced such a bad effect on public opinion that any hope of a League declaration vanished for the time.

Instead a conference of the Mediterranean powers was convened at Nyon, which was attended on behalf of Britain by Eden, Vansittart, and Lord Chatfield, the First Sea Lord. After a minimum of discussion it agreed to establish British and French anti-submarine patrols, an action reluctantly acquiesced in by Italy, with the result that the attacks ceased at once. 'I feel that the Nyon Conference, by its brevity and success, has done something to put us on the map again', Eden wrote privately to Churchill on 14 September.

'I was very glad to see that Neville has been backing you up, and not, as represented by the Popular Press, holding you back by the coat-tails', Churchill replied. 'My hope is that the advantages you have gained will be firmly held on to. Mussolini only understands superior force, such as he is now confronted with in the Mediterranean.' Unfortunately the lesson was not heeded. Although the sinkings stopped, Italian volunteers continued to serve in Franco's 'Nationalist' forces.

In spite of the Prime Minister's support over the Nyon agreement, his differences with the Foreign Secretary increased during the autumn. On 11 November, when they met, Eden strongly voiced his misgivings over what he considered the slow pace of British rearmament. Chamberlain thought his fears were greatly exaggerated, in effect refusing to listen to him and advising him to 'go home and take an aspirin'.

Shortly after this, Austen Chamberlain's widow Ivy went off on a private visit to Italy, having told Eden beforehand that she was going so that the Rome embassy could be informed of her visit. In the event she was fêted and entertained by Mussolini, Count Ciano and the other Fascist high-ups. Afterwards Chamberlain wrote in his diary:

She had written to me of the strong dislike and distrust with which Eden was regarded and the general belief that he did not want better relations. She said she had argued that the delays were due to Italian not British action and that she herself had been assured by Eden before she left London that he wanted to talk as soon as the coast was clear. All seemed in vain.

One day she met Ciano and he taxed her with not really believing what she said. It happened that she had just received a letter from me in which I had praised her efforts and said I was going to try again to over-come difficulties. The letter was meant for her alone but she read it to Ciano. The effect was magical for he was at last convinced. He reported what he had heard to Mussolini . . . who sent a message by Ivy assuring me of his genuine desire to settle everything between us. Unfortunately this episode seemed to produce in Anthony only further suspicions. If the Italians wanted talks there must be some catch in it, and we had better hang back.

Further trouble arose when Eden went on holiday to the south of France in January 1938, and Chamberlain temporarily took charge of the Foreign Office. During Eden's absence President Roosevelt sprang a surprise on Chamberlain and the Foreign Office 'by informing us', in the Prime Minister's words, 'that he proposed to issue a sort of world appeal to end international tension by a general agreement to abide by international law and order'. Roosevelt's communication reached Chamberlain on 13 January 1938, and in it he indicated that he would not publish his appeal unless the Prime Minister could assure him by 17 January of his 'whole-hearted support and co-operation'.

I was in a dilemma [wrote Chamberlain in his diary]. The plan appeared to me fantastic and likely to excite the derision of Germany and Italy. They might even use it to postpone conversations with us, and if we were associated with it they would see in it another attempt on the part of the democratic bloc to put the dictators in the wrong. There was no time to consult Anthony, for in view of secrecy on which Roosevelt insisted in emphatic terms I did not dare to telephone. Therefore after consultation with Wilson and Cadogan, I sent a reply deprecating immediate publication.

This produced what Chamberlain described as 'a somewhat sulky acquiescence in postponement and some strongly worded warnings against shocking public opinion' by giving *de jure* recognition of Italy's Abyssinian conquest.

Eden returned from his holiday on 16 January, and as it was the weekend he immediately went to see the Prime Minister at Chequers. When he heard what had happened, he was angry, taking the view – mistakenly, as it turned out – that Chamberlain had missed a great opportunity for enlisting American support. (In fact, nothing of the kind was even remotely envisaged in Washington.) He was still more angry that a decision on foreign policy had been taken without consulting him. Also he still objected to opening conversations with Italy at once, since (so he said) he did not trust Mussolini. Chamberlain even enlisted the assistance of Grandi, the Italian ambassador, whom he invited to meet him with Eden in the Cabinet room. They tried to find a satisfactory formula which would express *de jure* recognition once the Italian volunteers had been withdrawn from Spain. But Eden refused to alter his position and Chamberlain appealed to the Cabinet.

The Cabinet met next day, 20 February, and fourteen members unequivocally supported the Prime Minister against the Foreign Secretary. Only four had some reservations – Malcolm Macdonald, W. S. Morrison, Lord Zetland and Walter Elliott – and they were greatly outnumbered. In the result Eden said he had no alternative but to resign. But the rest of the Cabinet begged him to hold his hand and reconsider his position. This he agreed to do and the Cabinet adjourned until the following afternoon.

Before the adjourned meeting he and Chamberlain met and the Prime Minister asked him if he had changed his view. Eden replied that he had not. The Prime Minister remarked that when they met again Eden would have a lot of persuasion from their colleagues. 'No doubt that will be so', replied Eden, 'but they will not alter my decision. I hope that the meeting will not be too long, for it will only prolong the agony.'

According to Eden, after they had reached this conclusion, the Prime Minister observed that it was only fair that Eden should know that the Italians had now accepted his formula for the withdrawal of volunteers from Spain. 'Have they, Neville? I have heard nothing of it', Eden retorted. 'No word has reached the Foreign Office and I am still Foreign Secretary.'

The Prime Minister was visibly embarrassed. 'I cannot tell you how I heard it', he went on, 'but you may take it from me that it is true.' Chamberlain did not elaborate. However, it is now known that he had heard the news indirectly from Grandi, who gave it to the legal adviser to the Italian embassy (a British subject named Dingli), who in turn told the Director of the Conservative Research Department, Sir Joseph Ball, who passed it on to the Prime Minister.

'This will make no difference to my decision', said Eden, trying to conceal his astonishment. 'Anyway, my head on a charger ought to be worth more to you than a formula.' The Prime Minister smiled wryly but made no comment.

Downing Street was more crowded than on the previous day, since news of the Cabinet crisis had been the subject of much comment in the morning papers. Eden persisted in his refusal to budge. During a pause in the meeting, Kingsley Wood took him aside and begged him again to reconsider his decision. 'I know Neville well', he said. 'He has had his lesson and this will not happen again.'

'I don't see why you should be worried', Eden replied, remembering Kingsley Wood's remark about his pro-French policy a short time before. 'After all, you'll be able to improve your relations with Hitler now!'

There was a final attempt at compromise when it was suggested that Eden should accept the formal opening of conversations with Italy, provided Italy accepted the formula for withdrawing the volunteers. But, as Eden afterwards put it in his memoirs, this attempt failed as it was bound to do, since it was the formal opening to which he objected, 'as an imprudent concession to Mussolini and one likely to divide us from the French Government, which had not as yet even been consulted'.

After the meeting Eden returned to the Foreign Office to write out his letter of resignation.

It cannot be in the country's interest [he told Chamberlain] that those who are called upon to direct its affairs should work in an uneasy partnership, fully conscious of differences in outlook yet hoping that they will not recur. This applies with special force to the relationship between the Prime Minister and the Foreign Secretary. It is for these reasons that with very deep regret I have decided that I must leave you and your colleagues with whom I have been associated during years of great difficulty and stress.

The Parliamentary Under-Secretary, Lord Cranborne, and Eden's Parliamentary Private Secretary, J. P. L. Thomas, both of whom strongly sympathized with their chief and the line he had taken, sent in their resignations at the same time. To the Cabinet and the country at large these resignations came as a severe shock, particularly since both Eden and Cranborne were comparatively young ministers as well as being men of considerable promise and admitted integrity, who were greatly looked up to and respected by the younger and more progressive Conservatives in the House of Commons.

The Prime Minister himself felt the loss acutely. 'I have won through', he confessed to a friend at the time, 'but it has only been with blood and tears.' Nevertheless he had his devoted admirers on the Conservative back benches. One of these was Henry Channon, who also kept a diary. 'Chamberlain's stock soars', he noted a few days later, on 5 March. 'I think he is the shrewdest Prime Minister of modern times; and it is a pity he did not drop Anthony [Eden] months ago.'

VI

Eden was immediately succeeded at the Foreign Office by Lord Halifax. The objection voiced by the Labour Opposition to having a peer as Foreign Secretary was met by the Prime Minister's undertaking that, with the aid of Mr R. A. (later Lord) Butler, who took Lord Cranborne's place as Under-Secretary, he would answer for the Foreign Office in the House of Commons. Although he had a mind of his own, the new Foreign Secretary was very much a man after the Prime Minister's own mind and much more attuned to it than Eden had ever been. Time and again Chamberlain expressed his gratitude for having such a 'steady, unruffled Foreign Secretary who never causes me any worry' as Edward Halifax. And it so happened that he had already met Hitler.

A few months previously, in November 1937, Halifax had received a somewhat bizarre invitation addressed to him in his capacity as Master of the Middleton Hunt to visit Germany to 'shoot foxes' and attend a hunting exhibition in Berlin. The invitation was accepted as a pretext for seeing the various Nazi leaders, and in due course Halifax was taken to meet the Führer in his mountain retreat at Berchtesgaden. 'He struck me as very sincere, and believing everything he said', Halifax recorded of his somewhat disjointed three-hour talk with Hitler.

I definitely got the impression that apart from colonies there was little or nothing he wanted from us, and that as regards European problems he felt time to be on his side. The result was that, while I think he wants to be on friendly terms with us, he is not going to be in any hurry to consider the question of League of Nations return, regards disarmament as pretty hopeless, and in short feels himself to be in a strong position and is not going to run after us. He did not give me the impression of being at all likely to go to war with us over colonies; but no doubt, if he cannot be met on this issue, good relations, without which the present strain continues, would remain impossible.

Eden had made it very clear to Halifax both orally and by telegram that he should warn Hitler of the dangers likely to arise through German intervention in Central Europe. According to the German interpreter's record, Halifax spoke of England's interest 'to see that any alteration should come through the course of peaceful evolution'. But no doubt the phrase conveyed quite different meanings to the Führer and his English visitor. Anyhow Halifax's observations had no deterrent effect upon Hitler, who had secretly told his chief political lieutenants and military Chiefs of Staff of his aggressive plans, and there is no doubt that these plans depended upon a carefully worked out timetable.

Austria was to be the first victim. The coup against her was fore-shadowed when Hitler, who had just assumed supreme command of Germany's armed forces, met the Austrian Chancellor Dr Kurt Von Schuschnigg and his Foreign Minister Guido Schmidt at Berchtesgaden on 12 February 1938. In a browbeating and bullying mood the Führer threatened that Austria would be invaded by German troops unless the Austrian Chancellor agreed to the appointment of an Austrian Nazi, Arthur Seyss-Inquart, as Minister of Security in the Austrian Government, a general amnesty for all Austrian Nazis in detention, and other humiliating demands. Hitler warned Schuschnigg that he could expect no help from England, France or Italy. In fact, Hitler was uncertain of Mussolini's attitude until a few days later, since at the time of the murder by Austrian Nazis of Schuschnigg's predecessor Dollfuss in 1934, the Duce had moved troops to the Brenner Pass. Now Schuschnigg learned that it was too late to expect any help from that quarter. 'I will never forget Mussolini for this', said Hitler at the time. 'Never, never, never. . . . I shall stick to him whatever may happen, even if the whole world were against him.'

Schuschnigg tried to counter Hitler's tactics by ordering a plebiscite for 13 March. But Hitler forestalled his move two days before by ordering German troops to occupy Austria. The troops accordingly marched in to Austria on the 12th to be greeted with rapture by the mass of the population except the Austrian Jews.

It so happened that on that very same day in London Ribbentrop, the German ambassador, was preparing to leave to take up his appointment as German Foreign Minister, and Chamberlain and his wife gave a farewell luncheon for him and Frau Ribbentrop at No. 10 Downing Street. A dozen or more guests were invited including Churchill, who happened to be sitting beside Sir Alexander Cadogan, who had recently succeeded Vansittart as permanent head of the Foreign Office after Vansittart had been 'kicked upstairs' with the hollow title of Chief Diplomatic Adviser on account of his strongly anti-German sympathies. About half-way through the meal a Foreign Office messenger came into the room and handed Cadogan an envelope. Cadogan immediately opened it and when he had read the contents got up and walked round to the Prime Minister and showed it to him. It contained the alarming news of the Nazi invasion of Austria.

After lunch Chamberlain managed to get hold of Ribbentrop and took him into his study where he taxed him with the news. Ribbentrop simply could not understand why the British Prime Minister was so concerned. This was a local matter, he explained, and the so-called *Anschluss* between Germany and Austria a natural consequence of the desires of the Austrian people.

To Chamberlain it was now clear that the only argument which Germany understood was force. Yet he was determined to persevere with his policy of appeasement. 'Heaven knows I don't want to get back to alliances', he wrote at the time. 'But if Germany continues to behave as she has done lately, she may drive us to it.'

It is tragic to think that very possibly this might not have happened if I had had Halifax at the Foreign Office instead of Anthony at the time I wrote my letter to Mussolini....

For the moment we must abandon conversations with Germany, we must show our determination not to be bullied by announcing some increase or acceleration in rearmament, and we must quietly and steadily pursue our conversations with Italy. If we can avoid another violent coup – in Czechoslovakia – which ought to be feasible, it may be possible for Europe to settle down again, and some day for us to start peace talks again with the Germans.

The talks with Italy, which had caused Eden's resignation, began almost immediately and were brought to a successful conclusion on 16 April when an agreement was signed in Rome by Ciano and Lord Perth, the British ambassador. It included a declaration that neither Government would use propaganda to injure the interests of the other.

For her part Italy disclaimed any territorial ambitions in Spain and Spanish overseas possessions, while Britain undertook to raise the question of the recognition of the Italian conquest of Abyssinia at Geneva, provided (in Chamberlain's words) 'it was shown to be an essential feature of a general appeasement'. That in turn depended on the outcome of the Spanish Civil War, and the Prime Minister in common with the rest of the Cabinet continued to support the policy of non-intervention. Thus he defended himself and his policy in the House of Commons at this time:

Because I do not share the views of the Opposition that one has to take sides with the party they favour in Spain, they charge me with having a bias towards dictators. There is no foundation for the charge. But I have to deal with a world in which dictatorships exist. I have no interest in other forms of government, except in so far as they react on other countries. I have no bias in favour of Nazism, Fascism or Bolshevism, because all of them seem to me to be inconsistent with what is all important to me because *it is the root of my political creed, and that is individual liberty.* [Author's italics.]

Chamberlain believed that, if the Italian negotiations had been initiated earlier, Hitler's forcible annexation might have been avoided through Mussolini's moderating influence, and there is no doubt that as late as 18 February, on the eve of Eden's resignation, Grandi assured both the Prime Minister and the Foreign Secretary that no prior agreement on Austria had been reached between the two dictators. This is confirmed by Hitler's almost hysterical relief when he heard that the Duce proposed to take no action as the result of Hitler's Austrian coup. However that may be, Mussolini's wish to begin conversations earlier in the year was not because he disliked the idea of an *Anschluss* between Germany and Austria, but because Mussolini and Ciano thought that it would be easier to reach an understanding before Hitler pounced on Schuschnigg and made the *Anschluss* a reality. In the event it was not until November 1938 that the Anglo–Italian agreement which had been concluded the previous April was brought into force. By that time the Spanish Civil War was nearing its end, and Chamberlain had come to believe that Spain was not 'a menace to European peace any longer'.

Chamberlain's belief in rearmament, in spite of Eden's complaint about the slow pace at which it was proceeding, as a concomitant of his appeasement policy, has already been noted. Indeed he had realized this when he was at the Treasury, and it is only fair to credit him with the fact that the Defence White Papers of 1936 and 1937 were largely his production. Even Churchill had given him credit for this. 'When the late Government were at length convinced of the urgent need to rearm', Churchill acknowledged in 1937, 'no one was more active than Mr Chamberlain.' The greatest need was in the air, but without something like industrial conscription, which it was considered that the English people would not tolerate in peacetime, little could be done to increase production, particularly in the construction of military aircraft, than had already been done under Swinton, the Air Minister, and his industrial adviser Lord Weir.

In December 1937, an important decision was taken by the Cabinet on Inskip's initiative to shift the emphasis from the production of bombers to that of fighters, largely because fighters were cheaper to manufacture and to a lesser extent because of the need felt to strengthen the air defence of the United Kingdom. Inskip's view carried the day in the face of opposition from Swinton and the Air Staff. When the matter was debated in the Cabinet on 22 December 1937, the Prime Minister stressed 'the necessity of maintaining economic stability as an essential element in defensive strength', as indeed Inskip had advocated. 'In my view, this is a matter of first importance', Chamberlain remarked. 'It may be that in the next war our enemy would aim at a 'knockout' blow, but the evidence before me does not show that it would be likely to succeed. . . . If that view is correct, the factor of our staying power must be present in the minds of other Governments as well as ourselves. They must be asking themselves what are our chances in a long war.'

Mounting public criticism came to a head when the air expansion programme was debated in Parliament on 12 May 1938. Mr Attlee, speaking for the Labour Opposition in the Commons, had accused the Government of 'war mongering' four years previously. Now he boldly stated an unpalatable truth: 'At the present time not only have we not got parity with Germany, but we are getting further away from air parity every week and every month.'

The sequel occurred next morning when Chamberlain sent for Swinton and abruptly dismissed him. 'I want you to go', he said, without assigning any reason. Swinton turned down the offer of another Cabinet job and immediately resigned. He was succeeded at the Air Ministry by Sir Kingsley Wood, a particular friend of Chamberlain's, whose place as Minister of Health was taken by Walter Elliot.

One result of Hitler's takeover in Vienna was that the neighbouring state of Czechoslovakia was threatened. 'If Austria goes, Czechoslovakia is indefensible', Austen Chamberlain had warned in 1936. How true this was, the events of 12 March 1938 amply demonstrated, and the Prime Minister, the Chiefs of Staff and the Foreign Office experts had to take a realistic view of the new situation. 'You have only to look at the map to see that nothing that we or France could do could possibly save Czechoslovakia from being overrun by the Germans if they wanted to do it', Chamberlain wrote to Ida a week later. The Austrian frontier was practically open, the great Skoda munitions works at Pilsen were within bombing distance of the German aerodromes, and Soviet Russia, on whom the Czechs relied for help, was a hundred miles away.

Therefore we could not help Czechoslovakia – she would simply be a pretext for going to war with Germany. That we could not think of unless we had a reasonable prospect of being able to beat her to her knees in a reasonable time, and of that I see no sign. *I have therefore abandoned the idea of giving guarantees to Czechoslovakia, or to France in connection with her obligations to that country.* [Author's italics.]

Czechoslovakia came into existence in the closing stages of the First World War in 1918, when the Czechoslovak National Council, of which Dr Edouard Beneš was general secretary in Paris, was recognized by the Allies as the country's Provisional Government with Beneš as its Foreign Minister. It was made up of remnants of the old Austrian Habsburg Empire and embodied the districts of Bohemia, Moravia and Slovakia, but not in accordance with the principle of self-determination, since it contained a number of minorities of which the largest, forming about $3\frac{1}{4}$ million, was mainly concentrated in the German-speaking area in the region of Karlsbad known as Sudetenland. The remaining population consisted approximately of $7\frac{1}{2}$ million Czechs, mostly inhabiting Bohemia and Moravia, $2\frac{1}{3}$ million Slovaks in Slovakia, and a heterogeneous collection of Magyars, Ruthenians and Poles. Lloyd George has been blamed for 'creating' Czechoslovakia, unfairly so since it really created itself. In fact, the British Prime Minister is said to have had 'serious' misgivings about the new state, but was assured by Dr Beneš at the Paris Peace Conference that the minorities would be organized on a regional or cantonal system comparable with Switzerland. This assurance did not materialize, since a centralized Czechoslovak state was established, administered from the old Bohemian capital of Prague. The most vocal discontent was expressed by the Sudeten Germans, who complained with but little justification that they were treated as 'second-class' citizens; now encouraged by their leader Konrad Henlein they demanded complete autonomy. Similar demands for self-government were put forward by the other minorities, particularly the Slovaks.

On 21 May, a military coup planned by Hitler in support of an anticipated revolt was forestalled, at least for the moment, by a rapid mobilization of the Czech army. Hitler's reaction was to increase the strength of the *Reichswehr* to $1\frac{1}{2}$ million men under arms. 'The more I hear about last weekend the more I feel what a "damned close-run thing" it was', Chamberlain wrote to Ida on 28 May; he also felt that the coup was avoided, by the Czech military action already noted, and by Hitler deciding that the risks were too great 'after getting our warnings'. 'The incident shows how utterly untrustworthy the German Government is', Chamberlain added, 'and it illuminates the difficulties in the way of the peacemaker'.

Thenceforward the Sudeten Germans became increasingly provocative and their relations with the Prague Government rapidly deteriorated. In July Halifax, with Chamberlain's agreement, despatched Walter (by now Viscount) Runciman to Prague as an 'independent mediator' between the Czechoslovak Government and the Sudeten German Party. Although he did his best, Runciman must have realized from the beginning that his mission was doomed to failure. The most he hoped for was, as he put it on his arrival, 'a little accommodation on some practical problems', but even this was not forthcoming. Various concessions were reluctantly offered by the Prague Government, but the Sudeten Germans refused to negotiate under the pretext of minor incidents, in reality artificially created 'outrages'.

Runciman's efforts were further frustrated by a warlike and provocative speech delivered by Hitler to his legions at the annual Nuremberg Party Rally on 12 September. A few days later Runciman with the rest of his small mission returned to London, tired and dispirited.

In these circumstances [Chamberlain subsequently declared in the House of Commons] I decided that the time had come to put into operation a plan which I had had in mind for a considerable period as a last resort. One of the principal difficulties in dealing with totalitarian Governments is the lack of any means of establishing contact with the personalities in whose hands lie the final decisions for the country. So I resolved to go to Germany myself to interview Herr Hitler and find out in personal conversation whether there was yet any hope of saving the peace.

Here is how he described to his sister Ida, in more familiar language, his decision and its immediate result:

Two things were essential, first that the plan should be tried just when things looked blackest, and second that it should be a complete surprise.... On Tuesday night [13 September] I saw that the moment had come and must be taken if it was not to be too late. So I sent the fateful telegram [to Hitler]* and told the Cabinet next morning what I had done....

At last during the afternoon my anxiety was relieved. Hitler was entirely at my disposal, and would not Mrs Chamberlain come too! Afterwards I heard from Hitler himself, and it was confirmed by others who were with him, that he was struck all of a heap, and exclaimed, 'I can't possibly let a man of his age come all this way; I must go to London.'

* 'In view of increasing critical situation, I propose to come over at once to see you, with a view to trying to find peaceful solution. I propose to come across by air, and am ready to start tomorrow. Please indicate earliest time at which you can see me and suggest place of meeting. Should be grateful for very early reply.' Chamberlain to Hitler, 13 September 1938.

Of course, Chamberlain went on in the account he gave Ida, when Hitler considered the matter further 'he saw that wouldn't do, and indeed it would not have suited me, for it would have deprived my coup of much of its dramatic force'.

4

MUNICH AND WAR

I

TODAY, WHEN 'summit' meetings take place frequently between leading figures in totalitarian and democratic countries, an initiative akin to Chamberlain's would excite little or no surprise. But in 1938 what Chamberlain proposed was a startling innovation, and he was criticized on the ground that it lowered the dignity of a Prime Minister. Lord Halifax, the Foreign Secretary, who was not invited to accompany the Prime Minister, admitted when he first heard of it that it 'rather took his breath away'. In the event Chamberlain's sole official companion on the flight was a forty-six-year-old civil servant, Sir Horace Wilson, whose official position was Chief Industrial Adviser to the Government and who had become the Prime Minister's close confidant.

Chamberlain has been accused of taking Wilson away from the Ministry of Labour and using him for all sorts of purposes, principally to circumvent the Foreign Office. This is not so. Wilson had been seconded from the Labour Ministry by Baldwin for special service with the Prime Minister. Chamberlain had inherited him from his predecessor and decided to retain him as he found this extremely able civil servant both congenial and useful. But he never became the kind of 'grey eminence' that many people thought him. Although it is probably true to say that he had more influence with Chamberlain than many members of the Cabinet, he did not dictate policy. Chamberlain was always his own policy-maker, and although he no doubt welcomed suggestions from Wilson in this field he never accepted them unquestioningly. What he particularly liked about Wilson was his tidy, well-ordered civil service mentality, which made him suitable both as a confidant and occasionally as an emissary.

Chamberlain and Wilson left Heston aerodrome for Munich on the morning of 15 September. It was the Prime Minister's first journey by air; and, as he thought it would create a bad impression in Germany if he arrived in a Royal Air Force machine, he travelled in a civil aircraft of American make, a Lockheed Electra. At this time British aircraft manufacturers were all employed turning out aircraft for the RAF, which explains why the Air Ministry was unable to produce a civil machine of British manufacture. Another feature of the flight was that in the rush of preparing for his journey Chamberlain omitted to obtain the King's permission to leave the country, a constitutional convention about which other Prime Ministers, notably Churchill, have always been most punctilious. However, George VI graciously ignored the oversight.

After flying through a storm, the aircraft landed at Munich in the rain. But the weather did not damp the apparent enthusiasm of the well-drilled crowds which lined the route to the railway station where the Prime Minister and his party boarded a train for the three-hour journey to Berchtesgaden. They were welcomed by similar demonstrations when the train stopped from time to time on the way. Then followed the mountain drive to the Berghof, the Führer's retreat where Hitler was waiting to greet them, bareheaded and dressed in a khaki-coloured coat of broadcloth with a red armlet and a swastika on it and the military cross on his breast. 'His hair is brown, not black, his eyes blue, his expression rather disagreeable, especially in repose, and altogether he looks entirely undistinguished', was Chamberlain's first impression. 'You would never notice him in a crowd and would take him for the house painter he once was.'

According to Duff Cooper, Chamberlain later described the Führer to the Cabinet as 'frightful' and 'the commonest little dog you ever saw'. But the Secretary of the Cabinet Sir Edward Bridges was more discreet in the minutes: 'On a first view Hitler was unimpressive. There was nothing out of the common in his features.'

The Führer led the way to the large room with a huge window commanding a magnificent view towards Salzburg, but owing to the mist only the valley and the bottoms of the mountains could be seen. Tea was laid at a round table at which Hitler sat with his guests and interpreter Dr Schmidt. Chamberlain found his host shy and his features did not relax when the Prime Minister endeavoured to find some small talk.

'I have often heard of this room', Chamberlain remarked, 'but it is much larger than I expected.'

'It is you who have the big rooms in England', answered Hitler.

'You must come and see them some time.'

'I should be received with demonstrations of disapproval', Hitler countered.

'Well', said Chamberlain, 'perhaps it would be wise to choose the moment.' At which, noted Chamberlain afterwards, Hitler permitted himself the shadow of a smile.

After tea Hitler took Chamberlain to an upstairs room whose walls, noted the Prime Minister, like the downstairs reception room, were decorated with pictures of nudes, but were otherwise completely bare of ornament. Their talk, which lasted for three hours, was mainly concerned with the question of Czechoslovakia. At one moment Hitler became very excited. 'I want to get down to realities', he exclaimed. 'Three hundred Sudetens have been killed. . . . The thing has got to be settled at once. I am determined to settle it. I do not care whether there is a world war or not. . . . I am prepared to risk a world war rather than allow this to drag on.'

It was now Chamberlain's turn to become indignant, and he inquired with some asperity why the Führer had allowed him to come all the way to Berchtesgaden if in fact he were determined to reach a settlement by force. Eventually, after some further heated exchanges, Hitler quietened down, his whole manner changed, and he accepted Chamberlain's suggestion for the separation of the Sudeten Germans from the rest of Czechoslovakia after he (Chamberlain) had consulted his Cabinet and the French. 'My personal opinion was that on principle I didn't care two hoots whether the Sudetens were in the Reich or out of it according to their own wishes', Chamberlain afterwards admitted to Ida, 'but I saw immense practical difficulties in a plebiscite.' They then broke off their talk and agreed to resume it after Chamberlain had held his consultations. 'I am very sorry that you should have to make two journeys', said Hitler. 'However, next time I shall come to meet you somewhere near Cologne.' Chamberlain found him much more cordial when they parted. In the meantime Hitler undertook to stay his hand. 'I got the impression', Chamberlain noted after he had left to return home, 'that here was a man who could be relied upon when he had given his word.'

The British Cabinet argued the pros and cons but eventually agreed to accept the principle of self-determination and to give the Prime Minister the support he asked for. The French proved more difficult. Edouard Daladier, the French Prime Minister, accompanied by the Foreign Minister Georges Bonnet, came to London on 18 September. Daladier argued that Hitler's real aim was the domination of Europe, and if Chamberlain believed in Hitler's good faith, would he guarantee the proposed new truncated Czechoslovakia? The meeting took place in the Cabinet Room at No. 10 Downing Street, the British ministers in addition to Chamberlain being Halifax, Simon and Hoare, with advisers in the persons of Vansittart, Cadogan, and Wilson. Daladier and Bonnet also had their advisers with them. In the event it was agreed to send a telegram to Beneš in Prague announcing that in the considered view of the British and French Governments only the cession of the Sudetenland to Germany could avoid war, and that if he agreed, as he was strongly pressed to do, the British and French would guarantee Czechoslovakia against 'unprovoked aggression'.

The rest of the British Cabinet, faced with a *fait accompli*, again acquiesced. Only Hore-Belisha, the War Minister, indicated his apprehensions that the Army, being far from ready to fight, was now being saddled with a new continental commitment. Chamberlain sought to soothe his fears, assuring him (according to the Cabinet minutes) that 'it was not right to assume that the guarantees committed us to maintaining the existing boundaries of Czechoslovakia. . . . The guarantee merely related to unprovoked aggression. He appreciated the difficulty of seeing how we would implement the guarantee. Its main value would be in its deterrent effect.'

After first rejecting the Anglo–French proposals, President Beneš was eventually driven to agree to them on 21 September in face of the threat that if he did not do so Britain and France would stand aside and refuse to support him.

Next day Chamberlain set off by air for his second meeting with Hitler, this time at Godesberg on the Rhine. If the British Prime Minister imagined that he had merely to settle the details, he was speedily disillusioned. Hitler, no longer satisfied with the transfer of the Sudeten territory after negotiating the necessary details, now wished for immediate occupation. The Führer's difficult mood was no doubt buttressed by the knowledge that the Poles and Hungarians were making similar claims. No delay was possible, Hitler emphasized; a settlement must be reached within the next few days. The Czechs must withdraw their army, police and other state organs from all German-speaking areas forthwith, and the ceded territory would at once be occupied by German troops. He also refused to consider a non-aggression pact with the new truncated Czechoslovakia so long as the Polish and Hungarian minorities remained unsatisfied, no doubt under the impression that partition would quickly lead to disintegration.

Chamberlain's reaction was to issue a stern warning which he did in a letter despatched from the Petersberg Hotel, where he and his advisers were staying, to the Hotel Dreesen at Godesberg, where Hitler waited and perhaps pondered that it was from this hotel that he gave the orders for the 'blood bath' of 30 June 1934, which resulted in the slaughter of Ernst Roehm and many of his old comrades in the SA. 'In the event of German troops moving into the areas as you propose', Chamberlain wrote on 23 September, 'there is no doubt that the Czech Government would have no option but to order their forces to resist.'

The seeming deadlock was broken by Hitler promising not to act prior to 1 October, before which in any event he would not be ready. ('You are the only man to whom I have ever made a concession.') At the same time he produced a 'memorandum' for Chamberlain to take back with him to London. In this he demanded that the occupation of the Sudetenland should begin on 26 September and be completed three days later, while the evacuated territory should be handed over without so much as the removal of a single peasant's cow. The definitive frontier would be settled by a plebiscite in November. That was his last word, he said. In that case, Chamberlain replied, there was no purpose in negotiating any further, and he would go home with a heavy heart since he saw the final wreck of all his hopes for the peace of Europe. 'It's up to the Czechs now', he said to the newspaper reporters as he left Godesberg on the 24th, after he had assured Hitler that he would communicate the contents of the 'memorandum' to the Czechoslovak Government after he had laid it before his own Cabinet.

The Cabinet met the same night immediately after the Prime Minister had got back to Downing Street. The sense of the meeting was that the terms of the Godesberg memorandum were unacceptable, while at the same time it was clear that public opinion had been hardening against further appeasement. The Labour Party and the trade unions in particular were for resistance. Preparations were now hastily made for war. Primitive slit trenches were dug in the London parks, air raid shelters were improvized, while 38 million gas-masks were distributed to the adult population. A day or two later the Fleet was mobilized, on Chamberlain's initiative, and the Auxiliary Air Force called up.

On 27 September the Prime Minister broadcast a message to the nation and the empire, in which he declared that it was unreasonable that 'a quarrel which had already been settled in principle should be the subject of war', and although he could well understand the Czech rejection of the Godesberg memorandum, nevertheless he believed that, if only time were allowed, 'it ought to be possible for the arrangements for transferring the territory that the Czech Government has agreed to give to Germany to be settled by agreement, under conditions which would assure fair treatment to the population concerned'. Meanwhile he would not abandon his efforts for peace as long as any chance remained. 'I would not hesitate', he added, 'to pay a third visit to Germany if I thought it would do any good.'

II

On the previous day Horace Wilson had gone to Berlin as Chamberlain's personal emissary 'to keep the door open' by making a fresh appeal to Hitler. At first the Führer refused to be moved, but he later relented a little and wrote a personal letter to Chamberlain in which he gave certain assurances about the German occupation of Sudetenland and the subsequent plebiscite and offered to join in a guarantee of the frontiers of the new Czechoslovakia. The Prime Minister, in what he later described as making 'the last desperate snatch at the last tuft of grass on the very edge of the precipice', thereupon drafted a reply proposing 'to come to Berlin myself at once to discuss arrangements for transfer with you and representatives of the Czech Government, together with representatives of

France and Italy if you desire'. At the same time, he made a bid for Mussolini's support. 'I trust Your Excellency', he cabled the Duce, 'will inform the German Chancellor that you are willing to be represented and urge him to agree to my proposal which will keep all our peoples out of war.'

This message was a shrewd move on the Prime Minister's part, since in view of the recently concluded Anglo–Italian Agreement, Chamberlain had every reason to believe that the Italian dictator would use his influence with Hitler as a mediator for peace. Chamberlain was not disappointed. Next morning, 28 September, the Duce instructed Bernardo Attolico, his ambassador in Berlin, to advise Hitler to postpone mobilization for twenty-four hours and to accept Chamberlain's proposal for an international conference. Meanwhile Parliament had been recalled, and that same afternoon Chamberlain appeared in the House of Commons to give members a detailed chronological account of the events leading up to the crisis and his meetings with Hitler.

Chamberlain, who received a warm and friendly reception when he took his place on the Treasury Bench, spoke to a densely packed House, with members spilling over into the gangways and crowding before the Bar, while the galleries were filled with all manner of distinguished individuals, including Queen Mary. The Prime Minister had been speaking, in his usual calm and measured tones, for about an hour to a largely silent and tense House. Suddenly a sheet of Foreign Office writing paper was handed by a messenger to one of the Foreign Office staff in the civil servants' 'box' in the corner of the Government side of the House. It had come from Halifax who was sitting in the Peers' Gallery, and it contained the contents of a telegram which had just arrived from Berlin. The official signalled to Lord Dunglass (later successively Lord Home, Sir Alec Douglas-Home, and again Lord Home), the Prime Minister's Parliamentary Private Secretary, who passed it along the Front Bench to Sir John Simon, who was sitting next to the Prime Minister. In a moment or two Simon was seen to be pulling Chamberlain by his coat tails, just as he was describing his appeal to Mussolini and the latter's anticipated reaction. He paused to read the message on the paper, and when he faced the House again he was seen to be smiling. 'Shall I tell them?' he whispered audibly to Simon and several other colleagues. 'Yes', was their unanimous reply.

'That is not all', Chamberlain now continued his speech. 'I have been informed by Herr Hitler that he invites me to meet him in Munich tomorrow morning. He has also invited Signor Mussolini and Monsieur Daladier. Signor Mussolini has accepted and I have no doubt Monsieur Daladier will also accept. I need not say what my answer will be.'

'Thank God for the Prime Minister!' exclaimed one unidentified member, possibly Henry Channon, whose admiration of Chamberlain had always been near-ecstatic. This was the signal for a hysterical demonstration, the like of which has rarely been witnessed in parliamentary history. Members cheered wildly and waved their order papers in the air; others in tears crowded round Chamberlain and, with what Simon described as 'unrestrained emotion', grasped the Prime Minister by the hand. There was an outburst of hand-clapping in the galleries, in which Chamberlain's predecessor as Prime Minister, Lord Baldwin, joined, forgetting in the excitement of the moment the rule which forbids this kind of applause. Winston Churchill, however, was not quite so enthusiastic as some of his fellow members. 'I congratulate you on your good fortune', he said to Chamberlain. 'You have been very lucky.'

Early next morning Chamberlain again set off from Heston, telling the reporters waiting with the rest of the Cabinet to see him off, 'If at first you don't succeed, try, try again!' and expressing the hope that on his return he might be able to say, like Shakespeare's Hotspur in *Henry V*, 'Out of this nettle, danger, we pluck this flower, safety'.

The conference assembled in Hitler's Munich headquarters and lasted, with breaks for lunch and dinner, for some fourteen hours. Mussolini appeared ostensibly in the part of impartial mediator, but it has since been established that the proposals which he put forward had been drafted for him by Goering and the German Foreign Ministry. There was seemingly interminable wrangling over the question of compensation for Czech property in the Sudetenland, which so infuriated Hitler that at one moment he shouted at Chamberlain, 'Our time is too valuable to be wasted on such trivialities.' Eventually it was agreed that the question should be referred with others to the International Commission to be charged with settling the new territorial boundaries and similar matters. Otherwise Hitler's demands were adopted virtually unchanged, except for the fact that the evacuation was to be spread over ten days instead of immediately as required in the Godesberg memorandum. The new truncated Czechoslovakia was to be guaranteed by the four powers when the question of the Polish and Hungarian minorities had been settled, which matters were also left to the Commission.

Shortly after midnight the Munich Agreement, after protracted redrafting and irritating delays and arguments, was at last ready for signature. But when the moment came, it was discovered to the general embarrassment that the ornate inkpot which had been provided for the ceremonial signing was empty. As Chamberlain's biographer Iain Macleod was later to write, in retrospect it might be said that the Munich agreement itself was just as empty.

Next morning Chamberlain had a further meeting with the German Führer, this time in Hitler's flat in Munich. The Prime Minister described himself to Hitler as being 'oppressed by the thought of the increasing burden which was being imposed upon all countries by the expenditure upon armaments, which was eating up the capital which ought to be employed on building houses, on better food, and on improving the health of the people'. To this Hitler replied that, where disarmament was concerned, 'if a single nation refuses to agree all the others have to follow her example'.

Before they parted, Chamberlain remarked that 'he thought it would be a pity if this meeting passed off with nothing more than the settlement of the Czech question'. What he had in mind, he went on, was to suggest that it would be helpful to both Britain and Germany and to the world in general if they could issue some statement which showed the agreement between them on the desirability of better Anglo–German relations leading to a greater European stability. In fact, he had drafted a brief statement to this effect and they could sign it immediately if the Führer agreed. 'Ja! Ja!' said Hitler when Chamberlain's remarks were translated. The document which they signed is reproduced opposite.

When he arrived back at Heston later that day, Chamberlain waved this piece of paper before the eyes of the assembled Press men, exclaiming 'I've got it!' and he broadcast its contents before leaving the airfield to see the King. 'Come straight to the Palace', so ran the royal message which awaited him on touching down at Heston, 'so that I can express to you personally my heartfelt

We, the German Führer and Chancellor and the
British Prime Minister, have had a further
meeting today and are agreed in recognising that
the question of Anglo-German relations is of the
first importance for the two countries and for
Europe.

We regard the agreement signed last night
and the Anglo-German Naval Agreement as symbolic
of the desire of our two peoples never to go to
war with one another again.

We are resolved that the method of
consultation shall be the method adopted to deal
with any other questions that may concern our two
countries, and we are determined to continue our
efforts to remove possible sources of difference
and thus to contribute to assure the peace of
Europe.

[signature]

Neville Chamberlain

September 30. 1938.

congratulations on the success of your visit to Munich.' All the way
to the Palace, as the Prime Minister described the scene to his
sisters, the streets were 'lined from one end to the other with people
of every class, shouting themselves hoarse, leaping on the running
board, banging on the windows, and thrusting their hands into the
car to be shaken.' Halifax, who accompanied him in the car, begged
Chamberlain not to exploit the popularity which his success had
brought him by holding a General Election. The Foreign Secretary

also suggested that Chamberlain should reconstruct his Government so as to include Churchill and Eden and also the Labour leaders if they would join. The Prime Minister said he would think it over. In the event he was to accept the first piece of advice but to reject the second.

He and his wife, who had also met the plane at Heston, received a tremendous ovation when they reached Buckingham Palace and appeared on the front balcony with the King and Queen. Later the same evening he spoke from an upper window of No. 10 Downing Street to an enthusiastic crowd which sang, 'For he's a jolly good fellow!' On this occasion he was to use a phrase which he was later to regret and in effect retract, when he said: 'This is the second time in our history that there has come back from Germany to Downing Street peace with honour.* I believe it is peace for our time.'

His predecessor as Prime Minister hoped events would prove Chamberlain right. 'You have everything in your hands now – for a time – and you can do anything you like', Baldwin told him. '*Use that time well, for it won't last!*'

III

There is no doubt that Chamberlain's achievement in averting a general war was received with relief not only in Britain and the dominions but also in Europe as well. During the three weeks immediately after Munich Chamberlain received more than 40,000 letters expressing gratitude and admiration for what he had done, while Mrs Chamberlain received a further 12,000. These messages were frequently accompanied by gifts which ranged from flowers and poems to fishing rods and salmon flies. Four thousand tulips arrived from Holland, there were cases of Alsatian wines from France, and from Greece came a whimsical request for a piece of his umbrella to become a relic in an icon. King Haakon of Norway cabled his congratulations and King Leopold of the Belgians wrote in his own hand. 'You have done a wonderful piece of work and done it under the guidance and providence of God', wrote the Labour leader George Lansbury, expressing a sentiment which

* The first time was when Disraeli returned from the Congress of Berlin in 1878.

was echoed by the Archbishop of Canterbury, as he put it, 'at a time of almost unexampled crisis. I thank God for it.' So far as the mass of the ordinary British people were concerned, they did not see the sense of going to war, in the words used by the Prime Minister in his broadcast on 27 September, 'because of a quarrel in a far-away country between people of whom we knew nothing'.

With one notable exception the Cabinet endorsed the immediate result of Chamberlain's mission. The exception was Duff Cooper, the First Lord of the Admiralty, who resigned and declared that Great Britain should have gone to war, not to save Czechoslovakia, but to prevent one country dominating the European continent 'by brute force'. No one supported Duff Cooper in the ensuing Commons debate, although there was a sense on the part of some members that the country was weakened and humiliated. When the Labour Opposition divided the House, some thirty Conservative members abstained, including several of Chamberlain's close or formerly close political friends such as Churchill, Eden, Cranborne and Amery. 'Your speech moved me very deeply, and very, very nearly persuaded both myself and Anthony Eden to vote', wrote Amery to the Prime Minister after the debate. 'I only hope that the misgivings, which even you could not dispel today, will be disproved by the events of the near future.'

In his speech Chamberlain referred to what he had said about 'peace for our time' and hoped that members would not be disposed to read into words 'used in a moment of some emotion, after a long and exhausting day, after I had driven through miles of excited, enthusiastic, cheering people', more than they were intended to convey.

I do indeed believe that we may yet secure peace for our time, but I never meant to suggest that we should do that by disarmament, until we can induce others to disarm too....

I realise that diplomacy cannot be effective unless the consciousness exists, not here alone, but elsewhere, that behind the diplomacy is the strength to give effect to it....

One good thing, at any rate, has come out of this emergency [the Prime Minister remarked in the same debate]. It has thrown a vivid light upon our preparations for defence, on their strength and on their weakness. I should not think we were doing our duty if we had not already ordered that a prompt and thorough inquiry should be made to cover the whole of our preparations, military and civil, in order to see, in the light of what has happened during these hectic days, what further steps may be necessary to make good our deficiencies in the shortest possible time.

Chamberlain claimed that Munich was the first step towards a new system of peace in Europe and at the same time defended it as an excuse for buying time until Britain was better armed. As A. J. P. Taylor has pointed out, he was not being dishonest or two-faced. 'He reflected the muddle in most English minds. Munich sprang from a mixture of fear and good intentions. In retrospect, fear predominated.' Thus the clearest lesson to be learned from the Munich crisis was that Britain should keep out of Europe.

The deficiency on which attention was rightly concentrated in the greatest measure, both inside and outside Parliament, was in the country's defence against air attack, including civil defence. There were none of the newer anti-aircraft guns; only 1430 search-lights were available out of an approved programme of 4128; and only 140 barrage balloons out of 450, while in the whole of London there were only sixty fire pumps. There were hardly any modern fighter aircraft. Out of twenty-nine mobilizable fighter squadrons amounting to 406 aircraft, only five were equipped with Hurricanes and only one with Spitfires. Even the Hurricanes would have been ineffective above certain heights, for example 15,000 feet in summer, as no arrangements had yet been perfected for heating the Browning guns with which they were armed. The situation in Bomber Command was little better, particularly in respect of shortage of aircraft, crews and spares. Indeed Churchill was not exaggerating when he declared in the House of Commons at this time: 'The equipment of the Royal Air Force is deplorable.' No wonder Marshal Goering boasted that he was the master in the air ('*In der Luft bin ich der Herr*'), since he knew that the RAF simply could not have taken on the *Luftwaffe* with any prospect of success if at the outset of hostilities Germany had mounted an air attack upon Britain. 'If we had gone to war in September', Inskip's Parliamentary Private Secretary Austin Hopkinson told Harold Nicolson, 'our air force would have been wiped out in three weeks and our pilots would have gone to certain death.' The truth was, as a senior Air Staff officer in charge of supply and organization bluntly told the Air Council: 'We have during the past few years been building up a front line air force which is nothing but a facade. We have nothing in the way of reserves and organization behind the front line with which to maintain it.'

Hitherto the Home Office had been responsible for air raid precautions and other aspects of civil defence. Hoare, who was Home Secretary, told Chamberlain in October that 'the burden of ARP' was 'too heavy' for him with all his other work. Accordingly he suggested that Sir John Anderson (later Lord Waverley), a most experienced administrator who had considerable knowledge of the subject, should be put in charge of civil defence. The Prime Minister agreed, and to facilitate this he also appointed Anderson Lord Privy Seal with a seat in the Cabinet.* It was a wise appointment since Anderson quickly produced results. Expenditure on ARP went up from £9¼ million in the current year to £42 million in the ensuing financial year, in addition to a further £9 million for the fire services. So-called 'Anderson' shelters were distributed to give people protection in their homes against all forms of bombing attack except a direct hit. At the same time Walter Elliot at the Health Ministry concerted plans for the evacuation of school children and finding some 3000 emergency beds in hospitals. Although the latter fell far short of the total aimed at, in the event casualties from air attack when it came were to prove in the aggregate far fewer than had been anticipated, since the experts had originally forecast casualties of the order of 200,000 a week, of which 66,000 would be fatal. As for hospital beds, in the event never more than 6000 were required at any one time, although the authorities provided for several hundred thousands. Radar and other scientific methods of defence were also extended and improved.

In the twelve months between Munich and the outbreak of war in the following September, there was a substantial increase in British armaments. This was by no means solely due to the sense of alarm generated by the crisis over Czechoslovakia, but rather to defence plans which had originated long before and would have come to fruition whether Munich had happened or not. Some of them, such as the heavy bomber production programme, were not designed to mature until considerably later than the actual outbreak of war in 1939. Duff Cooper thought that Hitler should have

* In the reshuffle necessitated by Duff Cooper's resignation, Lord De la Warr, who had been Lord Privy Seal, replaced Lord Stanhope as Education Minister, while Stanhope was moved to the Admiralty.

been fought in 1938. However, Britain had already lost parity with Germany in the air by that date, so that strategically 1938 was about two years too late in which to challenge him successfully, whereas 1939 was about two years too soon. In other words, as Iain Macleod has put it in his biography of Chamberlain, 'either we should have fought him much earlier before his rearmament programme had got under way, or else we should have avoided fighting him until much later when the full flood of our own rearmament programme had reduced the ratios of his superiority'.

According to Inskip's PPS Austin Hopkinson, Chamberlain was inclined to blame Inskip for the deficiencies revealed by the detailed scrutiny of the country's defences which the Prime Minister ordered to be made after Munich. If there is any truth in this, it may explain Chamberlain's decision in January 1939 to replace Inskip by Admiral of the Fleet Lord Chatfield, previously First Sea Lord at the Admiralty, as Minister for the Co-ordination of Defence, although when the Prime Minister sent for Inskip and offered him the Dominions Office (which he accepted) he assured him that he had no criticism to make of anything he had done or had not done in his position. ('You took on a thankless job, and you have done a great deal of important work.') The fact is that Inskip had no executive power in the sense exercised by subsequent fully-fledged Defence Ministers – he was merely a 'co-ordinator'. But within this limit Inskip undoubtedly made a number of important proposals which, as Chamberlain also told him, had been accepted by the Cabinet and which had been 'most valuable'.

Chamberlain had made it clear to the Army chiefs early in 1937 that, if only on grounds of manpower shortage, there must be a radical change in the role and size of the Army, and the War Office had been obliged to accept his argument that Britain must 'renounce all idea of a Continental Army on the scale of 1914–1918 and continue to concentrate resources on building up the Air Force and the Navy'. Consequently when Chamberlain and Halifax went to Paris for the Anglo–French conversations which took place at the Quai d'Orsay in November 1938, Daladier impressed upon Chamberlain the need for a larger British contribution to land fighting in the event of a general European war. Hore-Belisha, supported by Halifax, now advocated the dropping of the doctrine of the Army's 'limited liability', and in the event Chamberlain recommended this course to the Cabinet. After staff talks had taken place with the French in the March following Hitler's occupation of Prague, it was agreed to raise the British Army to thirty-two divisions, and in the event of an emergency to provide a British Expeditionary Force for despatch to France as in 1914. At the same time Chamberlain informed the House of Commons that the Territorial Army would be brought up to war establishment and then doubled in strength. Plans were also concerted by the Cabinet to introduce a measure of compulsory military service and to create a Ministry of Supply.

Chamberlain attached particular importance to his visit with the Foreign Secretary to France, as he noted at the time. 'I felt it a good thing for many reasons', among which was 'to show France, and Europe too, that, if we were anxious to make friends with Germany and Italy, we were not on that account going to forget our old Allies'. He also hoped to be able to pay a visit to Rome early in 1939.

I feel that Rome at the moment is the end of the Axis on which it is easiest to make an impression. I don't believe that Spain is a menace to peace any longer – all the same I should immensely like to stop the con- flict there, and although Musso wasn't very forthcoming on the subject in Munich, I got the impression it would be worthwhile to take it up with him again, after our own Agreement had come into force. An hour or two tête-à-tête with Musso might be extraordinarily valuable in making plans for talks with Germany....

'In the past', he reflected at the same time, 'I have often felt a sense of helpless exaggeration at the way things have been allowed to drift in foreign affairs, but now I am in a position to keep them on the move, and while I am P.M. I don't mean to go to sleep.'

IV

Chamberlain, accompanied by Halifax and a party which included Cadogan, travelled to Italy by train, stopping briefly in Paris to call on Daladier and Bonnet at the Quai d'Orsay and arriving in Rome in the late afternoon of 11 January 1939. Union Jacks as well as Italian flags decorated the platform, where a company of Musso- lini's Blackshirts were drawn up. The Duce himself was waiting with Count Galeazzo Ciano, who was his son-in-law as well as his Foreign Minister, to welcome the British party. 'Mussolini greeted the Prime Minister warmly, and everybody was introduced to everybody else', Halifax noted afterwards. They were then driven to the Government guest house, the Villa Madama, where they were to stay for the three-day visit, 'the Prime Minister and Ciano in an open car leading, and the Prime Minister being the subject of a remarkable and evidently spontaneous demonstration by the people lining the route'. On the other hand, Ciano's recollection, as recorded in his diary, was that 'essentially the visit was kept in a minor key, since both the Duce and myself are doubtful about its utility'. Ciano continued:

The welcome of the crowd was good, particularly in the middle-class section of the city, where the old man with the umbrella is very popular. The welcome was colder on the outskirts, where the workers are less emotional. He undoubtedly still remembers the boos with which he was received some months ago in friendly France.

Incidentally the Villa Madama, which had been designed by Raphael for the Popes on the slopes of Monte Mario, provided the English visitors with grand and luxurious accommodation. However, as they believed (no doubt correctly) that every room had been 'wired for sound', they were obliged to converse in the most guarded terms.

After they had settled in at the 'bugged' villa, the Prime Minister and the Foreign Secretary drove to the Palazzo Venezia for their first conference with the Duce.

Here the feeling of the stage play came over me strongly [Halifax later recalled]. As I walked with Chamberlain to be received by Mussolini along a not very wide passage between lines of black-shirted young men, all standing rigidly to attention, with drawn daggers held out at shoulder height, I had the uncomfortable feeling that if I stumbed I must infallibly impale my throat on a dagger point; Chamberlain being shorter would fare better and fall between the dagger line. This danger over, Mussolini met us at the far end from our door of entry into his long and practically empty room, and installed us opposite to himself at a large refectory table.

Mussolini spoke in Italian and Ciano acted as interpreter. The conversation lasted for an hour or more, being conducted to a running accompaniment of loud cheering and shouting in the square below the windows, which sometimes made it difficult to hear what was being said. Halifax had the impression that the noise was under official control, since after a while Mussolini rang a bell on his table, and on a member of his staff appearing at the door Mussolini put his finger to his lips and pointed out of the window. In a few minutes the cheering suddenly died down, although Grandi, who was sitting in the next room with someone from the British embassy, assured him that the demonstration was entirely spontaneous, being due to the belief of the crowd that Chamberlain and Halifax had come to save Europe from war. However that may be, the talks which were resumed next day accomplished little. As Ciano put it in his diary, 'the recorded conversations gave an impression of tiredness' and 'both parties have betrayed their reservations' and 'effective contact has not been made'.

How far apart we are from these people! It is another world [Ciano's diary continued]. We were talking about it after dinner with the Duce, gathered together in a corner of the room. 'These men are not made of the same stuff', he was saying, 'as the Francis Drakes and the other magnificent adventurers who created the empire. These, after all, are the tired sons of a long line of rich men, and they will lose their empire.'

Even Halifax admitted that 'the conversations did not add much to our knowledge of Italian policy', although he thought that the visit had 'probably done a little good'. Cadogan begged the Prime Minister before they left to talk to the Duce on the subject of Hitler's intentions. 'We must take away from here some assurance that Musso will try to restrain Hitler', Cadogan urged, 'and leave behind us here the idea that if Hitler is not restrained there'll be a blow-up.' This Chamberlain did at an appropriate moment. Mussolini's explanation of Hitler's continuing policy of piling up more and more armaments as being purely for defensive purposes the English ministers found particularly unconvincing and said so. Halifax also had a talk alone with Ciano in the latter's office, chiefly on Spain. 'I repeated to him our point of view and he gave his', Ciano noted afterwards. 'But he does not seem to be very convinced, and at heart I think he would be glad if Franco's victory were to settle the question.' It is hardly surprising that Ciano should have handed over a complete transcript of the Anglo-Italian conversations to the German ambassador for onward transmission to the Foreign Office in Berlin. Ciano also telephoned Ribbentrop when the talks had ended that the visit was a fiasco ('a big lemonade') and 'absolutely innocuous'.

The visitors were taken on conducted tours and much time was spent at receptions and banquets. They also went to the opera to see a mixture of *Falstaff* and *La Boutique Fantasque*. Since Chamberlain and Halifax both wore morning coats on the formal occasions except in the evening, their dress contrasted so sombrely with the glittering uniforms of the Duce and his black-shirted henchmen that one observer remarked that the Prime Minister and the Foreign Secretary resembled a pair of undertaker's mutes. On the night before their departure, the British ambassador Lord Perth gave a dinner for their Italian hosts in the British embassy. Next day Chamberlain and Halifax were seen off at the railway station by the Duce and his son-in-law. 'The leave-taking was brief but cordial', noted Ciano. 'Chamberlain kept repeating his thanks for the treatment that was accorded to him during his stay in Italy.'

Naturally the British colony in Rome turned up at the station in strength to give the Prime Minister a rousing send-off. As they began to sing, 'For he's a jolly good fellow' Ciano noticed there were tears in Chamberlain's eyes. Mussolini turned to Count Grandi, who was also in attendance, and asked, 'What is this little song?' No doubt Grandi was able to answer this question. 'Old Chamberlain is a pleasant fellow', was Ciano's conclusion, 'and quite apart from any other consideration I can understand the cordial atmosphere which has grown up around him.'

In a mood of optimism next day, Chamberlain wrote:

I may say at once that I have achieved all I expected to get, and more, and that I am satisfied that the journey has definitely strengthened the chances of peace. To give my first impressions of Mussolini, I found him straightforward and considerate in his behaviour to us, and moreover he has a sense of humour which is quite attractive. . . . He was emphatic in his assurances that he intended to stand by his agreement with us, and that he wanted peace, and was ready to use his influence to get it.

A week or two later, Chamberlain drafted a speech he proposed to make when the House of Commons reassembled after the Christmas recess, referring to his Italian visit, and as an act of courtesy he sent a copy of the draft to Lord Perth to show to Ciano 'in order', as Ciano put it, 'that we may suggest changes, if necessary'. Ciano, who never did anything without consulting the Duce, immediately brought it to him for his approval. Mussolini approved it, with the characteristic comment: 'I believe this is the first time that the head of the British Government has submitted to a foreign government the outline of one of his speeches. It's a bad sign for them.'

Mussolini did better than Chamberlain out of the meeting, since the Duce got something concrete that he wanted, while the British Prime Minister secured nothing more than vague protestations of friendship and the feeling that in the long term Mussolini would exercise a moderating influence on Hitler. On 27 February the Chamberlain Government recognized Franco as the *de jure* as well as the *de facto* ruler of Spain. During the final stages of the Civil War it looked as if France might intervene on the side of the Republicans, but nothing came of this, although the Left in both France and Britain lamented what they considered as a betrayal of democracy. Before his visit to Rome Chamberlain had expressed the opinion that Spain did not constitute any threat to peace and, he might have added, to British interests. 'I think we ought to be able to establish excellent relations with Franco, who seems well disposed towards us', he wrote a few days before recognition was formally accorded, 'and then, if the Italians are not in too bad a temper, we might get Franco–Italian conversations going, and if they were reasonably amicable, we might advance towards disarmament.'

Thus, as late as the beginning of March 1939, Chamberlain still firmly placed his hopes for European peace upon the policy of appeasement. In the middle of the same month an event occurred which, if it did not positively put an end to this policy, certainly provided a shift of emphasis. After Munich the new Czechoslovak state became hyphenated as well as truncated. By mid-March it had completely disintegrated, when the Slovaks refused to acknowledge the authority of the central government in Prague any longer and, with German encouragement, proclaimed Slovakia an independent state. This provided Hitler with a pretext for bullying Dr Hacha, who had succeeded Beneš as President, into agreeing that Bohemia–Moravia should become a German protectorate, thus in effect being incorporated in the Reich. German troops followed by the Gestapo moved into Prague on the morning of 15 March; Hitler himself reached the old Bohemian capital in the afternoon and spent that night in the Hradčany Palace. An immediate consequence of Hitler's action was that the rich industrial part of the country passed into German hands, including the Skoda munitions works, which would henceforth be manufacturing arms for the German army. At the same time Hungary seized the Sub-Carpathian Ukraine, thus completing the dismemberment of the artificial state created twenty years before.

Public reaction in Britain was one of shock and disgust. Even *The Times*, which had always been in the van of appeasement, denounced Hitler's latest action as something for which no 'moral case' existed. And well it might, since Hitler had now begun to annex non-German peoples to the Reich, although at the time of Munich he had declared that this was 'the last territorial demand which I have to make in Europe'. ('I shall not be interested in the Czech State any more, and I can guarantee it. We don't want any more Czechs.') At first Chamberlain appeared undisturbed by the latest continental development and showed signs of irritation when answering questions both from his own supporters and the Labour Opposition in the House of Commons, speculating that the end of Czecho-Slovakia 'may or may not have been inevitable', while Sir John Simon with a suggestion of legal casuistry explained that Britain's previous guarantee could not be applied to a country which had ceased to exist.

Chamberlain came under such immediate fire both in the House of Commons and from the Conservative Party that his position as Prime Minister was seriously threatened. In the course of a talk he had with Halifax on the evening of 15 March, the Foreign Secretary urged him to speak out strongly against Hitler and to do this in a speech he was due to make on his home ground in Birmingham two days later. On reflection, the Prime Minister accepted Halifax's advice and in his speech, which he consequently re-drafted, he denounced Hitler's breach of faith as a personal affront to himself, while continuing to defend what he (Chamberlain) had done at Munich.

'Surely as a joint signatory of the Munich Agreement I was entitled, if Herr Hitler thought it ought to be undone, to that consultation which is provided by the Munich Declaration', he protested. 'Instead of that he has taken the law into his own hands. . . . Is this the last attack upon a small State or is it to be followed by another? Is this in fact a step in the direction of an attempt to dominate the world by force?' If this was so, Chamberlain continued, then Hitler must realize that 'this nation' would 'take part to the uttermost of its power in resisting such a challenge'.

Such a declared change in foreign policy did not mean that Chamberlain had finally despaired of appeasement, but rather a shift of emphasis to measures which it was hoped would act as a deterrent to any further aggressive designs on Hitler's part. An immediate result was that a visit by two British ministers to Berlin for trade talks was immediately cancelled, which annoyed Goering considerably, while Sir Nevile Henderson, the British ambassador in Berlin, was recalled to London for consultations, although he was not (as Halifax wished) to be withdrawn permanently from his post.

Soviet Russia now proposed a six-power conference to include France, Poland, Romania and Turkey, all thought to be possible objects of Hitler's hostile intentions, in addition to Britain and the Soviet Union. Chamberlain, whose 'profound distrust' of the Soviets has already been noted, rejected this initiative as premature, thus frustrating the possibility of an Anglo–Russian agreement, which might well have staved off the eventual outbreak of war later in the year. Instead he proposed that Britain, France, Russia and Poland should issue a declaration of common action in the event of signs of new aggression by Hitler. However, this plan was immediately blocked by Poland, whose hatred and suspicions of the Soviet Union were not diminished by the fact of her own exposed position.

In the face of renewed German threats demanding the amendment of the Polish corridor – at the same time Lithuania ceded Memel to Germany under threat of immediate occupation – and the handing over to Germany of the Free City of Danzig, Poland now appealed to Britain and France for help, although she had a long-standing military alliance with the latter. In the result Chamberlain and the Cabinet executed a remarkable *volte-face*. First, on 31 March, Chamberlain wrote out an assurance in his own hand that, if Polish independence were threatened, the British and French Governments 'would at once lend them all the support in their power', and he made an announcement on the same day to this effect in the House of Commons. Colonel Beck, the Polish Foreign Minister, accepted the British offer, but from a sense of pride demanded that the one-sided guarantee should be converted into a reciprocal agreement. This was done a week later when Beck came to London.

Such a guarantee was unprecedented in British history, since it involved Britain for the first time in Eastern European affairs. Unfortunately Britain had no means of fulfilling the bargain she had made. 'If war occurred tomorrow, we could not send a single battalion to Poland', Lloyd George thundered in the House of Commons, pointing towards the Government Front Bench. 'I cannot understand why, before committing ourselves to this tremendous enterprise, we did not secure beforehand the adhesion of Russia. . . . We have undertaken a frightful gamble.' Lloyd George was to be proved right, since once begun the policy of giving such guarantees had no end.

On 7 April, Good Friday, disregarding an important anniversary in the Christian calendar, Mussolini launched a lightning attack upon Albania, which was annexed to Italy the same day. Summoned back to London from his country home in Essex where he had gone for the Easter weekend, R. A. Butler, the Parliamentary Under-Secretary at the Foreign Office, called at No. 10 Downing Street for instructions. He was shown into the small room on the second floor overlooking the garden which the Prime Minister used as a private study. Butler noticed that the window was partly open, showing a small table for bird food suspended outside, from which Chamberlain was feeding the birds. Butler also noted that Chamberlain seemed irritated at his intrusion and surprised that the Under-Secretary should have been perturbed by Mussolini's coup. 'I am sure Mussolini has not decided to go against us', the Prime Minister remarked. When Butler (according to his account of the interview) started to talk about the general threat in the Balkans, Chamberlain dismissed him with the words 'Don't be silly! Go home to bed', and continued to feed the birds. ('At least he did not tell me', wrote Butler afterwards, 'as he had once advised Anthony Eden, to take an aspirin.')

The British Government officially reacted by offering guarantees of independence to Romania and Greece, followed in May by an Anglo–Turkish declaration that the two countries would take joint action against any aggression in the Mediterranean. 'A guarantee a day keeps Hitler away', said the cynics at the time. Moreover, some countries doubted the efficacy of such guarantees, and in fact they were rejected by the Netherlands, Switzerland and Denmark, although Denmark, like Esthonia and Latvia, signed a non-aggression pact with Germany.

While he still clung to the belief that war was not inevitable,

Chamberlain by now had become distinctly disillusioned with the policy of appeasing the dictators. Mussolini had sent him many assurances calculated to allay any fears or suspicions he might have, wrote Chamberlain after Italy had invaded Albania. 'But I am afraid', he added, 'that such faith as I ever had in the assurances of dictators is rapidly being whittled away.'

V

It was widely thought in Britain that Hitler had been 'hit on the head' by the announcement of the Anglo–French agreement with Poland, and the assumption was strengthened by the fact that for a time Hitler kept quiet apart from denouncing the Anglo–German Naval Agreement and also the Non-Aggression Pact he had concluded with Poland in 1934. In the words of the historian A. J. P. Taylor, 'the British lion had roared, and the sound cheered even those who had supported appeasement. It cheered Chamberlain. All public men like applause, and Chamberlain enjoyed his new role of strong man, almost as much as he had enjoyed that of appeaser.' At the same time Chamberlain was urged on many sides, including several newspapers and such politically diverse personalities as the Liberal Lady Violet Bonham-Carter and the left wing socialist Sir Stafford Cripps, to reconstruct his Government on a truly national basis, and in particular to bring in Churchill. However Chamberlain rejected all such suggestions, notably that of offering Churchill a Cabinet post. 'The nearer we get to war, the more his chances improve, and *vice versa*', Chamberlain wrote of Churchill in this context. 'If there is any possibility of easing the tension and getting back to normal relations with the dictators, I wouldn't risk it by what would certainly be regarded by them as a challenge.' Meanwhile the Prime Minister was quite content with his present Cabinet, the majority of whom he dominated and who took their lead from him. Only a handful of ministers was bold enough occasionally to raise their voices in disagreement – men such as Elliot, Hore-Belisha, Malcolm MacDonald and Oliver Stanley – and they were greatly outnumbered by their complacent colleagues.

Chamberlain's popularity with the public was increased by their fear of war, and it contrasted strongly with his rating in parliamentary circles. He was acutely conscious of this, as he wrote to his sisters at the time:

I often think to myself that it's not I but someone else who is PM and is the recipient of those continuous marks of respect and affection from the general public who called in Downing Street or at the station to take off their hats and cheer. And then I go back to the House of Commons and listen to the unending stream of abuse of the PM, his faithlessness, his weakness, his wickedness, his innate sympathy with fascism and his obstinate hatred of the working class.

The truth was that Chamberlain remained convinced that Britain was composed of two separate and distinct nations, not in the Disraelian sense of *Coningsby*, but in the sense on the one hand of those sound British people who trusted him and followed his lead, and on the other hand of the schemers and intriguers in Parliament and the corridors of political power and influence. While he resented domestic criticism and was often inclined to question the sincerity of those critics who impugned his motives and his actions, it is remarkable that he should have trusted the dictators for as long as he did before the scales dropped from his eyes and revealed the Führer and the Duce in all their stark duplicity.

As one of the Government's most persistent critics, Churchill was most scathing at the ministerial ignorance of the intelligence which must have been available, and in spite of which the Fleet was allowed to be dispersed over a wide area at the time of Mussolini's coup. 'I can well believe', Churchill declared in the House of Commons after Parliament had been recalled, 'that if our Fleet had been concentrated and cruising in the southern parts of the Ionian sea, the Albanian adventure would never have been undertaken.' He went on:

After twenty-five years experience in peace and war, I believe the British Intelligence Service to be the finest of its kind in the world. Yet we have seen, both in the case of the subjugation of Bohemia and on the occasion of the invasion of Albania, that Ministers of the Crown had apparently no inkling or at any rate no conviction of what was coming. I cannot believe that this is the fault of the British Secret Service.

Churchill's surmise was correct. The records of the Intelligence Service (SIS) are naturally not available for private research, but it is clear from the Cadogan diaries, which have recently been published, that the Foreign Office, and presumably also the Prime

Minister, were being constantly supplied with high-grade information by secret agents, but the warnings were ignored.*

Chamberlain, who had visited Hitler three times, brushed aside suggestions that he should make personal contact with Stalin. However, in response to parliamentary criticism, he did agree with the French Government to open discussions with the Soviet Union designed to conclude a pact of mutual assistance and a military convention. For various reasons the negotiations were conducted at a leisurely pace, being entrusted to officials who, however competent they might be, were not of sufficiently high standing to impress the Russians, who anyhow were still inclined to distrust the western powers and feared that an agreement with them might precipitate rather than avert a war with Germany. It was not until the end of July 1939 that Molotov, who had succeeded Litvinov as the Soviet Foreign Affairs Commissar, agreed to accept military missions from the two countries which had not been proposed before. As with the civilian officials, the composition of the British mission consisted of service officers of the second rank, although they had to negotiate with a team led by Marshal Voroshilov, the Commissar for War. Even the British mission's journey, which might have been completed in a few hours by air, was made by sea so that after cruising through the Baltic they did not reach Moscow until 11 August. Next day, unknown to the British, the Russians informed the Germans, who had been pressing through Hitler for an understanding with the Soviet Union contrary to his previously frenzied anti-Russian policy and propaganda, that they were ready to begin political talks.

Meanwhile back home in Britain, thanks in great part to Churchill's persistent prodding of the Government, defensive preparations were being pushed forward at a quicker and more thoroughgoing pace than hitherto. A measure of compulsory military service was introduced – the term 'conscription' was deliberately played down – but it only involved calling up men aged twenty and twenty-one for six months' training and it could have no effect upon increasing Britain's armed strength for some time. Nevertheless it was opposed by the Liberal, Labour and the TUC

* The head of the service, otherwise known as MI6, at this time was Admiral Sir Hugh Sinclair. He died in November 1939, aged sixty-six, and was succeeded by his deputy, Major-General (later Sir) Stewart Menzies. The secret service chief has always been known as 'c' from the initial of the surname of the first holder of the office, Captain Sir Mansfield Cumming, RN.

leaders. 'Looking back', Attlee wrote in his memoirs many years later – and his colleague Hugh Dalton agreed with him – 'I think our attitude was a mistake.' It was not applied to Northern Ireland in order to please De Valera who warned against the dangers which would follow upon any attempt to impose conscription upon the Nationalist minority in the north.

The appointment of a Minister of Supply, which Churchill had originally advocated in Baldwin's time, was eventually made in July, although he did not set up his office until the following month. To please the Liberals, who were also keen on it, Chamberlain appointed Dr Leslie Burgin, who was a National Liberal, to the job. The new minister's jurisdiction was not as wide as would have been liked, since the Navy and the Air Force insisted on preserving their independence in the supply field, so that the minister was little more than a purchasing agent, his responsibility being confined to the production of munitions, army clothing and other service stores.

Hitler was unimpressed by these preparations. He had already made up his mind to obliterate Poland and to use German claims upon Danzig as an excuse for further aggression, although (as he told his military chiefs) he preferred not to have to fight on two fronts. He professed to believe that the Anglo–French guarantee to Poland did not cover the Free City, which was administered by the League of Nations. Chamberlain made haste to correct this misinterpretation of the British pledge. In mid-July the Prime Minister defined the position in the following terms:

Danzig is, of course, at present the danger spot. I have told Musso plainly that, if Hitler tries to get it by force, it will mean starting the European war. To which M. replies 'let the Poles agree that Danzig goes to the Reich, and I will do my best to get a peaceful agreed solution.' But that is not good enough. That is just what we tried at Munich, but Hitler broke it up when it suited him. I doubt if any solution, short of war, is practicable at present, but if dictators would have a modicum of patience, I can imagine that a way could be found of meeting German claims while safeguarding Poland's independence and economic security.

Thus Chamberlain had no intention at this date of doing what the American journalists called a 'Polish Munich' which the Russians feared. Apart from Poland's expressed and understandable unwillingness to allow Soviet troops on her territory, an objection which produced an immediate deadlock in the Anglo-Russian military talks, Stalin considered that when it came to the crunch the British and French would back down. 'We formed the impression', Stalin was to tell Churchill when they met for the first time face-to-face in Moscow three years later, 'that the British and French Governments were not resolved to go to war if Poland were attacked, but they hoped the diplomatic line-up of Britain, France and Russia would deter Hitler. We were sure it would not.' In that event Germany and Russia would directly confront each other once Hitler had conquered Poland. Hence Stalin's decision to talk to the Germans, a decision which culminated in the Ribbentrop–Molotov pact, which stunned the western powers when it was announced on 25 August. Besides neutralizing Germany's eastern flank and sealing Poland's fate, a secret protocol was attached to the pact providing for the partition of that unfortunate State between the Reich and the Soviet Union.

Hitler likewise doubted Britain's determination to go to war over Poland, at least for a time, and this led him to postpone his plans to launch his initial attack which was to have taken place on 25 August, although in a letter which Chamberlain sent him on the previous evening – very different from his approach to the Führer at the time of Munich – the Prime Minister reiterated Britain's determination to honour her pledges, as an earnest of which Parliament had been recalled to pass an emergency powers bill and the Army and Navy and Air Force reserves had been called up. If Hitler thought that in consequence of the German–Soviet agreement Britain's intervention on behalf of Poland was 'no longer a contingency that need be reckoned with', then 'no greater mistake could be made', since his Government's obligation to Poland was one they were 'determined to fulfil', as they had stated in public 'repeatedly and plainly'. Furthermore, Chamberlain went on, the British Government was resolved that there should be 'no such tragic misunderstanding' of Britain's intentions as there perhaps was in 1914. Finally, Chamberlain warned Hitler that it was impossible to foresee the end of hostilities once begun. 'It would be a dangerous delusion to think that, if war once starts, it will come to an early end, even if a success on any one of the several fronts on which it will be engaged should have been secured.' There should be a truce to 'press polemics', followed by direct negotiations between Germany and Poland, possibly with the aid of a neutral intermediary. 'At this moment', Chamberlain concluded, 'I confess I can see no other way to avoid a catastrophe that will involve Europe in war.'

Hitler wavered. He summoned Sir Nevile Henderson, Britain's ambassador in Berlin, to meet him, and offered his support for the maintenance of the British empire in the shape of a defensive alliance, an offer which incensed Mussolini who first heard of it from the British. But on Danzig and Poland Hitler refused to move or compromise in any way. A similar, rather less attractive, offer was made to France. Meanwhile there was a number of mysterious comings and goings behind the scenes. Birger Dahlerus, a Swedish engineer, who knew Goering and had contacts in the British business world, made three trips between Berlin and London with messages from Goering. Then there was a suggestion, conveyed through British secret intelligence, that Goering might himself fly to England to see Chamberlain as Hitler's special emissary, and arrangements were made for him to land at a deserted airfield and be driven in conditions of secrecy to Chequers. But at the last moment Goering's visit was called off, apparently on Hitler's instructions, and nothing came of the other fleeting attempts to preserve the peace. Hitler eventually decided to strike which he did on 1 September, and to do so without being able to count on Mussolini's aid, since the Italians were not ready for war and anyhow did not wish to be involved in hostilities at that time.

The course of events, sometimes contradictory and confused, which directly led to the declaration of war by Britain and France, has been so frequently described by historians who now have access to enemy as well as British archives, not to mention the mass of documents introduced into the subsequent war crimes trials at Nuremberg, that it is unnecessary to repeat them in any detail here. But the Prime Minister's private account, which he confided to his diary a week after the outbreak of hostilities, deserves quotation:

The communications with Hitler and Goering looked rather promising at one time, but came to nothing in the end, as Hitler apparently got carried away by the prospect of a short war in Poland, and then a settlement. . . . They gave the impression, probably with intention, that it was possible to persuade Hitler to accept a peaceful and reasonable solution of the Polish question, in order to get an Anglo–German agreement, which he continually declared to be his greatest ambition.

What happened to destroy this chance? Was Hitler merely talking through his hat, and deliberately deceiving us while he matured his schemes? I don't think so. There is good evidence that orders for the invasion on the 25th August were actually given and then cancelled at the last moment because H. wavered. With such an extraordinary creature one can only speculate. But I believe he did seriously contemplate an agreement with us, and that he worked seriously at proposals (subsequently broadcast) which to his one-track mind seemed almost fabulously generous. But at the last moment some brainstorm took possession of him – may be Ribbentrop stirred it up – and once he had set his machine in motion, he couldn't stop it. . . . Mussolini's proposals were, I think, a perfectly genuine attempt to stop war, not for any altruistic reasons, but because Italy was not in a state to go to war and exceedingly likely to get into trouble if other people did. But it was doomed to failure, because Hitler by that time was not prepared to hold his hand, unless he could get what he wanted without war. And we weren't prepared to give it to him. . . .

Mussolini had proposed to invite Hitler to a conference if Britain and France would first agree. The British Cabinet, meeting in the afternoon of 2 September, insisted that all German troops must be withdrawn from Poland before a conference could be considered, the consensus being that an ultimatum should be sent to Hitler in the sense that the Germans should only be allowed until midnight to make up their minds, although Halifax had been negotiating on the basis of no time limit for withdrawal. In the event no ultimatum was sent, in deference to the French who wished for more time to complete their mobilization and move troops up to the Maginot Line. Also the Prime Minister appeared to think that there might still be some way out, in spite of the fact that the Polish Government had requested 'an immediate fulfilment of British obligations'.

On the previous day Chamberlain had seen Churchill and asked him to join the Government in the event of war. Churchill intimated that he would be glad to do so but he was puzzled by the delay. 'The Poles have now been under heavy attack for thirty hours', he wrote to the Prime Minister early on the morning of 2 September, 'and I am concerned to hear that there is talk in Paris of a further note. I trust you will be able to announce our joint declaration of war at *latest* when Parliament meets this afternoon.' At 7.30 p.m. Chamberlain went over to the House of Commons, which was fully expecting at least an announcement that an ultimatum to Germany had been despatched. Instead they were told

145

that the Government would only take action against Germany if the latter did not agree to withdraw her forces from Poland, and that Mussolini's project for a conference could not be entertained while Poland was subject to invasion. Meanwhile, said Chamberlain, discussions were proceeding with the French on the question of a mutually agreed time limit for the German withdrawal.

The House reacted in a mood of disappointment mingled with anger. Chamberlain sat down without a cheer, a scene very different from the reception he had had a year before as the prelude to Munich. When the Labour leader Arthur Greenwood rose to speak for the Opposition, in Attlee's absence due to illness, Leo Amery shouted across the floor of the House, 'Speak for England!' Greenwood did so. He was gravely disturbed by the delay, he said, since Germany had been at war with Poland for forty-eight hours and Britain's treaty obligations towards Poland had not been automatically put into effect. 'I wonder', he went on, 'how long we are prepared to vacillate at a time when Britain and all Britain stands for, and human civilization, are in peril.' The Prime Minister rose again to deny that there had been any weakening on the part of the Government and referred to the need to synchronize action with the French whose Cabinet was in session at that moment. Unfortunately for Chamberlain his reassurance failed to correct the impression caused by his original statement, and the House broke up in confusion and dismay.

As Chamberlain left the chamber, Greenwood followed him to his room and told him that unless the inevitable decision for war was taken before they met again next day 'it would be impossible to hold the House'. Meanwhile an indignation meeting of ministers – Simon, Hore-Belisha, Anderson, De la Warr and Elliot – was taking place in Simon's room behind the Speaker's Chair with the result that Simon was asked to go to Downing Street and demand that the Cabinet should meet again that night with a view to the immediate declaration of war. The Cabinet duly met at 11 p.m. The general mood was one of insistence that when the House met next morning the Prime Minister should be in a position to say that the country was at war with Germany. Chamberlain bowed to the inevitable and the decision was conveyed to the Quai d'Orsay by Halifax on the telephone to Bonnet, the only concession being that France could postpone her declaration of war until later next day. At 5 a.m. Henderson in Berlin was instructed to present an ultimatum to the German Government to the effect that, if no satisfactory reply was received to Britain's previous note by 11 a.m., this would be tantamount to a declaration of war. Henderson did so four hours later, the ultimatum being received with stunned surprise by Hitler, Goering and Goebbels. The Germans made no reply before the expiration of the ultimatum, and so Britain was at war. France issued her declaration at 5 p.m.

'So the war began after a short and troubled night', Chamberlain noted in his diary a week later.

Only the fact that one's mind works at three times its ordinary pace on such occasions enabled me to get through my broadcast, the formation of the War Cabinet, the meeting of the House of Commons, and the preliminary orders on that awful Sunday [3 September]...

'You can imagine what a bitter blow it is to me that all my long struggle to win peace has failed', the Prime Minister told the nation in his Sunday morning broadcast shortly after eleven o'clock. 'Yet I cannot believe that there is anything more, anything different, that I could have done, and that would have been more successful.' When he spoke in the House of Commons later the same day, he sought neither to excuse himself nor to reproach other members of the House 'not in possession of all the information we have'. Were he in their position he would very likely have felt the same as they did.

Inevitably he ended on a sombre note. 'Everything I have worked for, everything that I have hoped for, everything that I have believed in during my public life, has crashed in ruins', he remarked sadly. 'There is only one thing left for me to do: that is, to devote what strength and powers I have to forwarding the victory of the cause for which we have to sacrifice so much. I cannot tell what part I shall be allowed to play myself. . . .'

VI

'How can they fight this war?' asked Ciano when he heard the news that the ultimatum which Britain and France gave Germany had expired. 'The German advance in Poland is overwhelming.' As to the future course of the war, for once he did not see eye-to-eye with his father-in-law who forecast a rapid finish. Ciano wrote in his diary on the night of 3 September 1939:

In what way can France and England bring help to Poland? And when Poland is liquidated, will they want to continue a conflict for which there is no longer any reason? The Duce does not believe so. He believes rather that after a short struggle peace will be restored before the clash which in any case he considers impossible from a military point of view.

I am not a military man. I do not know how the war will develop, but I know one thing – it will develop and it will be long, uncertain, and relentless. The participation of Great Britain makes this certain. England has made this declaration to Hitler. The war can end only with Hitler's elimination or the defeat of Britain.

Before leaving Berlin for the eastern front, Hitler called Attolico, the Italian ambassador, to the Chancellery and asked him to convey his greetings to the Duce. 'He was, I am told, calm and optimistic', Ciano noted. 'He thinks that he will have Poland at his feet in four weeks, and in another four weeks will be able to concentrate his forces on the western front. . . . The Duce, who still prizes German friendship, was happy to know of Hitler's gesture.'

For his part Chamberlain was heartened by Italy's decision to remain neutral, and his feelings were shared by Count Grandi, who had recently returned to Rome and Mussolini's Cabinet as Minister of Justice, and who wrote to Chamberlain at this time to tell him 'how happy' he was by the decision. 'All that I have strived for during seven years of my mission in England, and during these last momentous weeks in Rome, has been saved.' In his reply, the British Prime Minister hoped that now the critical moment had been passed, that they would never be drawn into conflict. 'I place my hope', he told his sisters, 'and indeed my confidence, on the attitude of the Italian King, Church and people.'

In constructing his War Cabinet, Chamberlain did not follow the precedent set by Lloyd George after he succeeded Asquith in December 1916 when he chose a small number of ministers without departmental duties. Chamberlain's War Cabinet, nine in number as compared with Lloyd George's five, contained only two ministers without departmental responsibilities, Hoare (Lord Privy Seal) and Lord Hankey, who had been Secretary of the Lloyd George Cabinet and also Secretary of the Committee of Imperial Defence. Chamberlain was criticized for his action, but he defended it on the ground that his sole purpose was 'to find a Cabinet that would work, which means that personalities must be taken into account', and that in the event they were 'working together very harmoniously and successfully'.

Churchill went back to the Admiralty, the post he had held at the outbreak of war in 1914. Consequently Chamberlain felt he must include the other two service ministers, Hore-Belisha (War) and Kingsley Wood (Air), as well as Chatfield (Co-ordination of Defence), who all kept their old posts, as did Halifax (Foreign Office) and Simon (Exchequer). Hoare (Privy Seal), who with the Prime Minister, Halifax and Simon had belonged to the old inner ring of appeasers in the previous Cabinet, completed the Chamberlain War Cabinet. Eden returned to the Government as Dominions Secretary, replacing Inskip who became Lord Chancellor as Lord Caldecote, but he was not a member of the War Cabinet. However, with the exception of Malcolm MacDonald (Colonies) and one or two minor posts, the Government was essentially Conservative in composition, since both Labour and the Liberals refused to join. Churchill pointed out to Chamberlain at the time that the average age of the War Cabinet was over sixty-four, 'only one year short of the Old Age Pension!'

'I used to say to Annie before war came that if such a thing happened I thought I should have to hand over to someone else', Chamberlain was to write immediately after he left No. 10 Downing Street for good seven months later, 'for I knew what agony of mind it would mean to me to give directions that would bring death and mutilation and misery to so many. But the war was so different from what I expected that I found the strain bearable and perhaps it was providential that the revolution which overturned me coincided with the real thing.'

It is easy to be wise after the event, but in spite of the advantage of hindsight there can be no doubt that Neville Chamberlain should have resigned on the outbreak of the war instead of carrying on until, as will be seen, he was forced to submit his resignation to the King. He was too much a man of peace to lead a nation and inspire the British peoples of the Commonwealth to wage what was to be a long war.

While India and the colonies came in automatically on Britain's side as they had done in 1914, Chamberlain was encouraged by the support of the dominions, who immediately rallied to the side of the mother country with the solitary exception of Eire who remained strictly neutral. He was further encouraged by the us

Congress on the initiative of President Roosevelt amending the Neutrality Act so as to permit the sale of arms on a 'cash and carry' basis, of vital importance to a sea power like Britain, although there was a hard core of 'isolationist' opinion in America opposed to the United States becoming involved in any European commitment.

However, even if Chamberlain had resigned in September 1939, he would not have recommended the King to invite Churchill to take over from him. 'I would rather have Halifax succeed me than Winston', was always his opinion. Yet Halifax would only have been a stop-gap Premier, had he been sent for. Sooner or later Churchill's characteristic qualities, his popular appeal, and his knowledge of war would have inevitably raised him to the leadership. Meanwhile, from the moment he was installed in his old post at the Admiralty, Churchill proceeded to bombard the Prime Minister, somewhat to the latter's embarrassment, with letters and memoranda, many several pages long, which went considerably beyond his departmental responsibilities with suggestions for the conduct of the war. 'I can assure you that all your letters are carefully read and considered by me', wrote the Prime Minister in his sole reply to this avalanche of paper which daily descended upon him, 'and if I have not replied to them, it is only because I am seeing you every day and moreover, as far as I have been able to observe, your views and mine have very closely coincided'.

Chamberlain eventually sent for Churchill, on 2 October, and told the First Lord of the Admiralty that, if he were dissatisfied with any aspect of Government policy, the proper course was to raise the matter with the minister concerned or, if necessary, put up a paper to the War Cabinet so that the question could be discussed there and responsibility shared. The First Lord agreed, promising to write no more letters and assuring the Prime Minister that he was wholeheartedly behind him and that he did not desire any extended powers for himself. 'I believe all this was quite genuine', Chamberlain commented privately, while Sir Horace Wilson, who made notes of the interview, described it as 'friendly throughout'. A week later the Chamberlains dined with the Churchills at Admiralty House, where the First Lord had a commodious flat at the top of the building, and the evening was pronounced a great success.

Although Churchill and Chamberlain had been colleagues for five years under Baldwin in the 1920s, they and their wives had never met socially in this way before. By a happy chance Churchill turned the conversation to Chamberlain's early life in the Bahamas and drew him out on the details of the venture in which the Prime Minister's father had sunk £50,000 with no return. Churchill afterwards admitted that he was fascinated by the way Chamberlain 'warmed as he talked, and by the tale itself which was one of gallant endeavour'. Churchill thought to himself, 'What a pity Hitler did not know when he met this sober English politician with his umbrella at Berchtesgaden, Godesberg and Munich, that he was actually talking to a hard-bitten pioneer from the outer marches of the British Empire!'

Elaborate plans had been made in the event of emergency to disperse the various Government departments and move the Cabinet and the royal family to Canada. However, since there were no signs of a German invasion and the anticipated rain of bombs did not descend on London and other cities, few of these plans were put into operation, although a section of the Admiralty moved to Bath and the newly created Ministry of Food functioned from Colwyn Bay, despite the fact that food rationing was not immediately introduced. True, there was petrol rationing, but on a fairly generous scale. However, income tax was increased by two shillings from 5s 6d to 7s 6d in the £. The Prime Minister and the Cabinet carried on in Downing Street, while the King and Queen remained in Buckingham Palace, but Queen Mary, who had been living in Marlborough House since the late King's death, was induced to migrate to Gloucestershire as the guest of the Duke of Beaufort 'for the duration'. Thousands of children were also evacuated from London during the period known as the 'twilight' or phoney war. At the same time theatres, cinemas and other places of entertainment were closed, and while the blackout operated during the hours of darkness many people stayed at home and listened to the 'wireless'.

'One can already see how this twilight war is trying people's nerves', wrote Chamberlain after three weeks had passed. 'Without the centripetal force of mortal danger, all the injustices, inconveniences, hardships and uncertainties of war-time are resented more and more, because they are felt to be unnecessary.' Out of 2450 letters which the Prime Minister received in three days at the beginning of October, 1860 of them begged him to 'stop the war' in one way or another. Many of his correspondents took the line, 'You stopped war before, surely you can find a way out now, before we are all pushed over the precipice.' The peace feelers which Hitler put out, after he had occupied his share of Poland, Chamberlain could not accept. These peace feelers were first made through the Swedish go-between, Birger Dahlerus, who paid three visits to England in September and October. Dahlerus had spent most of 26 September with Hitler and Goering but he did not have much constructive to say when he reached London. The German 'terms' were as to be expected, noted Cadogan. 'Give us a free hand in Central and Eastern Europe and we will guarantee the British Empire.' When Chamberlain met Dahlerus with Halifax and Cadogan, the Prime Minister stressed that 'Germany must do some *deed* as evidence of good faith', since neither her assurances or promises or signatures were 'worth *anything*'.

Hitler's next gesture was made in public in a speech to the Reichstag on 6 October. Since Britain and France had failed to save Poland, he argued, they might as well make peace. Two days later Chamberlain wrote to his sister Ida:

I was, I confess, anxious when I read Hitler's clever speech and especially when the first American reaction was reported, viz. that he had made a very attractive series of proposals and that his tone had been surprisingly friendly to Great Britain. I refused to think about the speech that night but next morning I was clear in my own mind that it offered no real advance in mind or spirit towards a reasonable peace and that it must be rejected.

The difficulty is that you can't believe anything Hitler says ... the only chance of peace is the disappearance of Hitler and that is what we are working for.

Chamberlain replied publicly and appropriately on 12 October to the effect that it was not British policy to exclude from her proper place in Europe a Germany able to dwell in friendship with others. 'The peace which we are determined to secure, however, must be a real and settled peace,' he went on, 'not an uneasy truce interrupted by constant alarms and repeated threats. What stands in the way of such a peace? It is the German Government, and the German Government alone.'

The same night Goering telephoned Dahlerus in The Hague to say that the Germans did not intend to answer Chamberlain's statement. It was later characterized by the German Foreign Office as 'an outrageous insult to Germany'. There could now, said

Ribbentrop, be only a war of annihilation between England and Germany. Nevertheless, at his next meeting with Goering, Dahlerus received what he called 'new proposals' and he thought the atmosphere was more hopeful. 'This, after Goering's first reaction to PM's speech', noted Cadogan, 'means either that the Germans think they can still bluff us or that they really are in a tight corner. And I don't absolutely exclude the latter. . . . This rain *should* hamper a German offensive in the West!'

On 19 October, Dahlerus was reminded in a telegram from the Foreign Office which Chamberlain approved that Britain could not consider any proposals from the Germans which did not right the wrongs done to other nations and provide guarantees of reparation and protection against aggression. These objectives might require large internal changes in Germany, and if Dahlerus therefore felt it impossible to proceed as mediator on these lines, the British Government could only accept the position. Shortly after this, Ribbentrop ordered that Dahlerus's attempts at mediation must cease, 'since the British had clearly indicated their rejection of the German position'. This is in fact what happened, although as late as 23 November Dahlerus reported to London that he had found Goering 'allegedly anxious for peace and still desirous of meeting with the British and French on neutral ground'.

Chamberlain again wrote to his sister Ida at this time, showing that his views about Hitler had not changed:

> To my mind it is essential to get rid of Hitler. He must either die, or go to St Helena, or become a real public works architect, preferably in a 'home'. His entourage must also go, with the possible exception of Goering, who might have some ornamental position in a transitional Government. Having once got rid of the Nazis, I don't think we should find any serious difficulty in Germany over Poland, Czechoslovakia, Jews, disarmament, etc.

A month later, however, the Prime Minister was convinced by 'the general consensus of reports' that German morale, so far from weakening, had been stiffened by Goebbels's propaganda. 'I am beginning to wonder', he wrote, 'whether we shall do any good with them unless they first get a real hard punch in the stomach.'

Although German submarines scored some initial successes, sinking the aircraft carrier *Courageous* with more than half its crew and even penetrating Scapa Flow to torpedo the battleship *Ark Royal*, the gloves were still on so far as the British forces were concerned, and after the RAF had made one attack on the German Fleet the Air Force was restricted to dropping propaganda leaflets. Amery, whom Chamberlain had not included in his reconstructed Government, and who consequently remained on the back benches in the House of Commons, begged Kingsley Wood to drop incendiary bombs on the Black Forest, which was full of munitions and war stores, pointing out that it had been a very dry summer and the wood would burn easily. The Air Minister was horrified at the suggestion.

Meanwhile things remained static in France where the British Expeditionary Force had taken up defensive positions. Neither the French nor British Army was challenged by the Germans who at that period had little strength behind their own Siegfried Line. Chamberlain paid two visits to France before the end of the year, the first with Churchill for a meeting of the Supreme War Council in Paris, which pleased Churchill greatly. ('Winston was in the seventh heaven at being asked to come and declared that he had never enjoyed two days more.) The second was in December to visit the BEF and the Maginot Line and to attend another meeting of the Supreme War Council in Paris. 'It sickened me to see the barbed wire and pill-boxes and guns and anti-tank obstacles, remembering what they meant in the last war', he wrote to his sisters when he got back to London. 'I was glad when it was over.'

Christmas he spent quietly at Chequers with his wife. 'I find war more hateful than ever', he admitted to the Archbishop of Canterbury at this time, 'and I groan in spirit over every life lost and every home blasted.' A terrible feeling of weariness and despondency overcame him at this time. To a friend with whom he used to fish in Scotland and who sent him greetings on the occasion of his seventy-first birthday, he replied that he doubted if they would fish at Castle Forbes again. 'Perhaps we may do it somewhere else – if there is fishing there!'

He found the House of Commons becoming 'more and more ill-tempered', and when Parliament resumed in January 1940 he complained that he was 'continually interrupted with shouts, sneers and derisive laughter' and that his depression was increased by the partisanship and personal prejudice shown by the Labour Party. In the same month trouble he had been having with a departmental member of the War Cabinet, Hore-Belisha, came to a head.

The War Minister did not get on at all well with Lord Gort, who commanded the BEF, and to some extent Chamberlain's visit to France before Christmas had been designed to patch things up between them. After Hore-Belisha had complained that the defences which the sappers had constructed on the unfortified frontier between France and Belgium were inadequate, the generals did their best to undermine the minister's position. Chamberlain decided to remove him when a favourable opportunity came, rather than wait for another crisis. 'In war-time', he noted in his diary, 'nothing could be worse than perpetual friction and want of confidence between the Secretary of State and the C-in-C in the field.'

The opportunity was provided by the necessity of appointing a new head of the Ministry of Information when it came under fire in the Press and Parliament. Chamberlain proposed to offer the post to Hore-Belisha after he had taken a number of soundings. Unfortunately at the last moment Halifax blocked the appointment on the ground that 'it would have a bad effect on the neutrals both because H-B was a Jew and because his methods would let down British prestige'. Halifax suggested that Hore-Belisha should change places with Oliver Stanley at the Board of Trade instead, but this offer was turned down by Hore-Belisha after a painful interview between Chamberlain and the War Minister. Hore-Belisha thereupon resigned, to be succeeded by Oliver Stanley, while the Ministry of Information went to Lord Reith, the former Director-General of the BBC. Chamberlain hoped that he would eventually be able to get Hore-Belisha to serve again in some other capacity later on, but the chance of doing so never came and Hore-Belisha's political career was now virtually finished.

On 4 April 1940, the Prime Minister addressed a meeting of the Conservative Central Office in a remarkable mood of optimism, saying that after seven months of war he felt ten times as confident as he did at the beginning. This was an unreasonable assumption in the circumstances and was shortly to be proved so. In this context he used an unfortunate phrase, which he had previously used in his correspondence with his sisters but which he now employed publicly for the first time. By not attacking in the west up till then, he said, Hitler had 'missed the bus'. It was a phrase with which he was later to be taunted by his political critics, and which he was to regret.

Five days later, on 9 April, Hitler's forces invaded Denmark, in spite of the recent non-aggression pact between the two countries. Denmark was speedily overrun and compelled to submit to military occupation. On the same day, German forces were landed by sea and air at several key points in Norway, namely Oslo, Stavanger, Bergen, Trondheim and Narvik, in accordance with plans which had been under consideration since the previous autumn. Britain had made some counter-plans connected with helping Finland which had also been invaded by Russia because, unlike the other Baltic states – Lithuania, Latvia and Esthonia – she had refused her powerful neighbour the right to garrison the country. These plans included mining the narrow channel known as the leads in Norwegian waters so as to prevent or impede the shipping of iron ore to Germany out of Narvik. For various reasons, one of which was that this operation would have breached Norway's neutrality, it was not proceeded with until the eve of the German landings.

The War Cabinet wished to attack Trondheim, the country's ancient capital, but the Chiefs of Staff counselled caution and despatched troops instead to Namsos and Andalsnes, two fishing ports incapable of coping with landings in strength. A larger force was sent to capture Narvik, which it was eventually to succeed in doing after waiting for a month on the Lofoten Islands, in the face of contradictory orders from the War Office and the Admiralty, for the snows to melt.

Neither the War Cabinet nor the Chiefs of Staff reckoned with the effect of the Germans taking over the Norwegian airfields. Apart from the fact that the German Navy suffered heavy losses and the Royal Navy was able to evacuate the King of Norway and his Government to Britain as allies, the tale of the British expedition was a dismal one. The British forces withdrew from Andalsnes and Namsos on 1 May and 3 May respectively. Narvik was later similarly evacuated after being held for barely a fortnight. 'This has been one of the worst, if not *the* worst week of the war', Chamberlain wrote at the time:

We hadn't reckoned on the way in which the Germans had poured in reinforcements of men, guns, tanks, and aeroplanes. In particular this brief campaign has taught our people, many of whom were much in need of teaching, the importance of the air factor. . . .
I am thankful that at least we got our men out of Norway. . . . We could not give them what they wanted most, namely fighter aircraft,

because we had no aerodrome from which they could operate. I rather doubt whether our experts realised before the power of an unopposed air arm.

Public confidence at home in the Government was badly shaken by the failure of the expedition, and the Cabinet agreed to the Opposition's demand for a two-day debate in the House of Commons. The debate was to prove one of the most momentous and far-reaching in English parliamentary history.

5

VALE

I

THE HOUSE OF COMMONS debate, which began on 7 May 1940, was on the technical motion for the adjournment of the House, although in reality it was one of censure upon the Government. The Prime Minister opened the debate with a straightforward account of the Norwegian expedition and why it had failed. He was soon interrupted with taunts about 'missing the bus', which led him to digress in an attempt to explain the unhappy phrase. He went on to defend the character of the War Cabinet and to explain in particular his recent appointment of Churchill to preside over a Military Co-ordination Committee – Chatfield's office had recently been wound up – as the senior Service Minister concerned, although the committee was later chaired by Chamberlain, who thus admitted prime responsibility for the ill-fated Norwegian expedition. According to one observer of the scene he spoke haltingly and did not make a good case – 'in fact he fumbled his words and seemed tired and harassed. I realised at once the House was not with him, and though he warmed up a little towards the middle of his speech, the very crowded House was restive and bored and the Egyptian Ambassador even slept.'*

As the debate developed, the severest attacks on the Prime Minister were seen to come, not from the Labour Opposition, but from the Conservative benches behind him and also from the Liberals, although Attlee, the Labour leader, who immediately

* *Chips: The Diaries of Sir Henry Channon*, edited by Robert Rhodes James (at p. 244). Other vivid eye-witness accounts of this historic debate have been given by Sir Edward Spears in *Assignment to Catastrophe*, Vol I; Harold Nicolson in *Diaries and Letters*, Vol II; and Leopold Amery in *My Political Life*, Vol III.

followed the Prime Minister, criticized the War Cabinet for ineffi-
ciency in the conduct of the war, observing that its members, at
least some of them, such as Simon and Hoare, were the same men
who had had 'an almost uninterrupted career of failure'. Many of
the Conservatives were already in the armed services and some had
just returned from Norway, so that they could speak with first-
hand knowledge of troops being rushed into battle inadequately
trained and equipped, and also of the Government's failure to anticipate the enemy's plans. Admiral Sir Roger Keyes, the hero of
Zeebrugge in the First World War, dressed in the uniform of an
Admiral of the Fleet, with three rows of medals – 'questionable
taste', commented 'Chips' Channon, 'but it lent him dignity' –
denounced the Government for not ordering a big naval attack on
Trondheim, which he had pressed for. 'When I saw how badly
things were going', said the gallant Admiral, 'I never ceased impor-
tuning the Admiralty and the War Cabinet to let me take all
responsibility and lead the attack'.

The most powerful speech on the first day and the most damning
indictment came from another Conservative backbencher and former minister, Leopold Amery. He began with a devastating attack
upon Chamberlain. 'The Prime Minister gave us a reasoned, argu-
mentative case for our failure', he said.

It is always possible to do that after every failure. Making a case and
winning a war are not the same thing. Wars are won, not by explanation
after the event, but by foresight, by clear decision and by swift action. I
confess that I did not feel there was one sentence in the Prime Minister's
speech this afternoon which suggested that the Government either foresaw what Germany meant to do, or came to a clear decision when it
knew what Germany had done, or acted swiftly or consistently throughout the whole of this lamentable affair.

Amery summed up this argument with a story about a young
friend of his many years before in East Africa who went lion-
hunting. He secured a sleeping car on the railway and had it
detached from the train at a siding near where he expected to find a
man-eating lion. 'He went to rest and dreamt of hunting his lion in
the morning', said Amery. 'Unfortunately, the lion was out man-
hunting that night. He clambered up on to the rear of the car,
scrabbled open the sliding door, and ate my friend. That is in brief
the story of our initiative over Norway.'

'We are fighting today for our life, for our liberty, for our all',

Amery went on; 'we cannot go on as we are.' He concluded by quoting the terrible words used by Oliver Cromwell in dismissing the Long Parliament 'when he thought it was no longer fit to conduct the affairs of the nation'.

You have sat too long here for any good you have been doing. Depart, I say, and let us have done with you. In the name of God, go!

Afterwards Lloyd George told Amery that in fifty years he had heard few speeches to match his in sustained power and none with so dramatic a climax. 'Pardonable exaggeration, no doubt', was Amery's modest comment on this tribute, 'but pleasant for one who has never claimed more than a capacity for reasonably lucid exposition.'

Herbert Morrison, who opened the debate for the Opposition next day, though he made a hard-hitting speech, had little to add to Attlee's criticisms until the very end when he indicated that Labour would divide the House and he asked for a vote which would 'represent the spirit of the country'.

The moment Morrison sat down the Prime Minister rose to his feet to say that, at a time when national unity was essential in face of a relentless enemy, this challenge had made a grave situation graver. He went on:

I do not seek to evade criticism, but I say this to my friends in the House – and I have friends in the House. No Government can prosecute a war efficiently unless it has public and Parliamentary support. I accept the challenge. I welcome it indeed. At least we shall see who is with us and who is against us, and I call on my friends to support us in the Lobby tonight.

This reference by Chamberlain to 'my friends' was an unfortunate blunder, since it enabled speaker after speaker on the benches opposite to taunt him with fighting a vital national issue on narrow political lines, thus making a personal issue out of a question where national interest alone should have been paramount. No doubt, on the other hand, there was real anxiety behind the Prime Minister's appeal. The Government Whips had discovered that discontent was rife among the Conservative rank-and-file, as well as several prominent members of the Party, like Amery and Duff Cooper, and they were doing their best to stem the anticipated backbench revolt. Lord Dunglass, Chamberlain's Parliamentary Private Secretary, later met a number of the rebels and tried to persuade them to refrain from action on the understanding that the Prime Minister would see them next day and tell them of his plans for a dramatic reconstruction of the Government, which would include replacing Simon and Hoare. To no avail. They said they were sorry, they would be glad to meet the Prime Minister next morning, but they must vote against the Government that night.

Meanwhile the debate continued. Only a few weeks previously Kingsley Wood had had to give up the Air Ministry on health grounds, to be succeeded by the controversial figure of Sir Samuel Hoare, who had held the job three times in the past. Hoare now carried on the debate, giving an account of the brave exploits of the RAF in the face of the handicap of having no air base in Norway. But the House, whose attention was now concentrated upon the question of the Government's competence to conduct the war, showed little interest. Hoare was followed by Lloyd George with a speech, which was to be his last decisive contribution after half a century's membership of the House of Commons, in which he castigated the Government for 'the despatch of a half-prepared, half-baked expeditionary force'. On the other hand, he added, he did not think that Churchill was 'entirely responsible for what happened there'.

This immediately brought Churchill to his feet. 'I take complete responsibility for everything that has been done by the Admiralty', he remarked with characteristic pugnacity. But his intervention only enabled Lloyd George to drive his point home. 'The Right Honourable Gentleman', he observed, 'must not allow himself to be converted into an air raid shelter to keep the splinters from hitting his colleagues.'

'It is not a question of who are the Prime Minister's friends', the veteran leader in the First World War concluded. 'It is a far bigger issue.'

He has appealed for sacrifice. The nation is prepared for every sacrifice provided it has leadership. . . . I say solemnly that the Prime Minister should give an example of sacrifice, because there is nothing which can contribute to victory in this war than that he should sacrifice the seals of office.

Churchill had volunteered to wind up the debate for the Government, which (as he afterwards put it) was 'no more than my duty, not only in loyalty to the Chief under whom I served, but also because of the exceptionally prominent part I had played in the use of our inadequate forces during our forlorn hope to succour Norway'. In the face of continuous interruption, he did his best to regain control of the House for the Government, and he argued with considerable eloquence and skill, sometimes unable to make himself heard above the din from the Opposition benches. Yet all the time it was clear that Labour's wrath was directed not against him but against the unfortunate Prime Minister.

Churchill finished his speech a few moments before eleven o'clock. Immediately the division bells rang and members trooped into the lobbies. One Conservative in uniform was seen walking through the Opposition lobby with tears streaming down his face. Another confided in the Labour member Hugh Dalton that he had come straight back from Namsos to vote against the Government. 'I voted on behalf of my men', he said. 'We were bombed by German aircraft and had nothing with which to reply.'

When the tellers walked up to the table to announce the result, it was seen that the Government had won. But the figures which the Chief Whip read out came as a great surprise – 281 for the motion, 200 against. The Government majority, normally around 240, had fallen to eighty-one. Thirty-three Conservatives voted against the Government, including four ex-ministers (Amery, Duff Cooper, Hore-Belisha and Winterton), together with a handful of other members (National Liberal, National Labour and Independents) who usually supported the Government. About sixty Conservatives abstained or were absent unpaired.

When the Speaker repeated the figures, Chamberlain seemed momentarily stunned. There were cries of 'Resign! Resign!' from the Labour benches and one of their members began to sing *Rule Britannia*. The Prime Minister quickly recovered his composure, but as he walked to the door behind the Speaker's chair, he looked grave and sad. 'No crowds to cheer him as there were before and after Munich', noted 'Chips' Channon in his diary, 'only a solitary little man, who had done his best for England.'

Before leaving the chamber Chamberlain had asked Churchill to go to his room. When he went in, Churchill immediately sensed that the Prime Minister felt he could not carry on and that there ought to be a National Government. Churchill tried to comfort and reassure him. 'This has been a damaging debate, but you have a good majority', he told Chamberlain. 'Do not take the matter grievously to heart. We have a better case about Norway than it has been possible to convey to the House. Strengthen your Government from every quarter, and let us go on until our majority deserts us.' But Chamberlain was neither convinced nor comforted, and Churchill left him about midnight with the feeling that he would persist in his resolve to follow Lloyd George's advice 'if there was no other way, rather than attempt to carry the war further with a one-Party Government'.

'The debate was a very painful affair to many besides myself, and in particular for its exhibition of personal and Party passion', Chamberlain wrote to Ida afterwards. 'It was supposed to be about Norway, and I think it was recognised that the Government had a pretty good case there.'

But the long period of waiting without any real set-back to German prestige, and then the sudden and bitter disappointment over the hopes that had been so recklessly and unjustifiably fostered by the press, just boiled up, with the accumulated mass of grievances, to find expression. The serving members were acutely conscious of various deficiencies, not realising apparently that, though you can double your Territorial army with a stroke of the pen, you can't do the same thing with its equipment. The Amerys, Duff Coopers, and their lot are consciously, or unconsciously, swayed by a sense of frustration because they can only look on, and finally the personal dislike of Simon and Hoare had reached a pitch which I find it difficult to understand, but which undoubtedly had a great deal to do with the rebellion.

A number of those who voted against the government have since either told me, or written to me to say, that they had nothing against me except that I had the wrong people in my team. . . . They don't want to believe that the real reason is our comparative weakness, because we haven't yet anything like caught up the German start, but as that fact remains, whatever the administration, I am afraid they will presently be disappointed again.

One of the Conservatives who voted against the Government was the young member for Oxford City, the Hon. Quintin Hogg, later Lord Hailsham. 'God bless you in your present trouble', he wrote to Chamberlain afterwards. 'Your country is and always will be grateful to you for your devoted service and your splendid courage. . . . Whatever happens, you can be sure that you *have* friends even amongst those who did not vote with you.'

From the following morning, 9 May, events moved swiftly. About 9.30 Churchill telephoned Eden and asked him to come round to his house. When Eden arrived, he found Churchill shaving, and he learned from him of his talk with Chamberlain after the debate. Churchill now expressed the view that Chamberlain would not be able to bring in Labour and that a National Government must be formed. Later Eden had lunch alone with Churchill and Kingsley Wood, who had taken Hoare's place as Privy Seal and as a member of the War Cabinet was still much in Chamberlain's confidence. Wood thought that Churchill should succeed Chamberlain, but he warned that Chamberlain would want Halifax and he would also want Churchill to agree. 'Don't agree', Wood advised Churchill, 'and don't say anything.' Eden was shocked that Wood should talk in this way, since 'he had been so much Chamberlain's man'. On the other hand, it seemed to Eden to be 'good counsel', and he accordingly seconded it. In fact Churchill had already received similar advice from his friend Brendan Bracken.

'It did not take me long to make up my mind what to do', Chamberlain told Ida afterwards.

I saw that the time had come for a National Government in the broadest sense. I knew that I could not get it, but it was necessary to get an official confirmation of the Opposition attitude, if only to justify my resignation to my own Party. I had conversations with Winston and Halifax who I found agreed with my view, and I sent for Attlee and Greenwood that afternoon to ask the definite question whether the Labour Party would join a Government under me or if not under someone else. I did not name the someone else to them but I understand that they favoured Halifax and I had him in mind.

Churchill and Halifax met Chamberlain and Captain Margesson, the Government Chief Whip, in the Cabinet Room at 4.15. For once Churchill, following the advice of Bracken and Kingsley Wood, was silent and left Halifax to do most of the talking. It was clear that Chamberlain preferred Halifax as his successor, assuming Labour refused to serve under him in a National Government. However, Halifax maintained that it would be difficult if not impossible for him as a peer, sitting in the House of Lords, to conduct a war. It looked therefore as if the lot would fall on Churchill, although it was by no means certain that Labour, who had never forgiven him for Tonypandy,* would give him the necessary support. The matter was left unresolved and the two ministers were invited to return at 6.15 when Chamberlain had also asked Attlee and Greenwood to meet him.

Somewhat surprisingly, Chamberlain renewed the invitation he had extended to them the previous March to join him in a national coalition. After Attlee had made it clear that Labour's decision to serve in any coalition under any Prime Minister must depend on the approval of the Party Executive, then at Bournemouth for the Annual Party Conference, Chamberlain asked them to put two questions to their colleagues:

(1) Would they enter a Government under the present Prime Minister?
(2) Would they come in under someone else?

The Labour leaders promised to do this and let the Prime Minister know the result of their enquiries by two o'clock the following afternoon, but they left Chamberlain in little doubt as to what their answer to the first of these questions would be. 'Mr Prime Minister', said Attlee bluntly, 'the fact is our Party won't come in under you. Our Party won't have you and I think I am right in saying that the country won't have you either.'

That night Eden dined with Churchill who told him, according to Eden's diary, 'that he thought it plain N.C. would advise [the] King to send for him'. Halifax, Churchill went on, did not wish to succeed since he was a peer. Churchill indicated clearly that he hoped Chamberlain would stay on in the War Cabinet and lead the House of Commons and also continue as leader of the Conservative Party. 'W. would be Minister of Defence as well as P.M.' noted Eden. 'W. quiet and calm. He wishes me to take War.'

Next morning, 10 May, the dramatic news was received that the German Army had broken through the lightly held defences in eastern France and were overrunning Holland, Belgium and Luxembourg. Chamberlain's first reaction was to remain at his

* In November 1910 there was serious rioting and looting by Welsh miners on strike in the Rhondda Valley. The local authorities appealed to the War Office for troops to be sent to Tonypandy. On hearing of this, Churchill, who was Home Secretary, consulted Haldane the War Minister, and they agreed to send police instead, but to hold some troops in reserve nearby. Although the troops were not called upon to act, the legend spread in Labour Party circles that 'Churchill sent troops who fired upon the miners at Tonypandy'. The legend has persisted in spite of the fact that it was conclusively disproved at the time and subsequently.

post as head of the Government, at least until this fresh crisis was over, and the Whips' Office was told that this was what he intended to do. However Kingsley Wood, who had not begun his career in the insurance business for nothing, insisted that Chamberlain must go, and he strongly urged him to resign and advise the King to send for another Prime Minister.

Shortly afterwards the news arrived in Downing Street that the answer to the first of Chamberlain's questions was an emphatic 'No', and the answer to the second was 'Yes'. By this time he had also heard that 'the Labour Party had changed their minds and were veering towards Winston'. This was quite true, since Churchill's stalwart supporter Brendan Bracken had been in touch with Attlee and had learned from him that, though Labour preferred Halifax, they would not refuse to serve under Churchill. Chamberlain thereupon agreed that he would go to Buckingham Palace to tender his resignation and also 'put Winston's name to the King'.

Chamberlain went to the Palace shortly after six o'clock. 'I accepted his resignation, and told him how grossly unfairly I thought he had been treated, and that I was terribly sorry that all this controversy had happened', the King noted afterwards.

We then had an informal talk over his successor. I, of course, suggested Halifax, but he told me that H. was not enthusiastic as being in the Lords he could only act as a shadow or ghost in the Commons where all the real work took place. I was disappointed over this statement, as I thought H. was the obvious man and that his peerage could be placed in abeyance for the time being.*

On being asked for his advice, Chamberlain told the King that Churchill was the man to send for. The King agreed, and after he had said goodbye to Chamberlain and repeated that he would greatly regret not having him as his Prime Minister, he immediately sent for Churchill and asked him to form a Government. This Churchill said he would do and at the same time gave the King the names of some of the people he would ask to join his Government, including Chamberlain and Halifax as well as representatives of Labour and the Liberals. 'He was full of fire and determination to

* The King thought that some constitutional arrangement might be made to enable Halifax to speak in the House of Commons; but this would have involved legislation, which might not have been acceptable to Parliament at that time.

carry out the duties of Prime Minister', the King added in the note of the meeting he made at the time.

After he had kissed hands Churchill's first act, on returning to his office from the Palace, was to write and tell Chamberlain how grateful he was to him 'for promising to stand by me, and to aid the country at this extremely grievous and formidable moment'.

In these eight months we have worked together I am proud to have won your friendship and your confidence in an increasing measure. To a very large extent I am in your hands – and I feel no fear of that. For the rest I have faith in our cause, which I feel sure will not be suffered to fail among men.

II

Perhaps this is a convenient point at which to take a brief view of Neville Chamberlain in the context of his Premiership. His rule lasted for almost exactly three years, from May 1937 to May 1940, with one significant change. In September 1939, the twenty-one-strong Cabinet of Chamberlain's National Government, of which surprisingly no photograph exists, was transformed into a smaller War Cabinet of nine.

His first Government had a good administrative record, as might be expected from his previous reforms of local government and public assistance, and it was responsible for some important and useful legislation in the domestic field. Coalmining royalties, for example, were nationalized in 1938, despite strong opposition from the colliery owners in the House of Lords, foreshadowing the passing of the mines themselves into public ownership after the war. There were legislative measures affecting factories and housing, subsidizing slum·clearance and reducing overcrowding; provision was made for physical training, a pet subject of Chamberlain's; and plans were put in hand for the reform of the criminal law, another reform which was destined to come to fruition under the first post-war Labour Government. The Government also formulated plans to raise the school-leaving age to fifteen. Pensions in one form or another engaged the Prime Minister's personal attention. On a free vote he advocated a contributory pensions scheme for ex-Members of Parliament in need, which became law on the eve of the war. 'Your help is fully recognised by our side of the House', H. B. Lees

Smith, a Privy Councillor and later Acting Chairman of the Labour Party, wrote to him at the time, 'although this may not be expressed to you personally.' Furthermore, a promise he had made before the war was redeemed, in spite of war burdens, by reducing to sixty the qualifying age for pensions for women, and by introducing supplementary payments to other old-age pensioners who could show need.

Civil aviation was also nationalized, Imperial Airways and British Airways being fused into a single public corporation, the British Overseas Airways Corporation, under the dynamic rule of Sir John Reith who was persuaded to give up his old job at the BBC to become chairman of the new corporation. Although civil aviation, like merchant shipping, was taken over by the Government on the outbreak of the war, the foundations for the future internal, European and overseas services were laid.

Useful if unexciting as these measures undoubtedly were, Chamberlain must take a great share of the credit for their introduction, although this has now been generally forgotten. In A. J. P. Taylor's words, 'he was a meticulous housemaid, great at tidying up'. Above all, Chamberlain excelled in presiding over Cabinet meetings, wasting no time and disposing of the agenda in a characteristic brisk and businesslike fashion. Time and again Alexander Cadogan would later complain that Churchill would ramble on about a subject without a pause for over an hour, whereas Chamberlain would have settled it in six minutes. 'I *long* for poor old Neville Chamberlain again', Cadogan noted after a particularly aggravating and long drawn out meeting in February 1945. 'He *did* know how to conduct business!'

Unfortunately for Chamberlain's posthumous reputation it is in the field of foreign relations that he has been chiefly remembered and his policies judged. Nevertheless, even if some other politician had been Prime Minister from 1937 onwards, foreign affairs would have kept occupying the attention of Parliament and the Cabinet more and more. In the first year of the MacDonald National Government, the House of Commons devoted two days to debating foreign affairs and one day to the Disarmament Conference. In Chamberlain's first session (1937-8), foreign affairs occupied thirty-one full days of Commons debates, exclusive of the days allocated for the discussion of rearmament. At the same time, as A. J. P. Taylor has pointed out, more pamphlets and books on foreign affairs were published than at any previous time in English history, although the mass of the ordinary people of the country had little knowledge of the subject and had no idea of the dangerous imminence of war until the time of Munich.

Another Oxford historian, Robert Blake, has declared of Chamberlain that 'the verdict of history must be against him', because he 'risked the whole existence of the nation'. With all due respect to Lord Blake, this seems to be too sweeping a judgment. Who can say with any degree of certainty that the British people and the dominions, or for that matter the French, would have solidly supported a war before 1939? Certainly at the time of Munich the Commonwealth was not united, since South Africa as well as Eire had decided to remain neutral, Australia had declared against participation, and Canada showed no inclination to become drawn into the mother country's European involvements. So far as the Commonwealth was concerned, with the conspicuous exception of Eire there was unanimous support for the war in 1939, a change of heart which Hitler's rapacity over Czecho-Slovakia had undoubtedly helped to bring about.

Firstly, let Chamberlain be heard in his own defence. A fortnight after he handed over to Churchill, he wrote:

Whatever the outcome [of the war], it is as clear as daylight that, if we had had to fight in 1938, the results would have been far worse. It would be rash to prophesy the verdict of history, but if full access is obtained to all the records, it will be seen that I realised from the beginning our military weakness, and did my best to postpone, if I could not avert, the war. But I had to fight every yard against both Labour and Liberal Opposition leaders who denounced me for trying to maintain good relations with Italy and Japan, for refusing to back Republican Spain against France, and for not 'standing up to Hitler' at each successive act of aggression.

Undoubtedly Chamberlain never wavered in the belief that his combination of appeasement and rearmament was the correct one in the circumstances. One of his last attempts at self-justification was contained in a letter he wrote to Baldwin a few weeks before his death, in which he enlarged upon the words quoted above.

Never for one single instant have I doubted the rightness of what I did at Munich, given the violent and persistent opposition I had to fight against all the time. You remember how I, as Chancellor of the Exchequer, asked leave of the Cabinet to review the programmes put up by the Service Ministers, and submitted a programme which was accepted by you and the others which provided for a larger Air Force than Charley Londonderry had ventured to propose.

After Munich I still further increased that programme, and inaugurated all the A.R.P. measures which have developed since. I also introduced Conscription, but I had to fight for every one of these things. In September '38 we only had 60 fire pumps in London, which would have burned out in a week.

Some day these things will be known. My critics differed from me because they were ignorant, it is only fair to add wilfully ignorant in many cases.

There is some special pleading here which must be borne in mind when considering what the writer Ian Colvin, in his strongly anti-Chamberlain work *The Chamberlain Cabinet*, has argued in what he describes as the three broad issues upon which Chamberlain and his first pre-war Cabinet stand at the bar of history. These are that with a large parliamentary majority they 'failed to rearm in time'; that they surrendered over Czechoslovakia in 1938 when they need not have done; and that they failed to achieve an alliance with Russia, 'thus entering the war with less effective allies than could have been found in 1938'.

On the first charge, Chamberlain began to advocate rearmament in Baldwin's time, and his part in shaping the Defence White Papers has already been noticed. 'When the late Government were at length convinced of the urgent need to rearm', Churchill acknowledged in 1937, 'no one was more active than Mr Chamberlain.' But the expenditure involved was governed by the need for financial stability within the framework of balanced Budgets. Finally, when the Government were convinced of the need to rearm in order to catch up with Germany, the rate of rearmament was appallingly slow – certainly it so appeared to Churchill and his handful of supporters in the House of Commons.

It will also be recalled that in the 1935 General Election Chamberlain was branded by Labour as a warmonger because of his cautious advocacy of rearmament. Its slow rate of progress under his administration after 1937 was reflected in the Government's unwillingness to introduce any measures for the compulsory direction of labour, although the Prime Minister agreed with the policy of building shadow factories which had been inaugurated by Swinton and Weir. Later, it is true, he did introduce a measure of compulsory military service, but he was at first far from enthusiastic about it, and when the time came took it over from Hore-Belisha. He was much keener on civil defence and in this field he deserves credit for the appointment of Sir John Anderson to take the efficient charge he did of air raid precautions.

Chamberlain's own defence of the Munich settlement and the part he played in bringing it about has already been quoted. Others have defended it with foresight as well as hindsight, on the ground that it bought Britain some much needed time to strengthen her defences. Although Swinton, the former Air Minister, whom Chamberlain had peremptorily dismissed some months earlier, was now taking little part in politics, Chamberlain asked him at the time what line he was going to take over Munich. Swinton, according to his own account, said he 'thought it had been worth while buying a year's grace because in a year much of the air programme would come to fruition'. If he (Chamberlain) would do everything possible to advance rearmament, Swinton would support Munich on this count. 'But I have made peace', said Chamberlain. At the same time, the Prime Minister added, rearmament would go 'full steam ahead'. Swinton replied that on that understanding he accepted Munich but that he 'had no illusions about peace'. On the other hand Hoare, who had been close to him during the critical days of Munich, became more and more conscious of his work for peace as time went on. 'He was right to make the effort to save the world from a great catastrophe', Hoare assured Mrs Chamberlain after her husband's death, 'and history will give this verdict.'

Perhaps the best judgment of the second charge made against Chamberlain on the score of Munich has come from the late Sir John Wheeler-Bennett. 'Let us say of the Munich Settlement that it was inescapable', he wrote in his *Munich: A Prologue to Tragedy*;

that faced with the lack of preparedness in Britain's armaments and defences, with the lack of unity at home and in the Commonwealth, with the collapse of French morale, and with the uncertainty of Russia to fight, Mr Chamberlain had no alternative to do other than he did; let us pay tribute to his persistence in carrying out a policy which he honestly believed to be right. Let us accept and admit all these things, but in so doing let us not omit the shame and humiliation that were ours; let us not forget that, in order to save our own skins – that because we were too weak to protect ourselves – we were forced to sacrifice a small Power to slavery.

As Wheeler-Bennett has also pointed out, it is of no avail to say that Britain saved Czechoslovakia from the fate which was later suffered by Poland, and that, but for Munich, Bohemia and Moravia would have been devastated like Warsaw and Cracow were to be a year later.

In reality it was the Czechs who saved us, for had President Beneš elected to fight with Russian support and thus precipitated an Eastern European war, it is impossible to believe that Britain and France could have kept aloof, however reluctantly they might have been dragged into participation.

Thirdly, there is the charge that Britain dragged her feet over the projected and actual negotiations with Russia until it was too late. Chamberlain's 'profound distrust of Russia' seems to have been the result, not of any ideological motive, but rather of the views of the Chiefs of Staff that the purge of the Red Army in 1937 and 1938 had left the Soviet forces so weakened, particularly as regards the officer class, that Soviet Russia was in no position to render any effective military assistance in support of a treaty obligation. Her subsequent conduct of the campaign in Finland and the huge losses she sustained there lent some support to this view. There was the feeling too in the Foreign Office and the Cabinet that Russia was playing at power politics rather than making genuine efforts for peace.

It is worth noting in this context that the member of the Cabinet who was perhaps most anxious for an *entente* with the Soviet Union was the much maligned Sir Samuel Hoare. During the First World War Hoare had been a member of the British military mission to Russia, he spoke and read the language fluently, and he possessed a wide knowledge of Russian literature and of the Russian character and mentality. 'So far as my influence counted', he has recalled in his memoirs, 'I was persistently on the side of making every effort to bring Stalin over to the Allies, and if that was impossible, at least to keep him from throwing the weight of Russian power, whatever it might be, on to the enemy's side.'

In April 1939 Stalin had issued a clear warning that the appeasers by their policy might become warmongers, and that his aim was 'to be cautious and not to allow our country to be drawn into conflicts by warmongers who are accustomed to have others pull the chestnuts out of the fire for them'. Shortly afterwards Stalin told Joseph

Davies, the United States ambassador in Moscow, that in his view 'the reactionary elements in England, represented by the Chamberlain Government', were determined upon a policy of 'ultimately making Germany strong as against Russia', adding that in his opinion 'Chamberlain did not represent the English people and that he would probably fail because the Fascist dictators would drive too hard a bargain'.

Lord Swinton, the last survivor of the Chamberlain Cabinets, who died in 1972, regarded Neville Chamberlain as 'an outstanding example of the leader whom the current of world events carried out of his depth'. During the twenty years in which he sat with him in the House of Commons, and the dozen years he sat with Chamberlain in the Cabinet, Swinton had good opportunities of studying him at close political quarters. His assessment affords as good first-hand evidence of his qualities as one is likely to find.

He was the most pacific and honourable of men [wrote Swinton in *Sixty Years of Power*]: the vast expenditure of money on rearming was something which shocked him; his mind could not reconcile itself to the justification of a massive arms programme. This, combined with a personal faith that he could handle the dictators and make them see reason, is the fairest judgment I can make to explain Chamberlain, his motives, his ideals, his naivety, his courage, and his disastrous obstinacy.

III

Churchill's War Cabinet was small, having only five members, of whom only one, Halifax, who continued as Foreign Secretary, was in charge of a department as well. Chamberlain agreed to join as Lord President of the Council. Churchill wished him also to be Leader of the House of Commons and so relieve the Prime Minister of the burden of arranging day-to-day parliamentary business, and in fact Chamberlain in his farewell broadcast on the evening of 10 May actually announced this. But it was vetoed by Labour, notably by Attlee and Greenwood, who refused to serve in such an event, and consequently Churchill gave way. However, Chamberlain did continue as leader of the Conservative Party, an office in which Churchill greatly relied upon his help.

Of the two Labour members of the War Cabinet, Attlee became Lord Privy Seal, while Greenwood was Minister without Portfolio.

Churchill became Minister of Defence as well as Prime Minister. Other ministers were called in as occasion demanded, the most constant attenders naturally being the three service ministers, who each belonged to a different political party, Eden (War) being Conservative, A. V. Alexander (Admiralty) Labour, and Sir Archibald Sinclair (Air) Liberal. Kingsley Wood was rewarded for his part in the leadership crisis by being kept on as Chancellor of the Exchequer. There was no place in the Government for Hoare, who was shunted off to Spain as ambassador.

Hankey, who was in the Cabinet Room on the morning of 12 May, when Churchill was busy making up the new Government, gave a somewhat jaundiced account of the scene to Hoare later that day:

I found complete chaos this morning. No one was gripping the war in its crisis. The Dictator, instead of dictating, was engaged in a sordid wrangle with the politicians of the left about the secondary offices. N.C. was in a state of despair about it all.

The only hope lies in the solid core of Churchill, Chamberlain and Halifax, but whether the wise old elephants will be able to hold the Rogue Elephant, I doubt.*

In the event the two 'wise old elephants' had little chance of fulfilling Hankey's hope, Chamberlain because he was soon to retire through illness, and Halifax because the death of Lord Lothian, the British ambassador in Washington, resulted in the Foreign Secretary being appointed in his place.

Churchill owed a good deal to Chamberlain, as he has generously acknowledged. There was much about the new Prime Minister that rankled with many Conservatives, and when Churchill and Chamberlain took their places on the Government Front Bench together for the first time on 13 May, Chamberlain received a great ovation from his Party, while it was noticeable that the cheers for Churchill came mostly from the Labour benches. As for not being Leader of the House Chamberlain suffered no pangs of disappointment. 'I saw that it would involve me in much tedious sitting in the House, and very likely lead to ill-temper and bad manners', he remarked at the time. 'So I gave it up without a sigh.' As it was, Chamberlain had plenty to do as Lord President, his task being to

* According to A. J. P. Taylor (*Beaverbrook*, p. 411 note), Hoare dropped the letter from his pocket when he came to take leave of Beaverbrook on 12 May, and it was placed in the Hoare file among the Beaverbrook Papers where it still is.

co-ordinate domestic policy while the Prime Minister got on with the job of running the war with the Chiefs of Staff. Chamberlain also presided at Cabinet meetings when Churchill was absent, which the Prime Minister frequently was at the time of the fall of France and during the Battle of Britain. 'Very able and crafty', was the Labour leader Attlee's judgment of Chamberlain at this period. 'and free from any of the rancour he might well have felt against us. He worked very hard and well: a good chairman, a good committee man, always very businesslike. You could work with him.'

Attlee's opinion was endorsed by Churchill in an off-the-record interview which he gave to the editor of the *Manchester Guardian*, W. P. Crozier, on 26 July.

The newspaper editor began by putting a question to Churchill. 'I suppose that, as a matter of fact, it is a political necessity for you to have Chamberlain in the Government? He answers to you, so to speak, for the support of the Conservative Party?'

'Well, I owe something to Chamberlain you know', the Prime Minister replied. 'When he resigned he could have advised the King to send for Halifax but he didn't. And he consented to serve under me as Premier – not everyone in his position would have done that; Asquith, for instance, wouldn't serve under Lloyd George. But Chamberlain worked very well with me and I can tell you this – *he's no intriguer.*'

'The trouble is that when anything goes wrong', Crozier went on, 'a lot of people think – both here and in other countries – that it's Chamberlain and the Munich people working against you, and that makes a bad impression.'

'They don't', Churchill answered emphatically, 'and I can tell you that Chamberlain works hard and efficiently.'

'Then it isn't true that in matters of drive and effort in the war Chamberlain and Co are a brake on the wheel – I mean on your wheel?'

'No, it isn't true at all.'

'Well', said the editor, 'I'm glad of that, but there's another point even more serious, and it's this. Do Chamberlain and those friends of his use their influence in any Government question of policy in the direction of "appeasement", pushing it on you and the Government?'

'I give you my word of honour', Churchill repeated, 'it isn't true!'

It is possible that in asking those questions the editor may have heard something of the Cabinet meetings on 27th and 28 May, during the Dunkirk evacuation, when it appeared that Italy was on the point of coming into the war on the side of Germany, and under French pressure the Cabinet considered the possibility of buying off Mussolini, which might eventually lead to a negotiated peace. 'My own feeling', Churchill has recalled, 'was that at the pitch at which our affairs lay we had nothing to offer which Mussolini could not take for himself or be given by Hitler if we were defeated. One cannot easily make a bargain at the last gasp. Once we started negotiating for the friendly mediation of the Duce we should destroy our power of fighting on.' On the other hand, Halifax was in favour of opening negotiations and in this he was seconded by Chamberlain. However, the Prime Minister's arguments against seeking a negotiated peace through Mussolini carried the day. Churchill clinched the matter by summoning all ministers of Cabinet rank outside the War Cabinet to a meeting in his room at the House of Commons. 'Of course, whatever happens at Dunkirk, we shall fight on', he told them, to which his audience replied with cries of, 'Well done, Prime Minister!'

It is worth noting, too, that after the Dunkirk evacuation had been completed and the British stood alone in 'their finest hour', the Prime Minister, who appreciated Chamberlain's loyalty to him, exhorted Sinclair and the Labour ministers in the War Cabinet to suspend the heresy hunt against the members of the previous Government, particularly Chamberlain and Kingsley Wood. 'The truth is that Winston is about the only person who has an absolutely clean sheet', noted Halifax at this time. 'Both Labour and Liberals have to share with Conservatives the responsibility of being late with rearmament by reason of the great part they took in creating an atmosphere in which Stanley Baldwin, though I think wrongly, not unnaturally thought a large bill for rearmament was not politically practicable.'

Chamberlain, who had moved into No. 11 Downing Street at Churchill's express request, was already a sick man, although how ill he was he did not then know. In June he complained of 'considerable pain in the abdomen'. An X-ray examination revealed a partial stricture of the bowel, and on 29 July he went into a nursing home for a surgical operation. At first all went well, and after a fortnight or so he went down to recuperate at Highfield Park, a country place belonging to a relative which he had been lent at Heckfield, between Reading and Basingstoke in Hampshire.* 'My friends all say I look well', he wrote to his sister Hilda. 'But I have lost my spring and my spirits. All my recreations, flowers, fishing and shooting, country life, have been taken from me – and there is nothing to look forward to.'

Three weeks later he returned to London. 'I have still to adjust myself to the new life of a partially crippled man, which is what I am', he wrote on 9 September. 'Any ideas which may have been in my mind about possibilities of further political activity, and even a possibility of another Premiership after the war, have gone.' By this time he was aware that the cancerous growth which had caused the internal pain was inoperable and incurable. Less than a fortnight later he found himself unable to carry on, and at Churchill's suggestion he returned to the country where he continued to receive Cabinet papers and official telegrams. His return to Heckfield coincided with the later stages of the Battle of Britain. On their way back to their bases in France, some German aircraft jettisoned their remaining bombs to lighten the load in the neighbourhood of Heckfield, an action which led some of the villagers to conclude that the bombs were deliberately aimed at Highfield Park and its distinguished occupant. However, the bombing of Heckfield seems to have been quite accidental, since it is very doubtful whether the Germans knew that Chamberlain was living there at this time.

On 22 September, he wrote to Churchill resigning his office. At first the Prime Minister would not accept his resignation, hoping that he might be able to rebuild his strength by a further rest in the country. But eventually, on 30 September, when he was told how ill he was, the Prime Minister reluctantly acquiesced. On the same day Chamberlain wrote to the King:

I cannot contemplate the termination of my relations with you, Sir, as a Minister, without a good deal of emotion. Broadly speaking, I was your first Prime Minister and I shall always recall with gratitude the confidence which you have been good enough to give me, and the increasing intimacy of our conversations which were so encouraging and

* Highfield Park belonged to Mrs Lilian Cole (*née* Williams) who was then living in Canada. She had previously been married to Neville Chamberlain's uncle, Herbert Chamberlain. After his death she had married Alfred Clayton Cole, who was an uncle of Mrs Neville Chamberlain and owned West Woodhay in Berkshire, where she was brought up.

helpful to me during some of the most anxious and difficult periods which have ever faced a Minister in all our long history.

It has been my fate to see the failure of all my efforts to preserve peace, and the destruction of all the hopes which I had entertained that I might be able to steer this country into calmer waters, and gradually to raise the standards of life among the people. Yet I do not feel that I have anything to reproach myself for in my attempts to avoid the present war, which might well have succeeded if they had not come up against the insatiate and inhuman ambitions of a fanatic.

'For me too it will always be a pleasure to recall our intimate talks together', the King replied.

I have sympathised with you very much in seeing your hopes shattered by the lust and violence of a single man, and yet, as I told you once before, your efforts to preserve peace were not in vain, for they established, in the eyes of the civilised world, our entire innocence of the crime which Hitler was determined to commit. For this alone the country owes you a debt of gratitude.

On 14 October, the King and Queen drove from Windsor to Highfield Park to call on Chamberlain. They spent about half an hour together. 'A characteristic act of human kindness and sympathy', so Chamberlain described the visit. They found him a dying man. 'I am very sad about poor Mr Chamberlain and I know that I have lost a trusted friend', the King wrote that same day to Queen Mary after he had returned to Windsor. 'When he was P.M. he really did tell me what was in his mind, and what he hoped to do. I was able to confide in him, and even when he was Lord President of the Council we were able to have our talks.'

Churchill with the King's willing assent offered Chamberlain the Order of the Garter, but this the sick man respectfully declined, as he had previously refused to accept a peerage, preferring, as Churchill later told the House of Commons, to die, 'like his father, plain Mr Chamberlain'

'So I regret nothing in the past', he had the strength to write in a long letter to Baldwin on 17 October. 'I do regret that I should be cut off when I feel capable of doing much more were it not for my physical disability. But I accept what I can't help and hope I shan't cumber the earth too long. I doubt if I shall ever visit Brum again.' He never did, since the end came more swiftly than Lord Horder, his doctor, thought or at any rate told him he thought. Pressed by

his patient early in October to give him some idea of his expecta-
tion of life, Horder after much hesitation, according to Chamberlain, 'went so far as to say he would be surprised if I were not here
in 3 months but more surprised if I were here in 12 months'. In
fact, he died at Highfield Park during the afternoon of Saturday
9 November 1940.

Halifax paid him a visit there two days before, being the last of
his old Cabinet colleagues to see him. Mrs Anne Chamberlain
spoke frankly to Halifax before taking him up to her husband's
bedroom, and said it was 'only a matter of days', since he could eat
practically nothing on account of the nausea that continually overcame him and he was growing steadily weaker. Halifax found him
propped up in bed, with a little bed-table, on which there was a
bowl of blue gentians which some well-wisher had sent.

I began by saying something about what a rotten time he must have
had with his sickness, to which he replied that he had been a bit better
the last day or two. 'Approaching dissolution brings relief', he said with
a half laugh. Then he spoke of our work together, and what it had
meant to him in a way that moved me much. And then he was plainly
tired, and Anne looked in, and I said good-bye. He took my hand in
both his, and held it, and so with no more said with the full understanding of friends who go to different duties, we parted.

It was all quite natural, and no shadow of constraint. He was brave
and quite resigned. He had wondered, he said at one point, how best to
satisfy himself that Anne knew how bad he was, but he was happy now
that she knew everything, though he feared she would be lonely. I left
him with her.

As a result of the destruction of the House of Commons chamber
by German bombs, the House now met in Church House, Westminster. It so happened that the first occasion on which Members
assembled in this 'new, slightly shoddy "Annexe"', as 'Chips'
Channon called it, was on 12 November, to enable the respective
Party leaders to pay their tributes to the departed statesman. The
Prime Minister led off, followed by Attlee for Labour and Sinclair
for the Liberals. The general impression, according to Channon,
was that it was well done, dignified and sincere.

Whatever else history may or may not say about these terrible tremendous years [Churchill declared], we can be sure that Neville Chamberlain
acted with perfect sincerity according to his lights and strove to the
utmost of his capacity and authority, to save the world from the awful,

devastating struggle in which we are now engaged. This alone will stand him in good stead as far as what is called the verdict of history is concerned.

Chamberlain's remains were cremated. Two days later they were laid to rest in Westminster Abbey close to those of another former Prime Minister, Andrew Bonar Law, with whom he had much in common as a businessman and who appointed him to his first ministerial post. Churchill and the rest of the War Cabinet acted as pall bearers. Since little or no public notice had been given out in advance for reasons of security, the Abbey was far from crowded with mourners. 'There had been some uneasiness lest the Germans should stage a raid and get Winston and the entire Government with one bomb', noted Channon, who was present. 'However, nothing occurred, and there was no alert during the actual service, which was long, dignified and moving.'

There in the Abbey, and it angered me to see them, were all the little men who had torpedoed poor Neville's heroic efforts to preserve peace, and made his life a misery: some seemed to be gloating. Winston, followed by the War Cabinet, however, had the decency to cry as he stood by the coffin, and Mr Speaker and others too seemed deeply stirred. . . . The service was long, and the Abbey was cold, that terrible ecclesiastic cold known only to English churches.

Afterwards I heard that, after everyone had left the Abbey, poor Horace Wilson, the once all-powerful *eminence grise* of the Chamberlain regime, was seen alone, his face contracted with grief, praying for his dead friend.

Chamberlain chose his own epitaph from Leigh Hunt's poem 'Abou ben Adhem and the Angel'. The words were inscribed on the stone plaque which was later erected to his memory in Heckfield village church:

Write me as one that loves his fellow-men.

SELECT BIBLIOGRAPHY

A. MANUSCRIPT SOURCES

Neville Chamberlain's private papers, together with those of his elder half-brother Austen and their father Joseph, are in the Birmingham University Library. The other principal private manuscript sources include the Baldwin and Templewood (Hoare) papers in the Cambridge University Library, the MacDonald papers in the Public Record Office, and the Swinton papers and the Inskip diaries in Churchill College, Cambridge. The principal official papers in the Public Record Office are the Cabinet Minutes (Cab. 23) and the Prime Minister's private office papers and files (Premier 1).

B. PRINTED SOURCES

Amery, L. S., *My Political Life*, 3 vols, London, 1953–5.
Avon, Earl of, *The Eden Memoirs. Facing the Dictators* London, 1962. *The Reckoning* London, 1965.
Birkenhead, Earl of, *Halifax: The Life of Lord Halifax* London, 1965.
Blake, Robert, *The Unknown Prime Minister: The Life and Times of Andrew Bonar Law* London, 1955.
Cadogan, Sir Alexander, *Diaries* edited by David Dilkes, London, 1971.
Channon, Henry, *Chips: The Diaries of Sir Henry Channon* edited by Robert Rhodes James, London, 1967.
Churchill, Winston S., *The Second World War*. Vol. 1 *The Gathering Storm* London, 1948.

Ciano, Count, *Ciano's Diary* edited by Malcolm Muggeridge, London, 1947.

Colvin, Ian, *The Chamberlain Cabinet* London, 1971.

Cowling, Maurice, *The Impact of Hitler: British Politics and British Policy 1933–40* Cambridge, 1975.

Elletson, D. H., *The Chamberlains* London, 1966.

Feiling, Keith, *Life of Neville Chamberlain* London, 1940 and 1970.

Garvin, J. L., and Amery, Julian, *Life of Joseph Chamberlain*, 6 vols, London, 1932–69.

Halifax, Earl of, *Fullness of Days* London, 1957.

Harvey, John, *The Diplomatic Diaries of Oliver Harvey 1937–1940* London, 1970.

Hyde, H. Montgomery, *Baldwin: The Unexpected Prime Minister* London, 1973.

Jones, Thomas, *A Diary with Letters, 1931–1950* London, 1954.

Macleod, Iain, *Neville Chamberlain* London, 1961.

Macmillan, Harold, *The Past Masters. Politics and Politicians 1906–1939* London, 1975.

Nicolson, Harold, *Diaries and Letters* edited by Nigel Nicolson, 3 vols, London, 1966–8.

Petrie, Sir Charles, *The Chamberlain Tradition* London, 1938.
The Life and Letters of Sir Austen Chamberlain 2 vols, London, 1940.

Roskill, Stephen, *Hankey, Man of Secrets* 3 vols, 1970–4.

Simon, Viscount, *Retrospect* London, 1952.

Swinton, Earl of, *Sixty Years of Power* London, 1966.

Templewood, Viscount, *Nine Troubled Years* London, 1954.

Wheeler-Bennett, Sir John W., *Munich, Prologue to Tragedy* 2nd edn, London, 1963.
King George VI: His Life and Reign London, 1958.

INDEX